A HANDBOOK
of BASIC SKILLS
and STRATEGIES for
BEGINNING TEACHERS

A HANDBOOK
of BASIC SKILLS
and STRATEGIES for
BEGINNING TEACHERS

Facing the Challenge
of Teaching
in Today's Schools

Robert E. MacDonald

California State University, Chico

Longman

A Handbook of Basic Skills and Strategies for Beginning Teachers

Longman, 10 Bank Street, White Plains, N.Y. 10606

Associated companies:
Longman Group Ltd., London
Longman Cheshire Pty., Melbourne
Longman Paul Pty., Auckland
Copp Clark Pitman, Toronto

Senior editor: Naomi Silverman
Production editors: Camilla Palmer and Carol Harwood
Cover design: Kevin C. Kall
Cover illustration/photo: Anthony J. Alberts
Production supervisor: Kathleen Ryan

Library of Congress Cataloging-in-Publication Data
MacDonald, Robert E.
    A handbook of basic skills and strategies for beginning teachers: facing the challenge of
teaching in today's schools / Robert E. MacDonald.
        p. cm.
    Includes bibliographical references and index.
    ISBN 0-8013-0608-6
    1. Teaching—manuals, etc. 2. Student teaching—United States—Handbooks, manuals,
etc. 3. Classroom management—United States—Handbooks, manuals, etc. 4. Teachers—
In-service training—United States—Handbooks, manuals, etc. I. Title
LB1025.2.M29 1991   90-41893
371.1′02—dc20   CIP

        8 9 10-CRS-9695

To the memory of my father,
W. Earl MacDonald

Contents

Preface

This handbook is designed to be a practical field-experience guide and methods text for beginning teachers, K–12. It provides a concise, "reader-friendly" volume that addresses the developmental needs of new teachers as they encounter the complex realities of a contemporary classroom. It presents basic skills and strategies that will enable entering teachers to deal creatively and responsibly with the significant new challenges they face.

This book will be especially appropriate as a resource for teacher candidates during the student teaching experience. It may be used as an adopted text for student teaching seminars or as a self-help guide for student teachers while they are in the field. The individual chapters may be used as separate modules.

This text will also have application to introductory methods courses for teacher candidates prior to student teaching. As a third group, inservice teachers will find this handbook valuable as a refresher or a guide. It will be particularly useful to first-year teachers who are still becoming oriented to the classroom and to the school.

MAIN FEATURES

This book has several prominent features that make it a unique and timely addition to available field guides and other practical methods texts. These features include:

1. *A strong emphasis on learning to work productively with students in a current school setting.* Besides separate chapters devoted to classroom management, interactive teaching, and becoming established with new classes, this handbook treats the being-with-students condition as perhaps the most ubiquitous aspect of the role. This is one of the pervasive, though less advertised features of teaching described in the first chapter.

2. *An accent on "proactive" attitudes and behaviors that will help teachers function as creative professionals in a school environment,* including a comprehen-

sive set of strategies for making a healthy and productive accommodation to a modern school organization. The book emphasizes a teacher's need to achieve job satisfaction by rising above the mindless routine and boredom that have become increasingly prevalent in today's classrooms. It shows how positively empowered teachers can minimize job stress and avoid occupational burnout.

3. *Concentrated attention to the dynamics of live teaching*, including succinct descriptions of basic interactive maneuvers that allow teachers to both conduct learner-paced instruction and manage student groups effectively. Together with chapters offering guidelines for classroom motivation and teacher explanations, these sections provide beginners with a manageable, intuitively appropriate framework for building a repertoire of teaching behaviors.

4. *An implicit psychology of adult learning and positive teacher development.* An effort is made to feature teachers as self-motivating persons whose behavior is a function of their own basic needs and purposes. As such, this book attempts to address the perceived needs of developing teachers as they encounter the new challenges of public school teaching. Two initial chapters serve to assist beginners in accurately sizing up the nature of the work and in beginning to build attitudes and strategies for maintaining personal stamina and sense of purpose in an organizational setting. The book also incorporates a psychology of classroom management that sees class control as a means to an educational end that the teacher has fully internalized, and includes a final chapter that appeals to beginning teachers to take initial steps to be responsible for their own professional development.

5. *A rich store of practical strategies for achieving the proficiencies it features.* The book contains an abundance of professional tips to help beginners become skilled teachers. Each chapter evolves from a problem-solving frame of reference. Chapter titles and many of the section headings are action-based, appealing to the performance needs of new teachers in a language designed to get their attention.

Throughout the book the reader will encounter short verbatim commentaries of teachers at various levels of professional development. These statements, primarily from student teachers and first-year teachers, were obtained by the author from personal journals and personal interviews with the contributors.

ORGANIZATION

There are three parts to this handbook. Part One contains four chapters devoted to Preparing for Teaching, the first two chapters being primarily conceptual and orientational. Chapter 1 identifies basic but intangible features of modern teaching that will have an important bearing on a teacher's professional growth and job satisfaction. Chapter 2 focuses on the teacher's relationship to the system itself. It shows teacher development to be integrally related to the kinds of adaptations teachers are able to make to dominant organizational realities. Both chapters offer the new teacher suggestions for making positive accommodations to these prevailing conditions. Chapter 3 provides basic guidelines for preparing instructional objectives, whereas chapter 4 consists of fundamental ideas and strategies to help beginners organize for instruction.

Part Two, Conducting Classroom Activity, includes five chapters, each of which centers on a major dimension of skilled classroom performance. Chapter 5 focuses on the dynamics of teacher–group relations and offers entering teachers rules for developing sound working relationships with their classes. Chapter 6 explores ideas and tactics for engaging students actively and genuinely in school learning. It emphasizes motivational techniques that appeal to students' intrinsic motivations to learn. Chapter 7 focuses on the explaining behavior of the teacher. It features teacher explanations as basic ingredients of quality teaching and treats this fundamental skill in considerable depth. Chapter 8 details the specific interactive tactics good teachers use to establish effective two-way communication as a medium for in-depth classroom learning. Chapter 9 describes an approach to classroom management that would make the control function an integral part of a teacher's instructional pattern. It presents a series of low-profile maneuvers for achieving behavior control in the classroom.

Part Three, Following up Instruction, is devoted to three main follow-up or "support" activities that teachers perform in connection with their instructional duties. Chapter 10 provides a conceptual framework for approaching the evaluation of classroom learning together with practical methods for testing and grading. Chapter 11 introduces basic communication strategies for productive parent conferences and effective one-to-one interaction with students. The final chapter offers ideas for managing one's own professional development as a new teacher. It recommends techniques for self-evaluation and self-development in several important areas.

ACKNOWLEDGMENTS

I would like to express my appreciation to several people who have helped make this book possible. First, I am grateful to my teaching partners Elyot Johnson and Dan Stuempfig for their flexibility and support while the book was in progress. Another colleague, Andy Hanson, found time in his busy schedule to read and critique each of the chapters. His perceptive suggestions were especially beneficial. I also want to offer my sincere thanks to Longman senior editor Naomi Silverman for her commitment to this project and her strong efforts on its behalf. She deserves a good deal of credit for helping make the book a reality.

A MESSAGE TO TEACHERS IN TRAINING

You are entering teaching at a crucial time in the history of American education. As a classroom teacher you will likely be called on to design learning experiences for increasingly diverse, nonacademically oriented populations of young learners. From all indications, you will need to prepare yourself to teach greater numbers of nontraditional and educationally disadvantaged students than encountered by previous teachers. Consider the following demographic patterns:

1. The nation's overall birth rate has dropped below the replacement level, and the median age of the population is climbing. As the general population ages, the proportion of young who are members of minority groups—particularly African-Americans and Hispanics—will expand dramatically. Some states can expect to have a "minority majority" in their schools by the beginning of the twenty-first century. California is already at that stage in its elementary schools.[1]

2. The gap between rich and poor in the United States continues to increase. As this gap grows wider, a larger and larger percentage of children will fall below the poverty line. Forty percent of the poor in the United States are children, and this situation is likely to worsen because the median income of families headed by a person under the age of twenty-five has declined steadily over the last twenty years.[2]

3. Fewer than 5 percent of U.S. households now conform to the standard model family of past decades: a working father, mother at home, and two or more school-age children. Indications are that 60 percent of the children born in 1983 will live in one-parent homes before they are eighteen. As shifts in the traditional patterns of marriage and child rearing continue, fewer children will have the emotional and educational advantages of a two-parent family, parents who are themselves educated, and close supervision after school.[3]

These sociological trends will no doubt have some dramatic implications for American teachers of the future. For one thing, classroom teachers will need to possess a working knowledge of alternative learning patterns together with schemes for engaging nonacademically inclined youngsters in new learning. As we move toward the twenty-first century, teaching will require more personalized, learner-centered techniques for teaching the highly diverse mix of students who will enter U.S. classrooms.

Future teachers must be able to summon the personal stamina and resourcefulness to face an ever more complex and formidable set of teaching responsibilities. As a means of coping with the complexity of teaching you will need strategies for working within a present-day school organization that will allow you to avoid being devitalized by the system, patterns of professional involvement that will allow you to make best use of your creative energies.

This handbook is designed to help you anticipate the challenge facing you as a new teacher in today's schools. It will assist you in preparing yourself to work effectively and productively with the young people you will be expected to teach. It is also intended to help you cope with the demands of the school system so as to maintain high levels of professional competence and creativity in your work.

REFERENCES

1. M. Sandra Reeves, "Self-Interest and the Common Weal: Focusing on the Bottom Half." *Education Week*, April 27, 1988, p. 17.
2. Ibid.
3. Ibid.

PART ONE

Preparing for Teaching

CHAPTER 1

Having a Realistic View of Teaching

LOOKING BEYOND THE SURFACE FEATURES

One of the first requirements for success in any occupation is to have a good understanding of what that activity will require of you. Many people enter teaching with well-entrenched impressions and expectations of the work, but are dismayed to find the job significantly different from what they had anticipated. Having spent a good portion of their early lives in school classrooms, beginning teachers generally approach teaching with a feeling that they are reentering familiar territory. But as Lieberman and Miller describe it:

> After years of formal academic preparation, most teachers enter teaching and experience a common jolt. Equipped with theoretical understandings, they lack the practical knowledge that they need for survival.[1]

Some beginning teachers never fully recover from this initial jolt. As a result, the number of people who leave public school teaching in this country during the first several years of service continues to increase.[2] A significant number of those who end up making careers of teaching do so with diminished enthusiasm for the work, often expressing regret that they had not gone into some other occupation. The seriousness of this burnout problem among teaching professionals has become increasingly apparent.[3]

What is it about classroom teaching that makes it difficult for beginners to realistically anticipate and prepare for its impact? In the first place, there is the relative abruptness with which beginning teachers find themselves on their own in the classroom. Teaching is unique among professions in expecting new members to immediately perform the same responsibilities as people with ten or twenty years of service. In comparison with other occupations where novices initially spend longer periods of time in on-the-job training, and their job responsibilities increase with experience, teaching has turned out to be more of a "sink or swim" type occupation.

Furthermore, it is difficult to simulate live classroom dynamics or to prepare yourself subjectively for the teacher's role prior to having responsibility for a real classroom and a full schedule of teaching activities. Prior experiences such as observing and talking about teaching can help to prepare you intellectually but not emotionally for the real thing. There is a significant experiential gap between learning about and actually performing the work of a teacher. The flesh-and-blood realities of teaching must ordinarily be experienced in their full magnitude, in all-or-nothing fashion, for a would-be teacher to know their effects. Newcomers to the teaching profession often comment on the discontinuity between preparing to teach and being in charge of their own classrooms:

> Though I think I learned a lot from my preteaching seminars, nothing that was said or done in education classes could have prepared me for the gut-level aspects of day-to-day teaching. You can talk about it and do everything in your power to psych yourself up for the real thing, but the feeling of having complete control of a classroom full of students has to be a unique experience for someone just starting out.

> Managing your own classroom is totally different from helping in another teacher's class. I couldn't avoid feeling like a guest during my aiding and student teaching semesters. Now I'm feeling the full force of the responsibility for my own classroom. It isn't that my knowledge of teaching has increased that much, it's just that overnight I'm having to behave like a real teacher. Up to this point I've been a student.*

Finally, the standard occupational description tends to accentuate the most apparent and well-known aspects of the teacher's role, to the exclusion of other very important, but less tangible characteristics and requirements. For example, people cite the knowledge background required to teach school students; but they neglect to describe the personal qualities necessary to coexist with students in a school setting. Or, teaching is depicted as a job where you work with young people to help them "become something." But such a characterization gives little insight into the kind of becoming teachers themselves must undergo in order to excel at this type of work.

The following are underlying, but pervasive realities of public school teaching that you should be aware of if you are to be psychologically as well as technically prepared for this kind of work:

1. You will be spending your working hours in a confined setting with groups of young people for extended periods of time.
2. You must learn to manage multiple, fast-paced activities, and to continually perform control and maintenance functions.
3. You ordinarily work alone as a classroom teacher—making critical decisions, applying your professional skills, and experiencing the satisfactions and frustrations of the job in isolation from people who are doing essentially the same work.
4. You will need to take abstract, nonsituational knowledge and make it meaningful for young learners who will normally lack the motivation and life-experience to appreciate its import.

---

*As mentioned in the preface, the firsthand commentaries to be found at various points throughout the handbook were obtained by the author from personal journals of and personal interviews with the contributors.

5. You will be joining a *character-intensive* occupation—a kind of work that draws more heavily on your emotional and interpersonal resources than it does on your formal knowledge.

This chapter attempts to shed important light on these fundamental though less well-defined aspects of classroom teaching. Beyond that, the chapter offers tips and strategies for making reasonable and satisfactory adaptations to these realities of modern teaching.

BEING-WITH GROUPS OF YOUNG PEOPLE

One of the first and most important realities faced by beginning teachers is the need to continuously be with groups of young people for relatively long periods of time, usually under conditions of limited space and limited resources. Jackson notes that

> there is a social intimacy in schools that is unmatched elsewhere in our society. . . . Even factory workers are not clustered as close together as students in a standard classroom. . . . Imagine what would happen if a factory the size of a typical elementary school contained three or four hundred adult workers. In all likelihood the unions would not allow it. Only in schools do thirty or more people spend several hours each day literally side by side.[4]

Whether or not teachers and students treat one another with respect, whether or not they have productive times together, whether or not they come to care for one another as people—the certainty remains that they will be together again tomorrow, and the next day, and the day after that, same time and same place. The togetherness condition is such a widespread and fundamental feature of a teacher's work that it is often overlooked when considering job requirements. Yet, of the various job demands placed on public school teachers, there are good reasons for considering being-with-students to be even more fundamental to a teacher's work than the instructional or "bringing-them-to-know" requirement.

Also, what you manage to teach students will to a large extent depend on the way you coexist with them in the classroom. When your demeanor consistently reflects enthusiasm, inquisitiveness, and encouragement, you have a much greater chance of producing meaningful learning than when you deal with students listlessly, dogmatically, and disparagingly.[5]

The ability to consistently be-with young people cheerfully and respectfully calls for a special kind of resolve on the part of a classroom teacher. When people spend this much time together in prestructured relationships, it is easy for them to become tired of one another and the agendas that bring them together. Classroom groups are like families in that relationships among the members can easily reach the point where they become dull and matter-of-fact. The potential for teachers and students in today's schools to drift into apathy and gamesmanship is always present. When this happens routines and roles tend to dictate behavior, while personalities and interpersonal relations are deemphasized.

Maintaining a Positive Climate

For conscientious teachers, an important part of being-with young people is the ability to keep the classroom environment energized and upbeat. Often the best teachers are effective spiritual leaders before they are competent teachers of subject matter. These teachers realize that the group atmosphere out of which meaningful learning and positive human relations emerge is one that radiates respect for individual and group needs. What students learn from lectures, discussions, and assignments is invariably related to how they feel about themselves, one another, and the world around them. A healthy classroom environment reflects the notion that the quality of the student's personal being and being-with-others is the primary consideration. The formal knowledge these young people may come to possess is a derivative of this more fundamental condition. That is to say, if the first condition is not right, the second loses its significance.

To keep group relations from degenerating into stale routine is perhaps the toughest part of a teacher's job. The best teachers are able to maintain an interpersonal climate that brings the best out of the young people in their classes. They recognize when the group is losing its dynamic edge and are able to provide that needed spark, that injection of new energy, that keeps students interested and productive.

There is a definite art to being-with-students on an extended basis and continuing to foster a group atmosphere that is stimulating and constructive for both students and teacher. As a beginning teacher, it is important for you to learn to be-with-students in ways that are invigorating rather than monotonous, in ways that allow for periodic renewal of class atmosphere and learner motivation.

As an indication of your readiness to effectively meet the togetherness requirement of classroom teaching, you should take time to consider the following questions:

1. Although I may enjoy being in the company of young people, can I tolerate them when they are at their worst as well as when they are at their best? Do I presently have the patience and resilience to flow with the kinds of behavior I can expect when students are feeling irritable, nonresponsive, or needful of attention? Because the presence of peers tends to foster a wide variety of student behaviors, what can I do to prepare for the occasions when students will show off, use questionable language, or express dissatisfaction with my teaching? Will I be able to keep a sense of humor when I see behavior that indicates kids are simply being kids?

2. Will I be able to anticipate inevitable changes in group attitudes and intergroup relationships during the course of a school year? What do I know about group dynamics and group cycles? How will I know when my classes are ready to function as a group rather than as separate individuals. What are some main stages in the metamorphosis of classroom groups? How long will the "honeymoon" period last? Will I be able to recognize and adjust to normal stages in group development when students suddenly become critical and less cooperative? How can I avoid feeling depressed or insulted when classes suddenly become disinterested or preoccupied with things other than my lessons. How can I recognize times when groups are "peaked" to handle higher thinking operations or more challenging assignments?

3. Am I prepared to face the "overexposure problem" that is often created when people are together for extended periods and begin to tire of one another's voices, mannerisms, and personal agendas? Can I be sensitive to the fact that students as well as teachers have times when they need their privacy? Will I know when I am bearing down too hard or when I need to vary my style? What constructive measures can I take when I sense I might be getting tired of certain classes or particular students? Are there measures I can take to insure that teacher and students continue to respect one another's privacy and individuality? What are some effective renewal strategies I can use when I feel classroom relationships are beginning to lose their freshness?

4. What can I do to consistently model a positive and constructive approach to classroom business, even on days when I am feeling less than enthusiastic myself? Will I be able to leave distractive personal problems and agendas at home when I come to school in the morning? Can I consistently provide the positive initiative to get students back on track after a school vacation, a bad lesson, or a class interruption? Am I prepared emotionally to be "an adult with the young" in my own classes? What can I do about any inclination I may have to be a peer rather than an adult leader with my students?

5. Am I developing theories of human growth and development that will help me better understand the young people with whom I will be working? What social and emotional stages will my students likely be experiencing if they are seventh graders, seniors in high school, first graders, high school freshmen? At what grade levels are students most likely to exhibit strong emotional attachment to their teachers, be preoccupied with themselves and how they look, voice cynical attitudes toward adult authority, tend to say things they do not really mean, or exhibit a dominant need for acceptance and recognition by their peers? Do I have a basis for distinguishing between student behavior that is irritating but developmentally appropriate, and behavior that is both socially and developmentally unacceptable?

All of these considerations are explored in more detail later in this handbook (see chapter 5).

THE IMMEDIACY OF CLASSROOM EVENTS

In addition, you must prepare yourself to deal with the crowded atmosphere and rapid pace of classroom events that characterize both elementary and secondary schools. The fast tempo of school activity places a premium on a teacher's ability to make instant decisions, to monitor multiple events, and to maintain crowd control. The number of verbal transactions a classroom teacher performs during a typical day can be phenomenal. In his studies of schools and teachers, Jackson found that elementary teachers may engage in as many as 1,000 interpersonal exchanges in a day.[6] In fact, a teacher's job has been likened to that of a ringmaster in a circus. So it is not abnormal for beginning teachers to be apprehensive about their ability to control people and events as they take full responsibility for one or more classrooms. Such early anxiety is reflected in this comment of a first-year seventh-grade teacher:

> To some extent I like having to spring into action when the bell rings. But I can't think of any other job or even a fast sport where you have to be in control of all of your wits like you do in teaching. I find myself worrying that things might get out of hand. I know I'm spending too much time imagining scary situations and wondering how I'd deal with them. I've got to start thinking more positively because so far I've managed to stay on top of the action once it's underway.

The Need for Instant Decisions

With so much happening, and at such a lively pace, teachers rarely have time to think about what they are going to do next. They find themselves reacting to classroom situations before they are able to give deliberate thought to each of the many decisions they have to make. This is a practical reality of modern teaching that might call into question the widely held image of teaching as a rational process. In this connection, Jackson has discovered that most classroom teachers find it necessary to radically change their thinking processes as they move from planning to actual teaching:

> When grading exams, planning a lesson, or deciding what to do about a particularly difficult student, teaching looks like a rational process . . . When students are in front of him [or her], the teacher's behavior is more or less spontaneous . . . the teacher tends to do what he feels is right rather than what he reasons is right. . . . Amid all this hustle and bustle, the teacher often has little time to think.[7]

This gives us an insight into one of the main sources of stress for people just becoming acquainted with the world of classroom teaching. Their preparatory experience has fostered a rational approach to teaching and some sense of control over the teaching situations they will encounter. Now, as they enter the bustling world of the classroom, their sense of rational control is weakened. They feel themselves having to be dependent on their instincts and intuitions if they are to stay on top of fast-moving events.

The Need for Multiple Concentration

Because of the the complexity and abruptness of much classroom activity, you must be able to perform various tasks in quick succession and to manage a number of overlapping responsibilities. For example, while conducting a class discussion, you are called on to organize and present your own input, elicit and orchestrate student participation, attend and respond to student contributions, monitor the behavior of nonparticipating members, manage the time, and be able to integrate these different teaching behaviors into one smooth-flowing performance.

Jackson attempts to classify the ongoing managerial chores that compete for a teacher's time and attention in a typical elementary classroom. These tasks include: (1) deciding who shall and who shall not speak, (2) acting as a dispenser of supplies, (3) delegating duties and privileges, (4) serving as official timekeeper, and (5) directing movement within the classroom.[8]

To effectively manage these diverse responsibilities under classroom conditions involves a mental juggling act. It requires what one teaching authority has called *multiple concentration:*

> Multiple concentration is the ability to use many centers of the brain to process information, and based on that information, to reflexively act or speak with successful results. . . . It's the act of combining simple skills in a sequence or using several skills at the same time.[9]

The ability to perform complex teaching acts under busy classroom conditions seldom comes naturally for new teachers. Like most other compound skills, it is something that normally takes considerable practice before you can expect to be proficient (see chapter 12). However, there are several things you can do to help prepare for the rapid pace of classroom interaction.

1. Recognize that skillful interactive teaching is to a large extent a matter of effective mind control. There are some good readings available on this topic that are appropriate for teachers. One is Robert Nideffer's *Attention Control Training,* another is Timothy Gallwey's *The Inner Game of Tennis* (do not be misled by the title), and a third is Robert W. Travers' *The Making of a Teacher* (see chapter 4: Acquiring Affect, Poise, and Self-Control).[10]
2. Become involved in physical activities that require you to make instant decisions and to react spontaneously under pressure. Excellent examples are the martial arts, racketball, tennis, basketball, and other recreational activities that cause you to alternate between broad and narrow focuses of concentration while you are performing.
3. Continue to improve your powers of language and abstract thought through challenging reading, stimulating discussion, and other conceptual activities. The better you are with language, the more likely it is that your classroom input will be spontaneous and free-flowing. And the more capable you are of abstract thinking, the better grasp you will have of classroom processes and the more adept you will be at multiple concentration.[11]
4. Make a deliberate effort to exercise your skills of multiple concentration in social and formal group situations. Practice your abilities to structure conversation, to draw others into discussion, to respond to other's ideas, to attend to nonverbal behaviors, and to alternate between talking and listening all at one time. Your ability to do this in your everyday life should pay dividends as you are called on to apply multiple concentration in the classroom.
5. Find opportunities to observe the behaviors of performers, like talk-show hosts, whose job it is to orchestrate spirited group interaction under pressure. Make note of the kinds of mental acts they are able to perform in a relatively short space of time. What techniques do they appear to be using to help them remain poised and under control in pressure situations (e.g., breathing movement, humor)? Assess their abilities to think and make decisions on their feet. How good are their powers of multiple concentration? Also attempt to rate their languaging skills and their levels of self-confidence and personal assertiveness.

The Emphasis on Control

Another central fact of life in busy, crowded schools is the emphasis placed on management and control. This has a direct bearing on a teacher's job description, particularly in a modern high school. At the high school level the press of numbers and the desire for crowd control has led to an organizational approach that facilitates the processing of students. Lieberman and Miller describe this system as follows:

> Life in schools is life in crowds, for both teachers and students. Because of the large number of students in any given high school, "batch processing" is the order of the day. So that students can be processed in batches, schools divide their days into discrete units of time for the purpose of distinct subject matter instruction. Students and teachers move through the building in mass, and they move every 50 minutes or so on the average of six times a day. Most teachers teach 125 to 150 students in a day.[12]

This organizational feature accounts for the constant movement and the repetitiveness that characterize life in most high schools. It means teachers have to conduct at least five separate classes a day, making it difficult to maintain the kind of freshness necessary to perform at one's best.[13]

The school's preoccupation with control and maintenance often detracts from a teacher's ability to give full attention to actual teaching. The management system of the school requires teachers to take on a variety of noninstructional duties, tasks that contribute to the maintenance of the system. They include monitoring and recording student attendance and promptness, as well as supervisory responsibilities in school corridors, lunchrooms, study halls, and parking lots. As Lieberman and Miller point out, the need to spend so much time attending to the control function can create nagging priority conflicts:

> This recognition of the need for control places teachers in a contradictory position. On the one hand, they want to spend their time doing what they are trained to do, and that is to teach. On the other hand, in order for instruction to take place, order must be maintained. Teachers view this role as a necessary evil; it "comes with the territory."[14]

The system of processing students, designed to maximize order and control, can also have serious effects on what and how a teacher teaches. Teaching patterns become shaped by the tension between the contradictory goals of educating students and those of controlling them and moving them through the system.[15] In the case of secondary teachers, breaking the school day into fifty-minute class periods limits a teacher's ability to promote in-depth learning. Also, it can result in disjointed lessons and cause teachers to feel rushed. It assumes that students and teachers can effectively turn frames of reference on and off as they move from one class to another and from one subject to another. Liberman and Miller observe that

> as soon as students walk into the room, they are supposed to switch frames of reference. For teachers, a similar switch is necessary. Teachers are expected to put aside the concerns of the previous class and to concentrate on the one sitting in front of them at the present moment. . . . Every teacher makes a separate peace with this concern. . . . For some, the solution is to keep things routine.[16]

Every teacher, then, must come to grips with the problems and contradictions created when schools emphasize controlling and processing functions at the expense of teaching. There are some important things you can do to help insure that the control function is not allowed to dominate your teaching. Consider the following measures:

1. Develop a well-defined set of overriding objectives that allow you to keep your teaching priorities in proper focus (see chapter 3). Make teaching your number one priority and treat the organizational and managerial responsibilities as support activities.

2. Use motivational techniques that are learning-based rather than control-based. Make it a practice to stimulate learning activity by appealing to students' interests, curiosities, and problem-solving inclinations rather than to their fears, anxieties, and competitive instincts. Techniques for achieving this are discussed in chapter 6.

3. Find workable strategies for dealing with system-imposed interruptions, transitions, and time limitations. Attempt to provide the best possible learning environment in your own classroom, and be protective of your teaching space. Develop efficient techniques for getting students into proper learning "sets" after they come in out of the halls, and after breaks and interruptions. Find ways of making appropriate use of teaching sessions, whatever their length. (Chapter 2 is devoted to ideas and strategies for making a creative adaptation to the organizational structure of the school.)

4. Develop a system for achieving classroom control that supports rather than interferes with teaching. Adopt effective low-profile class management techniques that flow with your teaching, techniques that make the control function subordinate to teaching and learning. An in-depth treatment of ideas and strategies for accomplishing this is presented in chapter 9.

5. Create an effective system for handling the organizational and managerial tasks of teaching so they do not become preoccupations. Learn to approach required paperwork, supervisory responsibilities, and other bureaucratic chores in good spirit, but with the kind of efficiency and dispatch that allows you to devote your best energies to teaching. Chapter 2 provides more detailed strategies for achieving this goal.

6. Use the inevitable conflicts and distractions as a motivating factor for you in your teaching. Prepare yourself to face the organizational contradictions that are inherent to public schooling in this country (see chapter 2). Realize that in *character-intensive* occupations like teaching, successful practitioners are those who find the energy and commitment to rise above the built-in conflicts and resistances of the system. (The concept of *character-intensive* occupations is developed later in this unit.)

ALONE IN A BUSY WORLD

Although teachers spend a great deal of time interacting with young people in the school, they seldom develop close professional relationships with their peers. Gene Maeroff describes the situation in these succinct terms:

> More than many other occupations, teaching is practiced in isolation—an isolation that is crushing at times. Collegiality is nonexistent for many teachers, unless hurried lunches over plastic trays in lunchrooms are viewed as exercises in colleagueship.[17]

This is another fact of life in U.S. schools that should to be taken into consideration by anyone planning to make a career of teaching.

For purposes of instructional planning, solving classroom problems, and cultivating new skills, the tendency is for teachers to function in isolation from one another and from outside sources of new information. John Goodlad has attempted to document the extent and seriousness of the isolation problem among U.S. teachers:

> The classroom cells in which teachers spend much of their time appear to me to be symbolic and predictive of their relative isolation from one another and from sources of ideas beyond their own background of experience. . . . We compiled a substantial amount of data pertaining to teacher's links to sources of influence in their teaching and to one another. The teachers we studied had some association with others . . . but rather brief and casual associations. . . . There was little to suggest active, ongoing exchanges of ideas and practices. . . . A large majority said they never observed instruction in other classrooms.[18]

Teachers generally work alone in separate classrooms, and are responsible for their own lessons, evaluational devices, and managerial policies. But, even when teachers are together between classes or during lunch, the culture of the school tends to militate against the serious sharing of ideas relating to what they do in the classroom. Whereas they may find it easy to talk about external matters like politics or recreational interests, teachers are generally more reticent to discuss interests, problems, and strategies having to do with their own teaching. Lieberman and Miller comment on this reality of school life:

> While relations with students tend to be immediate, direct, and engaging, relations with peers may be characterized as remote, oblique, and defensively protective. The rule of privacy governs peer interactions in a school. It is all right to talk about the news, the weather, sports, and sex. It is all right to complain in general about the school and the students. However, it is not acceptable to discuss instruction and what happens in classrooms as colleagues.[19]

One of the reasons teachers are disinclined to share professional concerns with one another is the need to have a break from classroom business when they are away from students. Full-time teaching requires a good deal of time and energy, so most teachers look for relief from this highly involving activity when they leave the classroom. There is often an unspoken agreement not to "talk shop" when teachers meet between classes or on social occasions.

Another reason is the inevitable differences in motivation and skill level among teachers, which leads to subtle competitions and professional jealousies within a school faculty. Teachers who are struggling with teaching and control problems are normally reluctant to discuss or solicit help for their problems, particularly in the teacher's room, for fear of being perceived as incompetents. In the words of one early career teacher of secondary English:

> I'd like to know how other teachers in the school deal with some of these smart alecky seniors. I can't be the only one these kids wise-off to. But everyone seems to act so self-assured about their teaching when we're together in the teacher's room. I'm caught between wanting to share my problem and fearing the possible consequences of my honesty. I don't want to be seen as the weak sister in the group.

Similarly, highly competent teachers are often inclined to keep their success stories and teaching ideas to themselves, sensing that colleagues might view it as bragging.

One of the problematic effects of teacher isolation is its tendency to inhibit teacher growth and to discourage the joint efforts of teachers to work together for needed improvements in their schools. Goodlad's studies have shown this to be a nagging problem:

> The teachers we studied appeared, in general, to function quite autonomously. But their autonomy seemed to be exercised in a context more of isolation than of rich professional dialogue with a plethora of challenging educational alternatives. . . . Teachers rarely worked together on schoolwide problems. . . . Teacher-to-teacher links for mutual assistance or collaborative school improvement were weak or nonexistent. . . . Although outside resource people were available, they drew upon them only a little and said that they were of limited value.[20]

The relative isolation of classroom teaching can produce chronic feelings of loneliness for teachers who are not prepared to face this basic reality of the job. The need to continually plan and work alone in a human-service occupation like teaching is an emphatic test of a teacher's self-confidence and personal resourcefulness. New teachers, in particular, may experience periods of insecurity and self-doubt on realizing that the long-term responsibilities for teaching objectives, lesson content, student discipline, and other important decisions rest exclusively on their shoulders.

The following are steps you can take to overcome the professional isolation of classroom teaching:

1. Find opportunities to team teach periodically with other teachers in your school. This can ordinarily be arranged for one or more periods if two people have the will to make it work. Planning and sharing teaching responsibilities with a compatible colleague can be an enlightening and enjoyable experience. It provides you with an opportunity to share practical strategies for teaching, to observe a different teaching style, and to solicit constructive feedback on your own teaching patterns.

2. Ask a trusted colleague to visit one of your classes on occasion. This can be an opportunity to get constructive feedback and suggestions from someone other than an administrator. Offer to exchange visits if that is feasible. Besides being a chance to receive ideas that may add to your teaching, a visit from a fellow teacher can be an opportunity to show things that you do particularly well, to

unveil a classroom "act" that to this point has gone unappreciated by the other adults in the school.

3. Make arrangements to visit other teachers and other schools from time to time. Once having completed their preservice teaching requirements, many full-time teachers become mired in their own classrooms for extended periods of time without ever getting a glimpse of fellow teachers in action. Their professional frames of reference become limited to what they see and do in their own classrooms. By making arrangements to periodically observe other teachers and other school settings, you are able to achieve a broader, more up-to-date perspective on your own teaching.

4. Read several professional journals. Professional reading will allow you to keep abreast of major topics and issues in U.S. education as well as new ideas and developments in the areas that you teach. Use professional reading as a means of keeping yourself in touch with other active and inquiring minds within the profession.

5. Volunteer for curriculum development projects and other constructive professional activities. Take opportunities to attend educational conferences and meetings where you can share professional concerns with other educators. Make it a point to be involved in activities that will help you keep a fresh perspective on your teaching. School districts are generally willing to hire substitutes for teachers who wish to pursue professional growth activities on school time.

THE ABSTRACT NATURE OF FORMAL TEACHING

Another reality that makes a teacher's job uniquely challenging is the abstract nature of teaching and learning in a school setting. School learning tends to be quite artificial in comparison with the learning young people experience outside of school. As Gardner reminds us

> Authorities generally agree that, outside of schooled settings, children acquire skills through observation and participation in the contexts in which these skills are customarily invoked. In contrast, in the standard classroom, teachers talk, often presenting material in abstract symbolic form and relying on inanimate media such as books and diagrams in order to convey information. Schooling generally treats subject matter that one cannot readily see or touch, even as those sensory modes of taking in information seem singularly inappropriate for most school tasks.[21]

Most people, young or old, learn best when they are actively involved in real-life situations that call for new competencies or new understandings. They learn more effectively when their own perceived needs and purposes are at stake and when they can learn at their own pace. Formal education, however, is based on the premise that responsible participation in a complex society requires certain understandings and abilities that people cannot be expected to acquire through life experience. The only way young people can learn some things about the world is from a distance, or nonsituationally. They need to learn certain life skills apart from and prior to the occasions when they will have use for them.

This creates a difficult dilemma for the school. It has a responsibility to prepare young people for life outside the school, yet in attempting to accomplish this it finds itself working against the grain of human nature. By definition *nonsituational learning* is abstract learning because it is removed from the context in which it has application. In order for it to be meaningful, the learner must possess a sufficient backlog of ideas and experiences to make a personal connection with the new ideas. As Frank Smith maintains:

> Making sense of what is going on is something all school children must do if there is to be any chance that they will learn, and they must do this by relating the situations they find themselves in to prior knowledge. . . . So a primary concern of teachers must be with what children already know, if only to avoid making impossible demands on them by confronting them with nonsense.[22]

Nonsituational learning also places a premium on learner imagination and mind control, because learners must be able to construct mental images of objects, events, people, and situations that lie beyond the school environment, and be able to do this on cue. When teachers ask students to conceptualize happenings of the Civil War era or to appreciate a poem satirizing life in metropolitan New York, the students must instantaneously formulate mental representations of distant objects and events if they are to meaningfully process this kind of school learning.[23]

The more mature the learner, the more likely that person is to possess the necessary motivation, perception, imagination, and mental organization to profit from nonsituational learning. To the consternation of many adults, most precollege young people are not highly proficient abstract learners. They find it difficult to remove themselves mentally from their immediate environments and to occupy themselves with realities that have no concrete referents for them at this stage in their lives.[24] These students can be expected to have problems coping with instruction that is exclusively verbal. When they are forced to learn nonmeaningful material, they usually end up simply going through the motions. Under these conditions the learning becomes elusive and artificial, and the learner often becomes disinterested, frustrated, and a behavior problem for the teacher.

In order to make formal learning more than a mechanical and impersonal game, you must be prepared to offset the inherent deficiencies of nonsituational learning. A large part of your instructional task will involve building-in the context, incentive, perception, and feedback that is naturally present when people learn experientially through normal give-and-take with their environments. Techniques for accomplishing this should represent the basis of sound teaching methods. Chapters 6, 7, and 8 contain practical suggestions for making classroom learning less abstract and more meaningful for young learners at all levels.

In the meantime, the following are some central guidelines that you should keep in mind as you attempt to compensate for the abstract nature of formal teaching and learning:

1. Make an effort to provide as much context as possible when introducing new learning. Grounded understanding depends on the formation of new relation-

ships. People learn best when new learning makes a connection with existing perceptions, abilities, and understandings. You can help put students in a frame of mind or "mental set" to see those relationships when you begin lessons by providing relevant background information, by posing problems, or by challenging student's existing knowledge structures.

2. Give students practice in imaging and projecting themselves into life situations beyond the confines of the school. Students often need vivid imaginations to profit from abstract learning. You can assist them in cultivating such imagination by taking opportunities to apply visualization techniques and other devices that will help students identify with learning situations that lie outside the boundaries of the school.

3. Become proficient in the use of visual aids and other concrete props to help make your teaching less abstract. Use a wide variety of teaching supplements, including physical objects, newspapers, films, role plays, simulations, and so on, to provide concrete references and high-quality vicarious experiences for your students. Make every effort to bring the outside world into your classroom.

4. Personalize your teaching by consistently addressing student's existing perceptions, needs, experiences, and understandings as they relate to new learning. Develop a learner-centered teaching style that attempts as often as possible to proceed from questions and inquiries rather than from information and conclusions. Make it a practice to appeal to student's interests, ideas, and values in the second person, for example, "How will *we* know when . . . ," "What would *you* do if . . . ," "How does this look to *you?*"

5. Take steps to make school learning an active rather than a passive process. Outside of school we generally learn by doing, through constant transactions with our environments. Design your learning activities so students will have to use some of their own initiative, thinking ability, and problem-solving strategy; always attempt to structure lessons so students will have to give something of themselves to the new learning.

6. Provide continuous opportunities for students to practice new learning and to receive appropriate feedback on their progress. In out-of-school situations people normally learn things that have current relevance to their lives. This means they get ongoing practice and immediate feedback to determine whether or not the new learning works. In order to maximize school learning, teachers should attempt to simulate this out-of-school learning process as closely as possible.

TEACHING AS CHARACTER-INTENSIVE WORK

People frequently come to teaching expecting a more technically exacting type of work, the sort of activity where a skilled performance will ordinarily produce certain positive and measurable results. They assume that the knowledge base they acquired in college will be the main prerequisite to success in teaching. With formal education being an integral part of the "knowledge business," successful classroom teaching is widely thought to depend on the academic backgrounds and technical training teachers bring to it. The best teachers, so it is imagined, are highly knowledgeable people who are able to transmit their ideas and know-how directly to the uninitiated.

There is a problem, however in considering teaching to be knowledge-based or knowledge-intensive work in the same sense that engineering, television repairing, and accounting are knowledge-intensive pursuits. In these latter occupations, persons with the appropriate technical knowledge and ability to apply it can ordinarily be successful in their respective jobs. Job requirements normally entail a relatively direct application of that knowledge to materially manipulable and controllable tasks. These are occupations where other human qualities may also be necessary, but where special knowledge and/or skill is the most critical determinant of success.

Teaching is a fundamentally different kind of activity. It is a type of work where to a large extent success is often dependent on variables that are difficult to control through specialized knowledge, for example, the attitudes and behaviors of other people. Like some jobs in nursing, police work, social work, and certain other human-service occupations, modern-day teaching asks you to apply your knowledge in settings where the odds may often be stacked against you. The situations you are attempting to control or influence are human situations where you frequently must contend with the resistances, skill deficiencies, and differing agendas of the people you are serving.

Whereas a great many jobs are primarily physically or intellectually challenging, teaching is an occupation that also draws heavily on your inner resources. It will require the application of your total personality rather than simply the specialized knowledge or technical skill you have acquired. Lightfoot makes the point this way:

> It is difficult to disentangle teacher character from teacher competence. . . . The teacher is deeply engaged in his work as a whole person because an effect is required on the student as a whole person. . . . Teachers make use of powerful affective resources to motivate learning by developing empathetic relationships with students.[25]

Public school teaching tests the emotional maturity of an individual to a much greater extent than most knowledge-intensive jobs. It is the kind of activity that often involves interacting with other people under stressful conditions. So in addition to the more obvious knowledge requirements, it calls for substantial investments in patience, empathy, and human concern.

Good teaching requires an abiding strength of commitment to one's occupational mission, a kind of singlemindedness that allows a person to cut through distractions and bureaucratic tangles, refusing to be distracted by the conflicts, frustrations, and adversities that seem to go with the job. Arthur Combs defines accomplished teachers as those who are able to use themselves effectively to carry out their own and society's purposes in the education of others:

> Research has shown that effective teaching is the product of certain kinds of purposes. . . . The good teacher sees his appropriate role as one of commitment to the helping process. . . . He has trust in his own organism. He sees himself as essentially dependable, as having the potentiality for coping with events. . . . He is not exclusively concerned with details but can perceive beyond the immediate to the future.[26]

As a teacher, you can expect to see some of your best efforts go unrecognized and unappreciated. You must be prepared to give more than you can hope to get back in the way of social or material reward. This is in contrast to many knowledge- and skill-based occupations where outstanding performances are more visible and more highly remunerated, and where workers generally have a greater degree of personal control over the outcomes of their work.

With these considerations in mind, it becomes appropriate to regard teaching in its most fundamental sense as character-intensive work, a type of occupation in which what you are as a person counts for as much as what you know. Failure to recognize its character-dependent nature leads to an unfortunate misidentification of what it takes to achieve success and fulfillment as a teacher in today's schools.

In appreciating the character-intensive nature of teaching, there are a number of important things you can do as a beginning teacher to make a reasonable and productive accommodation to this prevailing feature of the work. Many relevant ideas and suggestions are presented in chapter 2 under the subheadings Maintaining Transsystem Perspectives, Staying Vital, Dealing with Conflicting Agendas, The Self-actualizing Teacher, and Coming to Terms with the System. In the meantime, here are some general recommendations for adapting to the character-dependent nature of classroom teaching:

1. Recognize that in a character-intensive occupation like teaching your major satisfactions will need to be internally rather than externally derived. Money, prestige, and material achievements are less available in teaching than in most other professions, so you should be cognizant of the more intangible or hidden benefits teaching has to offer. The remaining section of this unit examines some of these more subjective rewards and suggests steps you can take to avail yourself of teaching's special opportunities.

2. Accept the day-to-day challenges of classroom teaching and realize the positive byproducts to be derived from character-intensive work. Some of the important side effects of teaching can be increased self-confidence, a better command of language, and substantial increases in interpersonal skill. Teaching tends to be excellent basic training for a wide variety of other opportunities and challenges likely to be experienced in life.

3. Continue to cultivate your people skills as universal keys to success and fulfillment in teaching. Your skills at human interaction are fundamental to this kind of work. The ability to be a sensitive and articulate conversationalist pays high dividends in teaching. This includes the patience and empathy to be a caring listener, and the aptitudes for entering into genuine two-way communication with others (see chapters 8 and 12).

THE INTANGIBLE REWARDS

It may be said that teaching is an occupation with hidden challenges, but it is also a job that contains a number of intangible benefits for those who are able to appreciate them. Just as it is essential for you as a beginning teacher to be realistic about the challenges, it is also important for you to be aware of the nonmaterial rewards that accompany this sort of work.

One of those benefits is the personal growth opportunities provided by classroom teaching. In comparison to a great many other occupations, including most jobs requiring primarily technical skill, teaching is a totally involving kind of work that continually utilizes your emotional and interpersonal resources as well as your technical knowledge. Having made the classroom plunge, one is pressed to develop these resources at an accelerated rate in order to meet the demands of the job. Early career teachers have been known to make dramatic leaps in self-confidence, language and public speaking ability, and interpersonal competence after concentrated exposure to classroom teaching. With few exceptions, those who experience the exigencies of classroom teaching find themselves much better prepared for child raising, community service activities, alternative career opportunities, and other personal and interpersonal challenges.

Another occupational benefit that tends to be unique to teaching is the opportunity for a teacher to recharge during summers and other school vacations. This job perquisite is usually described simply as "having your summers and vacations to yourself," a characterization that may fail to convey the essence of what this time away from the classroom can do for you. Teaching is the kind of work that requires a constant supply of emotional and creative energy, thus you must be able to periodically step back and find ways to replenish these crucial resources. Also, in an activity like teaching where people are especially prone to becoming stale, it is necessary to occasionally recreate your approach to the job. Quality time away from school can allow you the opportunity to do these things.[27]

A third attractive feature is the opportunity to work with developing young people. You will have occasion to spend your working hours in the presence of people who are in the prime of life. Although these hours spent with the young can be personally demanding, they can also be gratifying and rejuvenating. Contrary to what their overt behavior may suggest, most students are still experimenting, caring, trusting, and searching for an accommodation to the world around them. You will ordinarily get them in school before they have become cynical and jaded, before they develop the ego barriers that make them unapproachable. In short, there is something refreshing and inspiriting about a job that entails working with young learners, however frustrating and exhausting it may be at times. Being in their company keeps you on the cutting-edge of what is new and vibrant in a society where many jobs tend to be lifeless and uninspiring.

Finally, an aspect of teaching that has been regarded as a liability, namely, the fact that you work apart from other adults, in some respects can be a positive feature of the job. For creative teachers, working alone turns out to be a blessing in disguise. Once you are in the classroom on your own, you have a private work space you can use to develop your own style. This enclave separate from the rest of the school may be thought of as a studio where you can develop your own unique talents and interests as they apply to teaching and learning. It is a place where you can do special things with your own students. Teaching, then, is an occupation where you can have considerable privacy to create an environment that is uniquely yours, and within that special environment, to perform the act of teaching largely to your own specifications.

As a new teacher, consider the following things you can begin to do to take advantage of teaching's latent rewards:

1. Recognize what it takes to continue to grow in this profession. Beginning teachers often make dramatic personal and professional gains during the first several

years, then settle into nongrowth patterns for the remainder of their careers. Chapter 2 offers ideas and strategies for overcoming serious occupational hurdles and achieving a "creative orientation" as a teacher.

2. Develop a life-style that supports your need for consistent renewal as a teacher. Use your summers and shorter vacations to accomplish recreation in the generic sense of the word. Teachers frequently fall into do-nothing patterns during their time away from school. The kind of recreation-style they adopt is often counterproductive in terms of their need for personal renewal. It can cause a teacher to come back to school feeling more lethargic and out-of-sync than before. An especially good source of ideas on the type of recreation we are talking about here is Bruno Hans Geba's *Being at Leisure: Playing at Life*.[28]

3. Allow yourself to experience the unique satisfactions that can come from working with young learners. Learn to savor those special moments in teaching when you are glad you have chosen to work with youngsters rather than adults. Accept the fact that you are forfeiting opportunities to be around people who are more knowledgeable, stable, and predictable, for the chance to work with those who are naive, restless, and unfinished. Make this one of your main reasons for being there.

4. Take advantage of the special things you can do *because* you have a classroom to yourself. Make the most of opportunities to rearrange the furniture, bring in exciting materials, and use unorthodox approaches, without having to get someone's else's permission. Short of exhibiting bad taste or becoming an impossible eccentric, allow yourself to do things in the classroom that represent your own special interests and talents.

SUGGESTED ACTIVITIES AND QUESTIONS

1. What are some of the things that appeal to you about teaching as an occupation? Do you think of teaching as a glamorous kind of work? What are some common misconceptions about the work of a teacher? How do these ideas become established?

2. What are some of the lingering images you have of teachers from your own days in school? Try writing a description of several teachers that continue to stand out in your mind from your school experiences. Do you have favorable or unfavorable recollections of these people? What kinds of roles do you suppose these teachers were attempting to play (e.g., stern taskmaster, everybody's friend, subject-matter specialist)?

3. How do you see your own role as you enter the field of teaching? Do you have particular objectives you want to accomplish in teaching? What kinds of role conflicts do you anticipate as a classroom teacher?

4. Find occasions to talk with six to eight classroom teachers about what they perceive their main roles to be. Which among these various role perceptions do you consider to be most realistic? Most idealistic? Why?

5. How do you feel about a job where one of the main requirements is being able to control groups of people? As you imagine yourself in a teaching situation, how would you attempt to resolve the potential conflict between your role as a control specialist and your responsibilities as a facilitator of learning? Have you been in other responsible positions in your life where you felt there were conflicting expectations placed on you (e.g., military service)?

6. What do you anticipate will be some of the main problems you encounter as a teacher? Attempt to identify things you can begin to do to help make these expected problems less severe.

7. What are your present thoughts and feelings about working in a school environment all day with groups of young people? What special qualities do you possess that would allow you to adapt well to the "togetherness condition" of teaching? Are there some specific things you might do to make it easier for you and your students to "live together" over the long stretch?

8. In terms of its pressures, teaching has been compared to the job of an air-traffic controller. How does this comparison strike you? Do you see any other points of similarity? What are the dissimilarities?

9. Try to remember times when you have found yourself in environments that were highly unfamiliar or when you have felt overwhelmed by busyness, noise, movement, and so forth. Attempt to describe the sort of shock you felt. What were some of the things you did to attempt to deal with the problem? How long did it take you to adjust to these situations? What did you learn on these occasions that can help you as a teacher?

10. Describe some of the ways people deal with the "stimulus overload" they experience in situations like teaching. What sorts of defense mechanisms do people typically rely on in these instances? Describe what you would consider positive adaptations to the shock we sometimes experience under these conditions. What would you regard as less constructive types of responses?

NOTES AND REFERENCES

1. Ann Lieberman and Lynne Miller, *Teachers, Their World, and Their Work.* Alexandria, Va: Association for Supervision and Curriculum Development, 1984, p. 7.

2. Kevin Ryan observes that "teaching increasingly is becoming a short-term career, with the average teacher leaving the profession in less than ten years. Teachers who have unsuccessful and unpleasant early experiences do not make strong commitments and often begin to look for ways to escape from teaching," (in Kevin Ryan, *The Induction of New Teachers.* Bloomington, Ind.: Phi Delta Kappa Educational Foundation, 1986, p. 8.). Recent figures show that 40 percent of all new teachers leave the profession by the end of the second year (report of the National Governor's Association, Center for Policy Research and Analysis, *Time for Results,* August 1986, p. 37.)

3. See Sara Freedman, Jane Jackson, and Katherine Boles, "Teaching: An Imperilled Profession." In Lee S. Shulman and Gary Sykes (Eds.), *Handbook of Teaching and Policy.* New York: Longman, 1983, pp. 261–99.

4. Philip W. Jackson, *Life in Classrooms.* New York: Holt, Rinehart and Winston, 1968, p. 8.

5. Richard C. Sprinthall and Norman A. Sprinthall, *Educational Psychology: A Developmental Approach,* 3rd ed. Reading, Mass.: Addison-Wesley, 1981, p. 393.

6. Jackson, op. cit., p. 11.

7. Philip W. Jackson, "Talking About Teaching." In Kevin Ryan and James Cooper (Eds.), *Kaleidoscope, Readings in Education,* 3rd ed. Boston: Houghton Mifflin, 1980, p. 229.

8. Jackson, *Life in Classrooms,* op. cit., p. 12.

9. Joseph Hasenstab and Connie Wilson, *Training the Teacher as a Champion.* Nevada City, Calif.: Performance Learning Systems, 1989, p. 75.

10. See Robert M. Nideffer and Roger C. Sharpe, *A.C.T. Attention Control Training.* New York: Wyden Books, 1978; W. Timothy Gallwey, *The Inner Game of Tennis.* New York:

Bantam Books, 1974; and Robert W. Travers and Jacqueline Dillon, *The Making of a Teacher: A Plan for Professional Self-development.* New York: Macmillan, 1975. In his book, Nideffer offers some premises that are basic to the attention control techniques he would advocate for teachers: "When you're anxious your ability to deal with a large amount of information is reduced. . . . Knowing *what* you should pay attention to is critical. When people feel uncertain in a situation, they tend to try to pay attention to everything. At that very time attention is narrow and you're least able to succeed. By taking time for some advance planning, you can stop the tendency to overload yourself" (p. 59).

11. Norman A. Sprinthall and Lois Thies-Sprinthall, "Educating for Teacher Growth: A Cognitive Developmental Perspective." *Theory Into Practice* 19, no. 4, pp. 278–85.

12. Lieberman and Miller, op. cit., p. 40.

13. See Stuart B. Palonsky, *900 Shows a Year: A Look at Teaching from a Teacher's Side of the Desk.* New York: Random House, 1986; and Theodore R. Sizer, *Horace's Compromise: The Dilemma of the American High School.* Boston: Houghton Mifflin, 1984.

14. Lieberman and Miller, op. cit., p. 41.

15. See Linda M. McNeil, "Contradictions of Control, Part 1: Administrators and Teachers." *Phi Delta Kappan,* January 1988, pp. 333–39.

16. Lieberman and Miller, op. cit., p. 42.

17. Gene I. Maeroff, "A Blueprint for Empowering Teachers." *Phi Delta Kappan,* March 1988, p. 474.

18. John I. Goodlad, *A Place Called School.* New York: McGraw Hill, 1984, pp. 186–87.

19. Lieberman and Miller, op. cit., p. 11.

20. Goodlad, op. cit., pp. 186–87.

21. Howard Gardner, *Frames of Mind: The Theory of Multiple Intelligences.* New York: Basic Books, 1983, p. 357.

22. Frank Smith, *Comprehension and Learning: A Conceptual Framework for Teachers.* New York: Holt, Rinehart and Winston, 1975, p. 10.

23. Rosemary A. Rosser and Glen I. Nicholson, *Educational Psychology: Principles in Practice.* Boston: Little, Brown, 1984, pp. 487–89.

24. N. L. Gage and David C. Berliner, *Educational Psychology,* 4th ed. Boston: Houghton Mifflin, 1988, p. 128.

25. Sara Lawrence Lightfoot, "The Lives of Teachers." In Lee S. Shulman and Gary Sykes (Eds.), *Handbook of Teaching and Policy.* New York: Longman, 1983, p. 250.

26. Arthur W. Combs, *The Professional Education of Teachers: A Perceptual View of Teacher Preparation.* Boston: Allyn and Bacon, 1965, pp. 71, 85.

27. It becomes important, though, for you to learn how to achieve personal and professional renewal during vacations from work. Just being away from the job does not guarantee it. For this reason, you should regard vacation time as a potential benefit to you in your professional life. It becomes an actual benefit when you are able to use it to further your professional growth.

28. See Bruno Hans Geba, *Being at Leisure, Playing at Life.* La Mesa, Calif.: Leisure Science Systems International, 1985.

CHAPTER 2

Learning to Work Creatively within the System

THE NATURE OF THE CHALLENGE

Probably the most formidable challenge facing you as a beginning teacher is being able to adapt to the demands and pressures of the school organization without sacrificing your initiative and creativity as a teaching specialist.[1] The sort of personal accommodation you make to the system itself can have an important bearing on whether you achieve a degree of professional autonomy in classroom teaching or settle for the role of functionary within the school bureaucracy. It helps to have a good initial understanding of how the system works and how it can affect your teaching patterns.

Most first-year teachers have to work their way through an initial *survival period* where their main concern is demonstrating to themselves and others that they are capable of being a teacher.[2] During this adjustment period their main energies are usually devoted to coping with class schedules, time pressures, class management problems, and other such urgencies. The survival stage is typically a short one, however. Novice teachers will ordinarily move rather quickly through this time of doubt and instability, arriving at a set of routines that allow them to reduce the pressures and make the job more manageable. Having become familiar with organizational patterns, they are inclined to be less security-minded and primarily concerned with adapting their workaday situation to align more closely with their own personal needs and preferences.[3]

This second level of accommodation, or *pragmatic orientation,* often turns out to be an occupational plateau from which many teachers never advance. By continuing to devote their best resources to the organizational and managerial aspects of teaching, a person may learn to play the role sufficiently well to keep a job, but never develop the autonomy, sensitivity, and classroom maneuverability that characterize a *creative orientation* to this work. The resulting occupational rut can lead to serious job dissatisfaction and professional burnout.[4] The task, then, is to arrive at a relationship to the system that allows one to continue to grow as a teacher.

This chapter offers insight into the requirements for creative teacher performance in a school organization. It discusses the factors that contribute to lifeless, routine-bound teaching and offers perspectives and strategies for achieving a transsystem orientation, for managing conflicting roles and agendas, and for maintaining one's vitality and integrity in the institutional setting.

Patterns of Accommodation

By recognizing the variety and sequence of accommodations teachers normally make to school systems, and by anticipating the institutional forces that can serve to inhibit teacher growth, you are in a better position to confront the organizational hurdles that must be surmounted if you are to achieve your potential as a public school teacher. This section describes in more detail the three levels of system accommodation already mentioned, namely the *survival orientation,* the *pragmatic orientation,* and the *creative orientation.*[5] By regarding these as stages of teacher development, you have a framework for conceptualizing the kind of professional growth you can realistically aspire to within a modern school bureaucracy.

The Survival Orientation.   As beginning professionals, teachers at the survival level find themselves preoccupied with personal adequacy and job security. They are concerned with getting and holding a job, controlling their classes, and satisfying students and supervisors. These concerns are apparent in the following statements of three first-year teachers:

> I'm enjoying my classes so far, but right now I'm a little nervous about the evaluation I've got coming up. I'll be cruising along just fine until someone comes in and sits down in the back of my classroom. I couldn't stand to get a bad evaluation at this stage.

> It's especially important to me that I get off to a good start with my classes. I want my students to like me. If they like you, they'll be more cooperative and you'll have a better chance of getting through your first year without serious discipline problems. So having good rapport with my students is one of my most important goals right now.

> At the moment I'm mainly interested in finding a job. I've been told that social science positions are quite scarce. But I've been in school too long to spend another year without work.

Survival-oriented teachers often feel overwhelmed by the enormity of their new responsibilities. Their first encounters with the complexities of classroom teaching tend to be disorienting, causing them to limit their fields of vision as they react frantically, sometimes mechanically, to the fast-moving, multiple agendas of a typical teaching day.[6]

Being predominantly concerned with their own performances, survival-oriented teachers often fail to attend to other critical aspects of the teaching situation. They may have difficulty keeping their fingers on the "pulse of the class," or reading and responding to cues that strategy adjustments are in order. As a result, teachers at this level can be expected to have some initial difficulty with classroom control.

The Pragmatic Orientation.   Teachers at the pragmatic stage have become socialized to the ways of the school and are no longer preoccupied with personal competence and job security. They have succeeded in reducing the complexity of teaching to manageable proportions through routines that enable them to satisfy major role requirements, while providing important measures of stability and predictability. These teachers have usually achieved orderly classrooms, systems for handling required paperwork, adaptations to the prescribed curriculum, and workable relationships with administrators and parents.

By reducing teaching to a set of dependable routines, the pragmatically oriented teacher is able to systematize the teaching process, simplify the teaching day, and avoid having to function continuously in a creative mode. This preoccupation with efficiency and manageability generally results in mechanistic approaches to teaching and learning. The teacher becomes essentially a presenter of content, often a very proficient one. He or she is disposed to view teaching as rule-governed behavior and frequently functions best with "teacher proof" materials. This teacher will tend to rely primarily on extrinsic forms of motivation.

Although survival is no longer a central concern for teachers at the pragmatic stage, they still devote a major share of their attentions to the nuts and bolts of their work. The ability to cope effectively with the system still tends to dominate their consciousness. They are occupied with time pressures, numbers of students, availability of materials, noninstructional duties, and the politics and economics of teaching. Here are typical statements representing the dominant concerns of two third-year secondary teachers:

> I'm going to have to find another system. I won't continue to take home this much paperwork. There has to be a way to get more of this work done during the school day. I'll just try to squeeze some of it in during lunch.

> If they want me to teach this many students, I'm going to expect fewer preparations. Also, I believe I've been here long enough to deserve a room of my own. I'm tired of moving.

At the pragmatic level, the teachers' absorption with the practical realities of working in a public school often makes it difficult for them to see beyond the system. As a result, they tend to confuse organizational agendas (means) for educational goals (ends). Their notion of teaching competence is more likely to derive from prevailing role definitions than from consciously applied principles of teaching and learning. For example, they will be inclined to look to such external indicators as test results, rather than to individual learning patterns, for evidence that teaching goals have been achieved.

The Creative Orientation.   Superior teachers develop patterns of working within the school organization that allow them to concentrate on objectives that reach beyond the system itself. They are able to bring transsystem perspectives to their teaching. These teachers are able to be productive and creative in the pursuit of human-service goals in spite of work loads and school climates that could serve to distract them from their primary mission. They are often motivated by the challenge of performing under hectic conditions. They have learned to cope satisfactorily with the exigencies of school life and they seem to enjoy the complicated juggling act that characterizes superior teaching.

The major concern of creatively oriented teachers is their impact on students. They tend to employ methods and objectives that reflect dynamic conceptions of human learning and development. These teachers ordinarily possess well-developed powers of communication and self-expression and will strive to promote forms of self-expression in their students as an overriding objective. They place a high premium on intrinsic motivation and on the inner-self development of young learners. This is revealed in the following exchange between two veteran sixth-grade teachers:

> TEACHER A: I'm going to do less with formal grammar this time around and put more emphasis on impromptu writing.
>
> TEACHER B: Yes, I'm with you on that. I believe these kids definitely need opportunities to form ideas before they get bogged down in rules.
>
> TEACHER A: This, of course, will mean more papers to read, but I'm willing to do that if I can begin to make a dent in some of the negative attitudes toward writing they bring into my class.
>
> TEACHER B: That's what we're here for. I don't mind the extra work either if I can see some improvement in their compositions.

Teachers who perform at this level tend to approach teaching as an art form. One of their most important identifying characteristics is their ability to function in an indirect teaching mode. They recognize that meaningful learning cannot be forced. As such, they will attempt to provide a solid foundation for new learning and to adapt their teaching to the learning styles and rhythms of their students. These individuals are inclined to put a great deal of themselves into their teaching.

Anticipating the Hurdles

A great many people with the potential to become better than average teachers have difficulty realizing that potential within the structure of a U.S. public school.[7] In response to the system forces they encounter, most teachers adopt a pragmatic accommodation early in their careers and remain at that level until they leave teaching. These teachers do a satisfactory job of meeting major role expectations, but they fail to develop a creative orientation toward their work. Their best efforts are devoted to meeting system requirements that are frequently at cross purposes with their development as skilled classroom performers.[8]

Also, the most likely candidates for occupational burnout are pragmatically oriented teachers whose routines have become stale, causing them to experience serious job frustration and dissatisfaction. According to Seymour B. Sarason, burnout among professional people "involves a change in attitude and behavior in response to a demanding, frustrating, unrewarding work experience." One of the negative changes is "a loss of concern for the client, and a tendency to treat clients in a detached, mechanical fashion."[9]

Other characteristics include "increasing discouragement, pessimism, and fatalism about one's work; apathy, negativism; frequent irritability and anger with clients and colleagues; preoccupation with one's own comfort and welfare on the job; a tendency to rationalize failure by blaming the clients or 'the system'; and resistance to change, growing rigidity, and loss of creativity."[10]

In a sense, we might say burnout occurs when teachers feel buried within the school organization.

DEVELOPING A CREATIVE PATTERN

It is imperative, then, that you give serious consideration to the quality of your relationship to the system itself if you are to achieve maximum effectiveness and satisfaction in your work.

By examining the patterns and dispositions of creatively oriented teachers, you can gain insight into the kinds of personal investments that will allow you to make the most of your opportunities in teaching.

Maintaining Transsystem Perspectives

In order to make a healthy adaptation to a modern school bureaucracy, you must be capable of standing above the organization conceptually and psychologically. You must be able to see the system for what it is and have the personal strength to resist being overpowered by it.

Teachers with a creative orientation to their work are able to recognize the limitations as well as the merits of institutionalized schooling in meeting the needs of individuals. They expect neither more nor less of these organizations than they are capable of delivering. Such teachers construe school systems as vehicles for achieving purposes that go beyond the school itself. They are not as likely to confuse the requirements of institutional maintenance with the imperatives of human growth and development.

This is a crucial distinction for you to be able to make, because major institutions like schools do tend to be self-justifying and self-perpetuating. Like other well-entrenched social organizations, they are inclined to take on a relentless momentum of their own.[11] Much of what students learn in school is deemed important because it prepares them for what they will learn in school next year or the following year. Some school learning remains in the curriculum because it has always been part of the schooling tradition, that is, "it's something any 'well-schooled' person ought to possess."

The reality of the U.S. school system is largely self-contained. It has its own goals and values, its own rules for how the game is to be played, and its own language for defining organizational agendas.[12] It is one thing for a representative of the system to accommodate to that reality as a means of pursuing broader educational goals. It is another thing to allow yourself to be encapsulated and perceptually disabled by it. Creatively oriented teachers are able to keep one foot in and one out of the system. They manage to keep themselves grounded in ordering principles that reach beyond the organization and its programs, as reflected in this comment by a veteran teacher of eleventh-grade U.S. history:

> I'm not satisfied just to have my students pass tests. I can't see requiring them to memorize names and dates if there's no carryover. They've got to practice historical thinking when they leave the school, otherwise I really haven't taught. This class should help them to see history in the making as they read newspapers and watch the news. It's vital that these young people develop a realistic sense of where we've been and where we seem to be going as a country.

The following are some important things you can do to help maintain transsystem perspectives as a teacher:

1. Take time periodically to reflect on your most important purposes as a teacher. Allow your frame of reference to reach beyond the boundaries of the school. Apart from the specific content objectives that appear in your daily lesson plans, what sorts of "overriding" objectives are important to you in your teaching?

Do they include human development and social development goals? In the ideal, what kinds of people do you see yourself as helping to produce through your teaching? In what specific ways can the school contribute to making a better community and a better society?

2. Make a consistent effort to keep the ends and means of the school in proper focus. Recognize the fallacy of using organizational concepts to evaluate the performance of the system itself. This practice tends to be self-justifying. Test scores, grade-point averages, daily attendance figures, and percentages of high school graduates may indicate that the system is functioning well internally, but they do little to demonstrate the effectiveness of the schooling process in enhancing life beyond school.

3. Avoid relying on system requirements as prods to get students involved in school learning. For a teacher to introduce a learning activity with the reminder that students will be tested over the learning product is to be preoccupied with the school's need to measure and grade student's performances. It shows less sensitivity to the learning and developmental needs of young people. Chapter 6 centers on an approach to classroom motivation designed to involve students actively in learning without having to use the system and its requirements as the primary form of incentive.

4. Develop a critical attitude toward the specialized language of the school labyrinth in this country. For example, by recognizing the value assumptions that underlie concepts like "performance objectives," "academic subjects," "scholastic aptitude tests," and "remedial classes," you are in a position to properly assess their appropriateness as educational means.

Staying Vital

Resourceful teachers refuse to allow the demands, the resistances, or the impersonality of the system to rob them of their creative edge. In order to function productively as a teacher in a modern school system, you must consistently bring fresh energy to the job. As a model for the kind of spirit and enthusiasm you would like students to exhibit, you should feel a strong need to keep yourself vital.

Considering the long hours, the repetitiveness of the work, and the feeling of fighting an uphill battle, it takes a special effort to consistently display a constructive and optimistic outlook with groups of young people. Exemplary teachers, however, find effective means for meeting this challenge. Like superior athletes and entertainers, they learn to pace themselves during the course of long performances and to apportion their energies appropriately. They develop a knack for using their personal resources constructively, being careful not to waste them brooding, complaining, or chastising. Other contributing factors are the abilities of exceptional teachers to lighten the task with quality humor and their dispositions to avoid taking themselves or the institution too seriously.

To regularly bring positive and creative energy to this type of work, you will need to develop reliable mechanisms for personal renewal. You should have dependable means of obtaining both psychic and conceptual revitalization when you sense you are beginning to go stale. The following are some strategies for achieving periodic renewal of teaching energies and perspectives:

1. Take opportunities to detach yourself from the practical realities of your work for a period of time. Time away from the job gives a person an opportunity to achieve a fresh vantage. Cultivate at least one good hobby or recreational activity that calls for different mental and physical skills than you are accustomed to using in school.

2. Make a concerted effort to keep yourself as physically fit as possible. Insist on the kind of sleep, diet, and physical exercise that will allow you to feel rejuvenated in the morning and that will maximize your endurance throughout the school day. Do not ignore the close relationship between your physical well-being and your ability to function mentally and emotionally as a teacher.

3. Allow yourself time for serious reflection on the nature of your work. To maintain their creative edge, most good teachers make it a practice to periodically review and perhaps reconstruct their fundamental views of education and teaching, taking into consideration their most recent experiences with these processes. In-depth professional or philosophical reading can often be the stimulus for new motivation (see chapter 12). One indication that teachers are growing with the job is the realization that their basic outlooks and motivations are undergoing a metamorphosis as their experience widens and deepens.[13]

Dealing with Conflicting Agendas

The role of a public school teacher is especially complex. It requires that teachers be able to manage multiple conflicting agendas. This can be frustrating and disconcerting for those who have not prepared themselves for the reality that dealing with contradictions and dilemmas is part of the teacher's job.

One potential conflict derives from the fact that the school is a primary agent of socialization while it also purports to be an agent of education as human enlightenment. It has an obligation to help young people make a smooth adjustment to society as it presently exists, but it also has stated commitments to promote the kinds of thinking skills and social ideals that would dispose people to become critical of the status quo. This dilemma is unique to the schools of open societies such as our own. Schools in monolithic, centrally controlled nations are, by definition, exclusively instruments of socialization.

The processes of education and socialization are not easily mixed. One tends to be a broadening or liberating influence, while the main thrust of the other is to promote conformity.[14] Pragmatically oriented teachers tend to alleviate the stress produced by these conflicting agendas by concentrating on one of these school functions and ignoring or simply giving lip-service to the other. Those who settle for the pragmatic accommodation have implicitly opted for the socialization requirement at the expense of the school's educational role.

Mechanical and superficial approaches to teaching and learning are not only easier to implement, but they also facilitate the testing, grading, and sorting of students for job placement or further schooling. They do little to promote meaningful learning or higher thinking processes in students. So although it is possible to rationalize its social maintenance function, this kind of teaching is difficult to justify from an educational standpoint.

Another source of role conflict is the fact that teachers find themselves in the position of being both executives and counselors in their relationships with students. The executive role is essentially supervisory, directive, and critical. The other, that of counselor, is essentially supportive, advisory, and facilitative of the student's pursuit of knowledge.[15]

Teachers with a well-grounded creative orientation are able to maintain appropriate tension between the requirements of the apparently contradictory roles they are asked to play. They strive to keep alive the educational mission of the school when it struggles to compete with the social adjustment emphasis. Such teachers also manage to maintain supportive and facilitative relationships with students in spite of forces that would cause them to be preoccupied with their executive responsibilities.

Here are some suggestions for dealing constructively with the conflicting agendas that are often part of the teacher's role:

1. Do not repress these conflicts when you find them to exist within the system. Make an effort to meet them head-on. Value conflicts and contradictions are part of the American way of life and can be expected to appear in our education systems. The problems they create for you and your students should not be thought to reflect personal weaknesses or inadequacies on your part. The tension you feel when you allow yourself to face-up to such conflicts can turn out to be energizing rather than debilitating for you.
2. Accept the reality of classroom teaching as character-intensive work in which those who make the most positive impact and achieve the most personal satisfaction are people who are able to avoid the path of least resistance. Realize that truly creative performance in most any endeavor involves a willingness to buck the odds and resist entrenched patterns.
3. Make it a point to periodically review your own priorities. By having clearly defined purposes and schemes for achieving them you are in a better position to see the logic of system patterns and to assess their compatibility with your own teaching needs. This allows you to maintain a sense of purpose and direction in the midst of institutionalized conflict or confusion.

Teaching Professional or School Employee?

Another potential conflict stems from your double role as both teaching professional and employee of a particular school system. As paid employees, workers generally have no decision-making authority beyond that granted them by their employers. On the other hand, trained professionals in public service occupations are typically allowed considerable autonomy when it comes to decisions that bear on their abilities to carry out their social service commitments. Whereas employees are obliged to perform in a manner that meets the expectations of a particular employer, professionals have an ethical commitment to the profession, or in effect to the larger society, to perform a social function that overrides the perceived needs of individual employers.[16]

For conscientious and reflective teachers this raises important questions about the basis of their authority. It causes one to ask: For whom am I really working? Is my first obligation to the teaching profession (i.e., to the society at large), or am I ultimately responsible to the particular school district that pays my salary? Who are my clients?

Are they the students in my classes, or their parents, or all of the people in the school district who contribute to my salary? If the students are my clients, what is my professional obligation to them? Do I have a professional responsibility to prescribe learning experiences that I deem appropriate for these particular clients? What is my responsibility in cases where my professional judgment is different from or in conflict with the prescriptions of the school system? If I allow the school system to dictate not only teaching objectives but also the means for achieving them, can I still claim professional status?

Teachers with a pragmatic orientation will generally refuse to struggle with the dilemmas posed by these questions. The authority question is not a live issue for them. They are satisfied to consider it a legal rather than a philosophical or moral question. These teachers see themselves as employees who have been hired by the local community to perform a task in which the boundaries are clearly defined. Their views of teacher authority tend to be system-bound.

By approaching the issue of teacher authority from an oversimplified "craft-mentality," pragmatically oriented teachers allow themselves to concentrate on the means and mechanics of teaching and to avoid the difficult questions having to do with purpose. One effect is to leave the schools more vulnerable to local parochialism, to the discretions of laypersons who can usually be expected to favor the socialization function over the educational function.[17]

Creatively oriented teachers have an acute sensitivity to the conflicting roles they are asked to play. As indicated, a distinguishing characteristic of teachers who are able to perform at this level is their commitment to purposes that lie beyond the school organization itself. These people are able to achieve a satisfactory resolution of this difficult authority issue, managing to live with the requirements imposed by the school system while at the same time doing justice to the professional standards that are manifest in their teaching.

The following are suggested strategies for approaching the authority question and the conflicting expectations surrounding it:

1. Take a personal interest in examining the authority base from which you work. The question of whether your decision-making authority derives from your commitment and knowledge as a teaching professional or from your contractual responsibilities to the school district carries important implications for your work and satisfaction as a public school teacher.

2. Realize that as a conscientious, critical-minded teacher there will be times when the expectations placed on you as a school employee may put you in conflict with your perceived responsibilities as a professional educator. Be prepared to face the dilemma that these conflicting notions of authority pose for you.

3. Take the initiative to assert as much influence as you can bring to bear in favor of your responsibilities as a teaching professional. Find the courage to challenge the system when you are convinced it is causing you to compromise your professional obligations. Use your best knowledge of educational ends and means to make your case in arguing for or against courses of action that will affect your ability to perform responsibly as a teacher.

4. Take the optimistic view that the system is susceptible to positive influence by competent and assertive people with genuine commitments to educational excellence.

The Self-actualizing Teacher

In the final analysis, it takes a good deal of psychological strength to work creatively and humanely in a modern school organization and not be dominated by the system. It helps to have achieved the personal adequacy and autonomy to be able to stand apart from the system and not depend on it for one's primary need satisfaction. Abraham Maslow's model of the *self-actualizing* person has much to offer as a basis for the creative orientation in teachers.

In describing the quality of detachment in self-actualizing people, Maslow makes the following observation:

> It is often possible for them to remain above the battle, to remain unruffled, undisturbed by that which produces turmoil in others. . . . It becomes possible for them to take personal misfortunes without reacting violently as the ordinary person does. They seem to be able to retain their dignity even in undignified surroundings and situations. Perhaps this comes in part from their tendency to stick by their own interpretation of a situation rather than to rely upon what others feel or think about the matter.[18]

Maslow describes a related characteristic, the attribute of autonomy, in these terms:

> One of the characteristics of self-actualizing people is their relative independence of the physical and social environment. . . . They are not dependent for their main satisfactions on the real world, or other people, or culture, or means to ends, or in general on extrinsic satisfactions. Rather, they are dependent for their development and continued growth on their own potentialities and latent resources. . . . This independence of environment means a relative stability in the face of hard knocks, blows, deprivations, frustrations, and the like. These people can maintain a relative serenity and happiness in the midst of circumstances that would drive other people to suicide.[19]

In effect, the self-actualizing person has an uncommon ability to function within two reality structures at once and not allow one reality to be obscured by the other. Exceptional teachers are able to insure that organizational needs and agendas do not cause them to lose sight of the ordering principles from which they work.

The following are steps you can take to become more self-actualized as an individual and a professional educator:

1. Find time in your busy schedule to be alone, a time for personal reflection and renewal.
2. Be able to locate your "personal center." Learn to trust the inner core of your personality for a sense of stability and direction.
3. Continue to develop your total self by making time for "whole brain" activities, for example, art projects, musical interests, outdoor activities, travel. These are activities that draw on your intuitions, your imagination, and your emotions as well as your logical and analytical processes.
4. Strive to be more than a specialist in your work as a teacher. If anything, see yourself as a human growth and development expert first and a subject-matter specialist after that.

5. Make an ongoing effort to understand your own internal needs and motivations. This includes knowing your own personal agendas and how they affect your work as a teacher. It is important to remain aware of your personal strengths as well as inner changes that will make you a better teacher.

COMING TO TERMS WITH THE SYSTEM— GENERAL STRATEGIES

As a summary of this chapter, the following are a set of general guidelines for making a healthy and creative accomodation to teaching in a modern school organization:

1. *Know where you are bound and where you are free.* Do not allow yourself to continually dwell on situations where you feel hassled or constrained. Identify the areas where you have latitude to exert your personal influence and devote your best resources to making a difference in these areas. Teachers are of course tightly bound to time schedules, assigned classes, record keeping chores, and other organizational requirements. They often feel somewhat looser contraints when it comes to such things as prescribed curriculums, schoolwide discipline procedures, or parent-conferencing policies. You can usually expect a good deal of freedom to develop a teaching style and to express your own personality in the classroom once the door is closed. Teachers have considerable leeway in most schools and in most teaching areas to take nonconventional approaches to teaching the subject matter of their assigned classes. In one of the areas where you can have considerable impact, namely, in your relationships with students, you will normally have a great deal of freedom to determine the nature of those relationships.

2. *Keep yourself focused on positive, constructive goals that have personal meaning for you.* Design ongoing projects, inquiries, or activities that you can pursue relative to your teaching, projects that represent your own special interests and aptitudes. For example, in experimenting with a significantly different method of working with nonachieving students, or in pursuing ways for extending student learning into some kind of community involvement, you can derive a sense of autonomy and significance that may be harder to achieve if your efforts and purposes are entirely system-determined.

   The fact that teachers are busy people working in a fast-paced environment is not in itself the thing that causes burnout and job dissatisfaction. Often it is the hectic pace in pursuit of agendas one has not chosen, the fact of constantly being in a position of reacting to someone else's stimuli. Creative teachers are inclined to be initiators and meaning-makers, proactive rather than reactive people. Their response to apparent constraint or adversity is to take initiative, to move to control situations rather than waiting for these situations to control them.

3. *Be capable of challenging the system when necessary.* Expect some dissonance between your own educational agendas and those of systematized schooling. Develop the courage to oppose courses of action that you find to be in funda-

mental disregard for your needs and those of your students. Become organized and articulate in representing your own educational purposes and commitments. Be able to support your agendas with sound and convincing rationales in which you truly believe.

The frequent impersonality, inflexibility, and mechanicalness of a modern school bureaucracy is best countered by the initiative, courage, and fresh perspective of vital, people-oriented educators with strong purposes. You may find strength and courage in John Stuart Mill's contention that "one person with a belief is equal to a force of ninety-nine who have only interests." Of course, the more support you can generate from like-minded colleagues, the better chance you have of influencing the system in a desired direction.

4. *Know the hidden agendas of the system and use them to your advantage.* Make yourself familiar with the inner workings of the organization and its prime agents. Learn ways you can use the system (in contrast to working against the grain of the system) to accomplish your purposes. For example, present-day school administrators tend to be preoccupied with the political and public-relations aspects of running a school, frequently finding less time to be interested in the substance of educational activity within the school. Realizing this, you can often gain needed support for personal projects or activities, that might otherwise fall on deaf ears, by featuring their timeliness, their potential visibility, or their political or economic value to the system. At the same time, do not be surprised to find less than genuine interest in the content of your personal agendas. Determine which administrators have a special interest in teaching and learning and which are preoccupied with the smooth functioning of the school organization.

It will behoove you to understand the personalities of those key people within the organization who can make your job more or less pleasant for you, including support personnel, counselors, and fellow teachers, as well as administrators. Insightful teachers know when and how to approach administrators with problems, requests, or a desire to share accomplishments. They know which people in the school can be counted on to support innovative efforts, those who can provide helpful political clout, and those to approach or avoid when you want to share a problem or interest (teacher's lounges are usually poor places to find constructive conversation about education and teaching). System-wise teachers have learned how to gain the support of school secretaries and custodians when they need a favor. They are able to use the "informal power structure" of the school (often consisting of an especially influential group of teachers, or perhaps a veteran secretary) to accomplish purposes that may not be achievable through more direct channels.

5. *Organize and pace your teaching activities to make the most of your personal resources.* There are a number of things you can do to pace your activity during a long teaching day to insure you are using your mental and physical energies to best advantage:
   a. Plan your teaching so you will not have to talk for most of the day. Break up your lessons with activities that allow you a degree of relaxation from a constant teacher-centered format.

b. Learn to flow-with the interpersonal atmosphere of the school when that is appropriate. Adopt an interactive style that allows you to work effectively with students in a less judgmental, less confrontational manner than most teachers are accustomed to (refer to chapter 8). A smoother, less-ego-charged interactional pattern can be a tremendous energy saver for you.

c. Make an effort to arrange your teaching schedule to accomodate your own mental cycles. If you are a morning person, lobby to have your most strenuous classes before lunch. Take measures to build-in relaxation times for yourself during the day, short periods when you can calm your mind and body. If possible, find a quiet spot in the school where you can engage in simple relaxation techniques.

d. Identify the best time to plan for your teaching. If it is morning, get in the habit of doing your planning before school. Do not leave it to the last thing in the day when your creative energy is at its lowest ebb. Adopt a planning routine that allows you to stay on top of a busy teaching schedule with a minimum of stress.

e. Be conscious of your own creative style. Are you one who formulates ideas and projects deliberately or do you depend on flashes of insight while relaxing, eating a meal, or driving in your car? If the latter is your style, you may need to adopt a relatively noncompulsive approach to planning your lessons (not to be confused with a ''seat of the pants'' approach to teaching). You will want to learn to take advantage of ''propitious moments'' for constructing teaching ideas, for example, by keeping a pen and notepad with you in your car, on your bedstand, at the dinner table, and so forth.

f. Try to complete as much of your work as possible before you leave school. By using ''prep'' periods to advantage and by using ploys like ''peer editing'' to provide feedback on writing assignments, student exchanges of papers for correcting short objective tests, or teacher aides to help with paperwork, you can cut down on the amount of homework left after a day at work.

g. Find an effective system for handling paperwork. School systems, like other modern organizations, depend heavily on paper flow as their main form of communication. Learn to sort your mail, return information to the school office, prepare evaluational materials, and so forth, promptly and efficiently so these organizational chores do not pile up and become nagging preoccupations.

6. *Maintain a transsystem perspective on your work.* Do not expect more of the system than it is capable of providing. Get to the place where you are not continually disappointed and dismayed by the failure of the institution to live up to your expectations. A healthy sense of humor, one that does not reflect resignation or cynicism, can do wonders.

Recognize the limitations of school organizations when it comes to meeting the inner needs of individuals. Learn to get satisfaction from some of the unplanned, intangible successes you experience during a typical week of teaching, for example, a note from a shy student expressing appreciation for your special efforts, a productive lunchtime sharing session with a like-minded colleague, the excitement of an indepth class discussion that refuses to end with the bell.

Maintain ideals that extend beyond the system itself, with the realization that in a character-intensive occupation like teaching the meaning and satisfaction you derive from your work will depend more on the personal effort and vision you bring to it than on what is provided by the organization.

SUGGESTED ACTIVITIES AND QUESTIONS

1. Arrange to do interviews with seven or eight teachers in schools where you are involved. Use these discussions to gain insight into such things as (1) the main concerns that occupy them as teachers, (2) the theories of learning they work from, (3) their approaches to the conflicting roles they face, (4) their attitudes toward the external demands and distractions they encounter in their work, and (5) the kinds of energy, enthusiasm, and creativity they apply to teaching. Based on your interviews, how would you characterize the present accomodations of these teachers to the school system? Do you find any veteran teachers who still exhibit a survival orientation? Would some of the teachers qualify to be considered creative teachers? What evidence are you using to support these judgments?

2. Take the opportunity to talk to as many school students as possible (at various levels) regarding their perceptions of "good teachers." What are the qualities most frequently associated with high-quality teaching in the minds of these young people? Do they square with the concept of creative teaching developed in this chapter?

3. Identify any creative projects you have undertaken in your recent life, apart from school assignments, that have turned out to be growth enhancers for you, that is, that have caused desired changes in specific habits, levels of awareness, personal sensitivities, appreciations, and so forth. Describe as precisely as you can the sort of positive growth you believe to have resulted in yourself. How effective do you feel you are in monitoring your own personal growth as an individual and as a teacher? How close are you to being a self-actualizing person?

4. Pinpoint one or more aspects of your personality or interpersonal style where positive change could improve your chances of becoming a creative teacher, for example, listening skills, self-expression, stress tolerance, critical thinking, multiple concentration. Design specific courses of action for making these strength areas rather than liabilities. For example, on deciding you are generally a better talker than you are a listener, take deliberate steps to remedy this imbalance by adopting strategies for improving your listening skills in everyday situations. As other examples, skills of critical thinking and self-expression can generally be improved by mak..ng time for more substantive reading and thoughtful discussion.

5. How would you characterize your present level of concern as a developing teacher? Are you interested mainly in completing teacher training and locating a job? Are you concentrating on finding a particular type of job that will allow you freedom to teach a certain way and accomplish specific purposes? Or are you mainly concerned for an opportunity to work with young people, while attaching less importance to the particular school situation?

6. What are some of the ideals you have set for yourself as a teacher? Do any of the ideals you have identified amount to your main reason for choosing teaching as a career? Do you anticipate that these ideals will change as your immediate needs and circumstances change, for example, as you achieve a full-time job, tenure in a school, a stable income?

7. Can you identify with the particular attitudes and patterns of the level two, or pragmatically oriented, teacher? Have you had many teachers with this approach to teaching during your years as a student? Can you imagine yourself performing at one or another of the teaching levels described in this chapter?

8. What kind of an "organization person" do you see yourself as being? Apart from your experiences as a student, have you had the opportunity to work or function for any period of

time in a highly structured organizational setting, for example, the military, a government job, a youth camp? How do you handle situations where a good share of your time and behavior is structured by impersonal rules and regulations? Do you consider yourself a person who accepts authority easily? What ideas can you offer for maintaining individuality and creativity in a bureaucratic environment?

9. Do you subscribe to the idea that highly competent classroom teachers must be self-actualizing people? Give reasons to support your opinion.

NOTES AND REFERENCES

1. See Stuart B. Palonsky, *900 Shows a Year: A Look at Teaching from a Teacher's Side of the Desk.* New York: Random House, 1986, see chapters 3 and 7; Theodore R. Sizer, *Horace's Compromise: The Dilemma of the American High School.* Boston: Houghton Mifflin, 1984, see Part IV; and John I. Goodlad, *A Place Called School.* New York: McGraw-Hill, 1984, see chap. 6.

2. Francis F. Fuller, "Concerns of Teachers: A Developmental Conceptualization." *American Educational Research Journal,* 6 (1969), pp. 207–26.

3. Ibid., pp. 211–12.

4. See Herbert J. Freudenberger, *Burn Out: The High Cost of Achievement.* Garden City, N.Y.: Doubleday, 1980.

5. The three levels of system accommodation developed here reflect my own unpublished studies of teacher growth patterns in combination with notable work that has been done on teacher developmental stages and the changing concerns of teachers as they become stabilized in teaching careers. See Sharon Feiman and Robert Floden, *What's All This Talk About Teacher Development?,* Research Series No. 70. East Lansing: Institute for Research on Teaching, Michigan State University, February 1980, pp. 94–107; Paul R. Burden, *Developmental Supervision: Reducing Teacher Stress at Different Career Stages.* Paper presented at the Annual Conference of the Association for Teacher Educators, Phoenix, Arizona, February 1982; and Gene E. Hall and Susan Loucks, "Teacher Concerns as a Basis for Facilitating and Personalizing Staff Development." *Teachers College Record,* 80 (September 1978), pp. 36–53.

6. See Thomas L. Good and Jere E. Brophy, *Looking in Classrooms,* 3rd ed. New York: Harper and Row, 1984, chap. 2.

7. See Jack Frymier, "Bureaucracy and the Neutering of Teachers," *Phi Delta Kappan,* September 1987, pp. 9–14; and Patrick Welsh, *Tales out of School.* New York: Penguin Books, 1986, see chaps. 8 and 10.

8. See Goodlad, op. cit., chap. 6.

9. Seymour B. Sarason, *The Culture of the School and the Problem of Change.* Boston: Allyn and Bacon, 1982, p. 203.

10. Ibid., p. 204.

11. See John Gall, *Systemantics: How Systems Work.* New York: New York Times Book Co., 1975, pp. 29–31.

12. See Barbara Benham Tye, "The Deep Structure of Schooling." *Phi Delta Kappan,* December 1987, pp. 281–83.

13. See John W. Gardner, *Self Renewal.* New York: Harper and Row, 1965, especially chap. 10.

14. See Neil Postman, *Teaching as a Conserving Activity.* New York: Delacorte Press, 1979, see chap. 1; and Ira Shor, *Critical Teaching and Everyday Life.* Boston: South End Press, 1980, see chap. 2.

15. See Linda M. McNeil, "Contradictions of Control, Part 1: "Administrators and Teachers." *Phi Delta Kappan,* January 1988, pp. 333–39.
16. See Myron Lieberman, *The Future of Public Education.* Chicago: University of Chicago Press, 1960, especially chap. 8.
17. Ibid., pp. 72–75.
18. Abraham Maslow, *Motivation and Personality.* New York: Harper and Row, 1954, p. 212.
19. Ibid., pp. 213–14.

CHAPTER 3

Designing Appropriate Learning Objectives

OWNING YOUR TEACHING GOALS

As a teacher it is important that you be able to structure what takes place in your own classroom. You will want to feel you are controlling classroom events instead of allowing them to control you. However, in your efforts to cope with the hectic pace of modern teaching, it is easy to fall into a pattern of simply reacting to classroom situations rather than one that involves moving activities in some clearly established direction. At times you may find yourself confusing ends and means, and engaging in activity for the sake of activity. The best way to insure that this does not become a regular occurrence is to have a firm grasp of your teaching goals. In order to be a proactive teacher, an initiator rather than a reactor, you need to be aware of your main purposes and priorities as an educator. At any point in your teaching, it is important to be aware of what you are attempting to accomplish with your students.

You can usually obtain some initial guidance in formulating instructional objectives from course and program descriptions, curriculum frameworks, and other teachers. And whereas the structure you obtain from such external sources is often helpful and necessary, you cannot rely on it to give you the basic sense of direction you need to become a self-sustaining professional. To attain this sense of direction you need to start by giving serious attention to the long- and short-range objectives that will guide your teaching. You must focus on what you want your students to achieve in your classes. In short, you will need to "own" the learning objectives you work from in order to proceed confidently and autonomously in your planning and in your relations with students, parents, and school administrators.

Implicit and Explicit Purposes

One of your reasons for coming into teaching is undoubtedly a concern to have a positive impact on students. That is, you have certain goals you want to achieve in your teaching. In all probability, at this point, the goals you have set for yourself and your students are implicit rather than explicit. In other words, you believe in the value of education, you want to help young people develop their potentials as human beings, and you want them to acquire certain skills and understandings in the areas you will be teaching. However, if you are like most beginning teachers, you have not had occasion to analyze these broad goals and to transform them into workable learning objectives for your students.

When you begin to examine your teaching goals, along with the goal statements from curriculum guides and programmed materials, you realize that whereas they may serve as worthwhile points of departure, they are too general to be functional in structuring specific learning activities. For purposes of planning classroom learning, they need to be converted to precise and measurable terms. For example, a teaching goal that aims ''to promote student's powers of self-expression'' must eventually be reduced to pointed descriptions of what students will actually do to demonstrate increases in self-expression before the objective can be used as a basis for designing lessons or determining student achievement.

Also, when you are able to get these various statements of purpose on paper, some prescriptions may appear incompatible with others. A goal like ''students will develop skill at democratic processes'' could turn out to be in conflict with one that prescribes unquestioning acceptance of existing institutional patterns, for example, ''students will learn to accept authority in preparation for future roles in the world of work.''

It will be necessary, then, for you to make certain decisions regarding the educational goals you adopt for your teaching.[1] You will need to decide what your major objectives are, how they are to become manifest in your day-to-day teaching activities, how compatible your various teaching objectives are with one another, and how they align with externally provided goal statements for the classes you teach.

This chapter is designed to help you with this decision-making process. It also provides practical strategies for preparing learning objectives, and calls your attention to some of the major considerations that should enter into the development of teaching goals. More specifically, the content of the chapter serves to assist you in (1) making necessary distinctions between different types and levels of learning objectives, (2) establishing teaching objectives that represent your most important purposes and priorities as a teacher, (3) writing highly specific objectives for use in teaching situations where they are appropriate, (4) classifying instructional objectives into three major domains of learning as a basis for specifying a variety of learning outcomes, and (5) anticipating potential problems and areas of controversy regarding the formulation of learning objectives.

Educational Goals and Behavioral Objectives

As suggested earlier, you should know that learning objectives can vary widely from highly general statements of educational goals to very specific and detailed descriptions of behaviors students are expected to demonstrate following instruction. Educational goals, or global objectives of the school, describe the broad purposes of formal education in this country. The following are some examples:

Education should develop the whole child
Students will learn to think independently
Social studies should teach good citizenship

Students will develop an appreciation for art and beauty
The school aims to promote character development

Large-scale descriptions of educational purposes are often formulated by national committees or commissions that usually include educational leaders as well as interested laypersons. They are deliberately general, serving more as statements of educational philosophy than as precise teaching objectives.

Broad goals such as these do have an important function in that they give educators a place to start. They provide reference points from which to develop school curriculums. Educational goals can be used as general statements of purpose and as screens for determining the appropriateness of specific elements within school programs. For example, if one main objective of a teacher or a school is to promote independent thinking, this gives us a basis for questioning the value of activities where students are being spoon-fed ideas with no opportunity to reflect on their implications. Educational goals, then, are important to you at stage one in your organization for teaching because they serve to provide a broad framework for teaching and learning.

At the other extreme are the highly specific learning objectives that describe expected learning outcomes in precise and measurable terms. These explicit statements of what students should be able to do following instruction as evidence of learning are often called *behavioral objectives*. You may also hear them referred to as *performance objectives,* or *terminal objectives.* Here are some examples of behavioral objectives:

The learner will be able to list the fifty states in the United States
The learner will be able to identify the twelve cranial nerves
The learner will be able to tell how a first class lever works
The learner will master the multiplication tables so he can recite to nine times nine correctly from memory
The learner will be able to compose three different salutations for a personal letter

Behavioral objectives have been the source of considerable controversy in educational circles. Some educators claim that they are essential to any sort of organized teaching; others believe that they hamper creativity and in-depth learning if used too compulsively. Some main arguments for and against the use of detailed, performance-based objectives are considered in a later section of this chapter. In the meantime it is important for you to be able to identify general goals for your teaching and to have the capability for transforming these large-scale purposes into clearly stated learning objectives for specific groups of students.

IDENTIFYING BROAD LEARNING GOALS

Subject-specific Goals

The first and most obvious kind of broad goals you will be working with are the learning goals that encompass the particular subject or subjects you will be teaching. These are the major objectives that will serve as reference points for your large-scale planning;

they will provide valuable structure for your subject-level and unit-level organization. The following are examples of subject-specific goals:

> Students will develop an appreciation for modern art forms
> Students will be able to identify significant periods in U.S. history
> Students will understand the essence of scientific method
> Students will understand the requirements of physical fitness
> Students will become familiar with high-quality literature

For your reference, broad goal statements for various subject areas can usually be found in state and district curriculum guidelines as well as in textbooks and programmed materials for your teaching areas. You can normally expect to have considerable leeway when it comes to interpreting and adding to these subject-specific goals.

In actuality, you will have some fundamental choices to make here. Your subject goals should reflect what you think is most important for students to achieve in a general sense in the classes you are teaching. Whether these educational goals are entirely your own or largely provided for you, it is important for you to have a good idea of what is appropriate in the way of broad goals for particular teaching areas. This will help you avoid getting bogged down in subject-matter fragments and losing sight of large purposes for learning.

As a history teacher, for example, what are some ultimate goals for students of history? Should they be learning to think like historians? Should they become disposed to recognize historical antecedents for significant national and international events as they occur in their lives? Or in the case of science, what broad learning outcomes should it produce? Should students learn the facts of science or the application of the scientific method? Should they have a working knowledge of basic differences between empirical and intuitive modes of thought in their everyday lives? If you are to own your teaching goals, these are the sorts of fundamental considerations you will need to entertain.

Overriding Teaching Goals

The second type of educational goals, *overriding goals,* is especially important as you attempt to establish your own purposes and priorities in the classroom. These are the group process and human development objectives you set for your classroom and the young people in it, those that reach beyond subject-matter learning. In the first instance, they specify the kinds of intergroup behaviors and relationships that allow you and your students to function together in ways you consider educationally and interpersonally necessary. You might think of these as your *enabling objectives* because they enable teaching and learning to proceed in a reasonable, cooperative, and humanly justifiable manner. Some examples are:

> Class members will (learn to) acknowledge one another's rights to an opinion
> Class members will (learn to) address one another respectfully
> Class members will (learn to) honor group time commitments
> Class members will (learn to) honor one another's rights to attend to class
>   proceedings

When your enabling objectives are not being met, they should become your most immediate priorities. For example, in a classroom where name calling or class interruptions have become prevalent, your interpersonal and group process objectives should take precedence over your academic objectives. Under the circumstances, it will be less important to teach subject matter than to concentrate on more fundamental social and interpersonal skills.

Your overriding objectives should also reflect the most important concepts and ideals you hold for human growth and development, the ultimate goals you are striving to achieve with the developing young people in your classes. Here are some examples:

> Students will show sensitivity to the various forms of life around them
> Students will come to accept responsibility for their own behavior
> Students will become inclined to share in decision-making processes that affect their own lives
> Students will develop dispositions to approach personal problems confidently and rationally

In short, your overriding objectives are those that allow you to achieve purpose and direction in your teaching, and make it all worthwhile. They are the goals you look to when you are confused or when you sense a conflict in your teaching pattern. As one pair of teacher educators have described them, your overriding objectives are your *superobjectives*. They are the goals that permeate your teaching performance and hold it all together.

> The superobjectives give coherence and meaning to a teacher's performance. . . . A teacher who does not have superobjectives can manifest only a patchwork of unrelated skills and disjointed activities. . . . The acquisition of superobjectives is just as important an aspect of teaching as is the acquisition of specific skills. A teacher who acquires only the specific skills is like an actor who has learned his lines but who does not understand the part.[2]

Transitory and Dispositional Learning

In contrast to the more immediate learning objectives you will be focusing on in your day-to-day teaching, you should think of your broad goals as long-range prescriptions representing the basic understandings and dispositions that you want to become a part of the learner. To fully appreciate their significance, it might be helpful to consider for a moment the ideal progression of school learning from the memorization of simple facts to the development of useful life habits. Too often what we teach in school ends with the transfer of information, with simply telling students things (e.g., good writing requires careful proofreading, advertisers often use illogical means to sell products). With the exception of skill-based classes like writing, physical education, and shop, school curriculums frequently feature the transmission of facts rather than the development of skills. For our purposes we can think of this as *transitory learning,* because it tends to dissipate rather quickly if it is not put to some functional use. It infrequently takes students to the next level, which would entail the ability to use this information (i.e., to become proficient at proofreading or at discerning logical fallacies in TV and newspaper ads).

Furthermore, even when schools do promote skill acquisition, unless students are influenced to practice these skills in many contexts they are rarely advanced to the level of everyday habits. They seldom become manifest in life patterns, or what we might call *dispositional learning*. For example, students who are told that proofreading is important, and may even have learned how to proofread in school, often are not inclined to give a second reading to things they write on their own time. They have acquired a good deal of information, and perhaps some school-related skills, but they lack the readiness to actualize this new learning. Although they may have "learned a lot," it has been mostly learning in the weak rather than in the strong sense, because what they have learned tends to have remained at school. It does not become an integral part of their behavioral patterns.

Dispositional learning, on the other hand, goes beyond simply knowing about and/ or being able to do and affects what the student actually does do.[3] Learning in this stronger sense penetrates to the *being* of the learner. When learning reaches the *being-level,* students have not only learned about certain things and how to do certain things, but they have learned to be certain things: They have learned to be inquiring, to be thorough, to be caring, to be patient, and so on. When you attempt to incorporate dispositional or being-level goals into your teaching, your focus is on the kinds of life habits you want to foster in developing young people, on the behaviors and attitudes you would encourage to the point where they have a chance to become second nature for your students. Here are some examples of being-level goals:

Students will learn to disagree without being disagreeable
Students will come to respect their own life-space and that of others
Students will be disposed to take pride in the work they produce
Students will show evidence of carryover of school learning to their everyday lives, for example, being inclined to see "history in the making" in newspapers and other media, being disposed to take physical education home with them in the form of personal exercise programs, being inclined to apply rational and scientific principles to solve personal problems

Dispositional learning requires that the learner adopt certain attitudes and values in addition to understanding certain things. When teachers systematically attempt to promote the learning of attitudes and values, they find themselves prescribing learning goals in what is called the *affective domain* (discussed in a later section of this chapter).

In designing learning objectives that would foster specific life habits and values in students, it is important for you to be aware of the controversy surrounding the teaching of values in U.S. schools. There are those who maintain that values and attitudes are best developed in the home and the church. Some people believe teachers are violating a student's fundamental right to freedom of choice when they attempt to promote certain value preferences.[4] But, according to the position being taken here, you must inevitably foster certain basic human values to the exclusion of others whenever you set out to manage and instruct a classroom full of students. It is not a matter of whether you should or should not attempt to teach human values in your classes. Instead, it is a question of what kinds of values and attitudes you should be fostering in your students, and how you justify your choices.[5] You are encouraged to further examine both sides of this controversy, and to make your own enlightened decision regarding the role of values in the school curriculum.[6]

Application Exercises

1. Test your ability to recognize three types of teaching goals, namely broad educational goals, subject-specific goals, and overriding teaching goals, by labeling the following goal statements BEG, SSG, or OTG:
   a. Students will understand how values are formed.
   b. Class members will demonstrate respect and support for one another during times of individual vulnerability (e.g., solo class performances).
   c. To develop the whole child.
   d. To understand the importance of the Civil War in U.S. history.
   e. To prepare young people for the world of work.
   f. Students will learn to work cooperatively and productively in small groups to accomplish assigned group tasks.
   g. To acquaint the student with good dramatic literature.
   h. Students will take pride in a job well done and consistently give their best efforts to projects calling for creativity and self-expression.
   i. To instill an appreciation of the requirements of democratic citizenship.
   j. Students will adapt constructively to minor frustrations and disappointments they encounter in an organizational setting.
   k. Students will develop the abilities to solve mathematical problems encountered in day-to-day life.
2. Specify one or two subject-specific goals for the grade level and curricular area (or areas) you presently teach or hope to teach. Provide a rationale for your goal selection. Why are these goals important to the individual and/or to society?
3. Attempt to specify at least three overriding classroom goals that you will seek to achieve in your teaching. These may include *group-process* or *enabling* objectives as well as *dispositional* or *"being-level"* goals that are particularly important to you. In deciding on being-level objectives, a good place to start is by taking inventory of some of the positive human qualities and interpersonal dispositions that you *yourself* possess and would like to model for your students (e.g., basic trust, empathy toward the underdog).

MOVING FROM BROAD GOALS TO SPECIFIC OBJECTIVES

As indicated, our broad educational goals are not intended as objectives for daily lesson planning. A problem arises when we try to use general goal statements as lesson objectives. They are not specific enough, and they are subject to too many different interpretations to be useful in prescribing measurable learning outcomes. With these things in mind, it will facilitate your planning to be able to move from these more global statements of purpose to highly specific learning objectives.

Intermediate Objectives

As will be discussed in chapter 4, the progression from general educational goals to precise learning objectives is enhanced by establishing *intermediate objectives* or *narrowing* objectives that are primarily for teacher use in conceptualizing appropriate applications of the broader goals. They are considerably more explicit than goal statements, but less explicit than behavioral objectives. These intermediate-level objectives are useful for unit planning and long-range organization. They can help teachers focus on main understandings, attitudes, or learning processes they want to promote, without having to specify the precise learning behaviors that it will be necessary to stipulate in daily lesson planning. The following are examples of intermediate-level teaching objectives:

> Students will understand the main causes of big-city air pollution
> Students will visit a local fire station and interact with firemen
> Students will appreciate the need for safety in woodshop
> Students will learn to multiply double-digit numbers
> Students will write short essays on a topic of their choice

So if one of your subject-specific goals should be for students "to understand how their federal government works," a more explicit intermediate objective might be that students "know how a bill becomes a law," whereas a highly precise behavioral objective would be for students to "be able to list, in correct order, the steps a bill follows through Congress, specifying the requirements for passage in each step." As another example, if you should be working from an educational goal that says "students will become proficient in written English," a possible intermediate objective would specify that students "be able to write compositions that are grammatically sound," leading to a behavioral objective that stipulates, "students will compose two-to three-page autobiographical sketches, demonstrating proper subject-verb agreement and correct spelling in each sentence."

WRITING BEHAVIORAL OBJECTIVES

Once you have established a framework of broad goals and intermediate objectives for your teaching, you are in a position to begin developing more specific instructional objectives for the classes you will teach. We have seen that educational goals are broad statements of intended outcomes for student learning. In contrast, behavioral objectives are specific statements of what learners will be able to do during and/or after instruction that they cannot do before that instruction. Although there are a number of ways to write behavioral objectives, there are some general rules to observe in meeting the requirements of highly specific, measurable learning objectives. They include:

RULE 1. Describe the expected behavior of the student rather than the teacher.

RULE 2. Describe observable behavior in terms of an outcome verb that the student will perform (e.g., list, identify, arrange, weigh, describe).

RULE 3. Describe the criterion for evaluating an acceptable performance of the behavior (e.g., name at least four colors of the rainbow, hammer three nails one-inch deep, run a mile in six minutes).

RULE 4. Specify important conditions under which the student will perform the behavior (e.g., run a mile before breakfast, kick three field goals in a championship game, solve a quadratic equation during a classroom session).[7]

The following are some examples of objectives that meet these criteria:

Learners are to spell with 95 percent accuracy, the dictated words in each spelling lesson

Given a reference manual, the student will write a job application letter in correct form with no grammatical errors

Given the name of a note and the scale, a member of the chorus should be able to sing the note accurately nine out of ten times

On a level surface, the student should be able to do thirty push-ups in three minutes

Using no references, the student should be able to write five ways that socialist and capitalist countries are alike and five ways they differ

When presented with pairs of paintings, the student should be able to choose the paintings of the impressionist period seven out of ten times

As you examine these objectives, you will notice that each contains a descriptive verb or "action word" that leaves little doubt about the kind of behavior the student is to exhibit in satisfying the learning requirement. With correctly worded objectives it is easy to see how the teacher can tell if the objective has been reached. When writing behavioral objectives, verbs that are vague, ambiguous, and not measurable should be avoided. Words such as *know, understand, analyze, appreciate, comprehend,* and *realize* are not action verbs. Whereas they may represent important concepts in the area of human learning and behavior, they are not observable actions and thus cannot be used when writing performance or behavioral objectives. They can, however, be used in describing goals or intermediate-level objectives.

Also, each of the aforementioned objectives makes clear the performance conditions and the degree of accuracy expected.[8] One quick way to test a learning prescription to determine if it is specific enough to qualify as a performance objective is to ask yourself whether several independent learning evaluators would see the same thing. In the case of an ambiguous, intermediate-level objective like "students will have a knowledge of their multiplication tables," it is quite conceivable that different teachers would arrive at different determinations in assessing student's knowledge of multiplication. When we are concerned with the precise measurement of student performance in particular teaching areas, nonspecific objectives provide no solid basis for defining and evaluating learning outcomes.

Application Exercises

1. Classify the following as a subject-specific goal (SSG), intermediate objective (IO), or behavioral objective (BO):
   a. Students will evaluate the effectiveness of their experiments.
   b. When dissecting a frog, students will identify organs of the digestive system.
   c. Given a worksheet containing twenty addition problems requiring regrouping, students will correctly solve seventeen during class.
   d. Students will gain knowledge of the electoral system.
   e. Students will understand the process for electing a president.
   f. Students will become familiar with several varieties of modern art.
   g. Given a work of propaganda, the pupil will be able to spot the propaganda devices and fallacious logic in the piece.

2. From the following items, identify those that state an identifiable behavior or an observable performance:
   a. The student will appreciate the music of Bach.
   b. From memory, the student will name the Allied countries of World War II.
   c. The learner will describe the function of baking powder in the making of bread.
   d. The learner will know the Constitution and its amendments.
   e. The student will learn to write properly.
   f. The student will learn the names of six common tools in metal shop.
   g. The student will understand how paper is made.
   h. The student will write a short essay demonstrating proper use of the eight major punctuation marks.
   i. To show the effects of smoking on the individual.
   j. The student will draw a diagram of the combustion engine.

3. Examine each of the following statements and determine whether it meets the conditions necessary to be considered a behavioral objective. Rewrite any improperly written objectives in the proper form.
   a. At the end of the course the student will understand the fundamental concepts of long division.
   b. The student will learn about the structure and organization of Congress.
   c. Students will be able to state orally the correct time for any clock settings.
   d. Students will develop a clear understanding of the biological principle of photosynthesis.
   e. The student will be able to identify the major parts of speech in several unfamiliar sentences.

MAIN CATEGORIES OF EDUCATIONAL OBJECTIVES

Cognitive Learning

Up to this point in our discussion of learning objectives, we have focused on school learning tasks associated primarily with traditional subject-matter learning. For example, memorizing multiplication tables, learning to spell, comparing national economies, and writing job applications all involve essentially mental or intellectual processes. These learning activities and others of a similar nature that call for memorizing, analyzing, formulating, reasoning, judging, and so forth are called *cognitive learning* tasks. The educational psychologist Benjamin Bloom and his associates describe learning objectives in the cognitive domain as:

> objectives which emphasize remembering or reproducing something which has presumably been learned, as well as objectives which involve the solving of some intellectual task for which the individual has to determine the essential problem and then reorder given material or combine it with ideas, methods, or procedures previously learned. Cognitive objectives vary from simple recall of material learned to highly original and creative ways of combining and synthesizing new ideas and materials.[9]

Classifying Cognitive Objectives. Bloom's group has developed a useful taxonomy (or classification system) of cognitive objectives that allows teachers to better understand the kinds of cognitive tasks they are prescribing for their students. It contains six cognitive levels, ranging from simple and concrete to more complex and abstract mental operations.[10] Consider the following summary of these six cognitive levels:

1. Knowledge. Knowledge is defined as the remembering of previously learned material, from specific facts, such as dates, events, persons, and places, to basic principles and generalizations. All that is required is the bringing to mind of the appropriate information. Knowledge represents the lowest level of learning outcomes in the cognitive domain.

2. Comprehension. This is generally considered to be a minimal kind of "understanding." It entails the ability to grasp facts or ideas and make use of them without relating them to each other (e.g., paraphrasing or even interpreting something gained from reading or listening). At this lowest level of understanding, students in a foreign language class should be able to translate a paragraph from Spanish to English, while students in a social studies class might explain in their own words the causes of the Civil War. Also at the comprehension level, the learner may be able to extend thinking beyond the data by making simple inferences. As an example, students in science would be able to draw conclusions from a simple demonstration or experiment.

3. Application. This intellectual skill involves the use of information in new and concrete situations. The information may be in the form of general ideas, concepts, principles, or theories that must be remembered or applied. The science student, for example, who draws conclusions from a particular experiment at the comprehension level is now able to apply the basic principles to related experiments or scientific happenings. The social studies student can relate concepts or principles concerning the separation of powers to current problems.

4. Analysis. This skill entails taking apart information and making relationships in order to discover hidden meanings and the basic structure of an idea or fact. The student is able to read between the lines, to distinguish fact and opinion, and to assess degree of consistency or inconsistency. Thus, the science student is able to distinguish between relevant and extraneous materials or events. Also, the social science student is able to detect unstated assumptions that can be inferred only by analyzing statements within a document.

5. Synthesis. At this level, the learner is able to put together old knowledge in new ways. It involves the analysis and recombination of bits of knowledge to develop a structure or pattern the students did not have prior to learning (a creative behavior). The learner draws on elements from many sources in addition to those of the particular problem under consideration. For example, the science student may propose a unique plan for testing a hypothesis. The mathematics student may make a discovery or generalization not evident from the given communication.

6. Evaluation. This is considered the highest of all mental processes. It involves the ability to judge the value of material (e.g., a statement, poem, research report) for a given purpose. The judgments are to be based on distinct criteria for such decisions. As examples, students in an English class should be able to judge the merits of a story or a play, whereas students in social studies should be able to appraise how well our country's democracy works.

Psychomotor Learning

Although cognitive learning has received most of the emphasis in formal education, it is obvious that school learning often involves more than just mental or intellectual operations. In fact, there are areas within our school curriculums that heavily depend on the learning of coordinated physical movements as the main basis for student achievement, for example, physical education, typing, drawing, woodworking. Here we are concerned with *psychomotor learning,* or learning tasks that involve physical skills and often complex mind–body interactions, for example, handwriting, shooting a basket, playing a musical instrument. In contrast with cognitive learning tasks, which involve mental processing of information, learning objectives in the psychomotor domain are, as Bloom and his associates describe them, "objectives which emphasize some muscular or motor skill, some manipulation of objects and materials, or some act which requires a neuromuscular coordination."[11]

There is a cognitive component to most psychomotor objectives, but their basic purpose is to describe physical behavior.[12] We tend to separate cognitive and psychomotor objectives because they usually require different practice conditions. The outcomes of cognitive learning are ordinarily inferred from verbal behavior, whereas in psychomotor learning changes in the speed, accuracy, integration, and coordination of body movements are more directly observable.

Goals and objectives in the psychomotor domain are especially important to elementary teachers. In the lower grades, merely teaching a youngster to hold a pencil or crayon may constitute an initial objective and using the pencil or crayon properly can become a more advanced behavioral objective.

To help you distinguish between cognitive and psychomotor learning tasks, examine the following behavioral objectives and attempt to determine which are psychomotor objectives:

1. Given six equations with one unknown, students will be able to solve at least five.
2. Students will be able to march around the room three times in step to a military march.
3. Students will give examples, in their own words, of recent legal decisions regarding equal rights.
4. Students will be able to type an average of sixty words per minute for five minutes with fewer than four errors.
5. Given a situation in which a faulty conclusion is presented, students will analyze the data and identify the errors in logic.
6. Students will be able to print the letters of the alphabet, duplicating the model in the writing manual.

You will generally find that such physical behaviors, with and without objects, are easy to describe in behavioral terms because the required competence is always tied directly to a clearly defined overt behavior. For example, skill in throwing a baseball is a directly observable action. It does not require some extraneous behavior such as writing an essay or making marks on a true–false test as indirect evidence of achievement.

Classifying Psychomotor Objectives.   Like objectives in the cognitive domain, psychomotor objectives can also be classified according to behavioral levels from simple to complex. One classification system developed by Kenneth Hoover provides an easily grasped model for designing learning objectives in the psychomotor domain.[13] The model consists of a four-stage sequence of skill development tasks that will be useful to you at points in your teaching where your focus is on a performative skill:

1. Observing.   At this level, the learner observes a more experienced person performing the activity. The learner is usually asked to observe sequences and relationships and to pay particular attention to the finished product. Sometimes reading directions substitutes for observation, although often reading supplements direct observation. For example, the beginning tennis student may read a manual and then watch the instructor demonstrate certain techniques.

2. Imitating.   By the time learners have advanced to this level, they have acquired the rudiments of the desired behavior. Individuals follow directions and sequences under close supervision, making a deliberate effort to imitate the model. The total act is not important at this stage; neither is timing nor coordination. The tennis player, for example, may practice a prescribed stance or stroke.

3. Practicing.   The entire sequence of steps is performed repeatedly at this level. Conscious effort is no longer necessary once the performance becomes more or less habitual in nature. At this level, we might reasonably say that the person has acquired the skill.

4. Adapting.   This fourth stage of skill development is often referred to as "perfection of the skill." Although some individuals develop much greater skill than others in certain areas, there is always room for improvement. The process involves adapting minor details that, in turn, influence total performance. These modifications may be initiated by the learner or the teacher. This is the process engaged in, for example, when a good basketball player becomes a better player.

Affective Learning

Human learning can entail not only mental achievement and the development of physical skills, but it almost always involves feelings and attitudes. *Affective learning* is the term used to identify the feeling, valuing, and attitudinal components of learning processes. When students indicate that they have enjoyed reading a particular book, what they are really saying is that they have learned to value the work of the author. As teachers, we become sensitive to the difference between this and a situation where a person merely says to us, "I can read." The act of reading itself is essentially a cognitive skill. Coming to enjoy reading or valuing a particular book involves the affective domain of learning.

Affective learning would also encompass personality development. One of a teacher's goals might be to lead an overly shy student who never raises a hand in class to join actively in classwork. This is a good example of an affective goal. Consider some other instances of affective learning:

Willingly obeys the playground regulations
Enjoys listening to chamber music
Becomes interested in community problems
Shows willingness to comply with health regulations
Recognizes form and beauty in art, dress, and architecture
Is sensitive to human need and pressing social problems

Each of these statements reflects a behavioral disposition that goes beyond knowing about something and indicates an attitude toward or an inclination to be involved with some situation.

Notice also that each statement designates a learning outcome that is not observable as stated. Just as thoughts or thought processes cannot be directly observed, such is also the case with feelings, values, and attitudes. Terms like *appreciates, enjoys,* or *shows interest,* are acceptable for communicating broad goals or intermediate objectives in the affective domain, but are inappropriate when the need is to describe affective behavior in precise terms.

Affective conditions must be inferred from observing the student's behavior. But because the affective domain encompasses such intangibles as emotions and attitudes, behavioral objectives are even less easy to specify than cognitive objectives. The indicators we use to decide whether or not students know certain elements of school subject matter are better established than those we have for determining whether students do in fact appreciate or value aspects of school learning.

When analyzing an affective goal like "the learner will enjoy history," teachers of history would use essentially the same procedure in reducing the goal to behavioral terms as they would with cognitive objectives. They would attempt to identify in precise terms the sorts of behavioral indicators that would allow them to infer students were enjoying history. Students might, for example, do some or all of the following: (1) opt for a front-row seat and be especially attentive during history class, (2) talk impromptu with other students about history, (3) carry around a history notebook, (4) spend their own money on historical paperbacks, (5) come to school early to ask questions about the history they are reading, or (6) regularly browse in the school library for historical material.

A list such as this does illustrate that, given a certain amount of effort, affective goals can be expressed in behavioral terms. It takes a good deal of observation, direct and indirect, to permit a decision on whether an affective goal has been attained. Direct observation, of course, is what the teacher personally sees. Indirect observation is what other people—the student's classmates, the librarian, the guidance counselor—tell the teacher.

Classifying Affective Objectives.   Krathwohl, Bloom, and Masia produced a taxonomy for categorizing affective objectives that is similar to the one Bloom and his associates devised for classifying cognitive goals.[14] This system of classifying affective objectives describes a continuum of affective behaviors in terms of degree of internalization. Early in this process, one can be only peripherally involved with a particular idea or object, aware of its existence, but not investing strong emotion in it. Farther along in the taxonomy, we see how one becomes more deeply involved, as in responding to the object or idea, developing positive feelings for it, or even making it a whole way of life. The following is a summary of these five levels of affective learning:

1. Receiving (attending).   At this first level, the learner becomes aware of an idea, thing, or process and is willing to listen to a given communication. From a teaching standpoint, the concern is with getting, holding, and directing the student's attention. The student may advance from a purely passive role of captive receiver to one of directing attention to the communication, despite competing or distracting stimuli. For example, the student listens for rhythm in poetry or prose as it is read aloud.

2. Responding.   This involves displaying an interest in the subject. At this low level of commitment, the student displays an interest in the learning object, but has not yet learned to value it. From obedient participation, the student may advance to making a voluntary response and finally to having a pleasurable feeling about, or sense of satisfaction with, the subject matter. This matter may be expressed by the goal ''Reads poetry for personal pleasure.''

3. Valuing.   As the term suggests, at this level the student has come to value a thing, phenomenon, or behavior. Or, it might be said that the learner ''holds the value.'' At this level, individuals are motivated by their commitment to the behavior. At the lower end of the valuing continuum, learners might hold a belief somewhat tentatively; at the other end, their value becomes one of conviction. In fact, one who holds the value strongly may attempt to persuade others to adopt this way of thinking. Instructional objectives commonly classified under attitudes and appreciations are appropriate at this level.

4. Organization After having become committed to the value, the learner organizes personal values into a value system. Finding that more than one value may apply to a situation and sometimes values conflict, the person finds it necessary to gain a better understanding of the values and then to organize them into a system of dominant and subordinate values. At this level learners will be able to defend their value choices according to an established rationale. Objectives relating to the development of a philosophy of life would fall into this category.

5. Internalization. At this level of the affective domain, individuals have a value system that has controlled their behavior for a sufficiently long time that they can be said to have developed a characteristic life-style. Values have become integrated into some kind of consistent system. Instructional objectives concerned with the student's general patterns of adjustment (personal, social, emotional) would be appropriate here.

The Benefits of Classifying Objectives into Domains

It is, of course, not to be imagined that these three learning domains are mutually exclusive. Most of the time you are teaching you will be operating in several domains at once. Whereas some learning behaviors may be more easily classifiable into one or another of the three domains, others entail a complex interplay among the three types of learning. A student reciting Lincoln's Gettysburg Address is demonstrating cognition, affect (if the student feels any emotion or anxiety about reciting), and psychomotor skills (by standing, gesturing, and speaking). Emotion is an essential aspect of intellectual processes, and motor and mental skills have an affective dimension. Yet, some behaviors are more intellectual than emotional, whereas others are more emotional than intellectual. Still other action requires more mental and physical dexterity than anything else. As a teacher, you should remember which domain is important to you at the moment and set your behavioral objectives accordingly.

An ability to analyze learning in these three areas helps to clarify our thinking about what we are attempting to teach. Some believe the most important effect of this classification system has been to increase the emphasis given to higher-level cognitive activities.[15] There is a tendency for teachers to concentrate on lower-level skills within the cognitive domain to the exclusion of the higher-level skills.[16] In other words, we may be more inclined to ask students to remember a specific date from the Civil War period than ask them to analyze causes for the war. It is important to get beyond these lower-level skills in teaching, thus the classification of objectives in the taxonomy allows a check to see that we have objectives at the various levels of complexity.

In addition, this taxonomy of educational objectives serves to remind us of the complexity of productive learning, allowing us to see it in several important dimensions while pointing up the fallacy of emphasizing one type of learning process to the neglect of important accompanying processes. Thus, although we may feature the learning of history or mathematics as essentially cognitive processes, an enlightened perspective on learning should move us to ask whether it is realistic to neglect the affective domain in teaching areas where motivation is a perennial problem. Or, for any of us inclined to view physical education classes in terms of isolated skill development, an ability to view learning in broader terms would help us to recognize the need for the addition of some important cognitive and affective learning objectives in an area where psychomotor tasks have often been allowed to predominate.

Moreover, classifying objectives in this way highlights important relationships between these different types of learning. It becomes evident that goals in one domain are often reached through another domain. For example, good teachers frequently attempt to develop interest (affective goal) in a particular area so the student will learn it (cognitive goal). On other occasions, new cognitive learning is responsible for changing student attitudes. Outstanding teachers have the ability to reach cognitive goals through the affective domain. It turns out that the most liked and respected teachers are often described by students as those who take a deep interest in them, who challenge them, who understand their anxieties, who respect their opinions and do not embarrass them, who maintain high interest, and who instill a love of the subject.[17] These attributes are affective in nature.

Finally, recognizing basic differences between cognitive and affective objectives allows teachers to skillfully use each type of objectives to best advantage. Cognitive objectives can be used as teaching tools for purposes of informing and guiding the learner. We might think of the main function of these objectives as facilitating communication between teacher and student. On the other hand, the function of an affective objective is quite different. It is intended to be used by the teacher to identify those learner behaviors that indicate whether the learner values what is being taught. When there is good evidence that students do not value certain learning experiences, this might signal a need for the teacher to reexamine her teaching approach and her relationships with students. While a cognitive objective will indicate the extent to which students understand a subject, an affective objective will indicate whether students value the subject sufficiently to make contact with the subject, particularly outside of class.

Application Exercises

1. Classify the following objectives as representative of the Cognitive, Affective, or Psychomotor domains:
   a. The student will voluntarily read outside material related to current events.
   b. Learners are to develop skill in swimming so that they can, using any stroke of their choice, swim fifty meters within two minutes.
   c. The student will recognize the differences between facts and opinions.
   d. Given a model of a hypothetical cell, the student will identify the cellular structures.
   e. The student will correctly operate the duplicating machine.
   f. Students will express an interest in visiting a local art museum.
   g. The learner will show an appreciation of outdoor sports.
   h. Students will be able to list some of the characteristics of social insects.
   i. The student will correctly focus the microscope.
   j. When given ten Spanish sentences, students will be able to translate at least seven into English without error.
   k. The student will volunteer to remain after class to help clean up the classroom.

2. Consider the following samples of learning behaviors and determine which level of cognitive learning each represents (i.e., knowledge, comprehension, application, analysis, synthesis, or evaluation):
   a. Describes in own words the three major causes of the War of 1812.
   b. Composes a short musical score.
   c. Employs principles of nutrition and a list of foods to plan three menus for well-balanced meals.
   d. Names the fifty states of the Union.
   e. Judges a presidential decision.
   f. Compares the actions of characters from a short story.
   g. Provides an example to support an idea.
   h. Generalizes a solution to a problem from accumulated data.
   i. Recalls the parts of a lathe.
   j. Chooses from several alternatives.
   k. Translates a paragraph from Spanish into English.
3. Examine the following affective objectives and decide which level of affective development each represents (i.e., receiving, responding, valuing, value organization, or value internalization):
   a. Science students will develop a commitment to the need for clean air and water and will become active in encouraging others to do so.
   b. Students will listen patiently and good-naturedly to the opinions of peers who may have different points of view.
   c. Students will entertain an interest in poetry, and during a free reading period will select a book of poetry as one of their choices.
   d. Students will learn to value honesty and will show this by consistently monitoring their own behavior on tests and assignments and by discouraging others from cheating.
   e. High school students will accept responsibility for establishing career choices by seeking and organizing relevant job information at a career fair.

MAKING YOUR OBJECTIVES RELEVANT

One of the main reasons for using behavioral objectives is to enhance communication between the teacher and the learner. Clear and unambiguous statements of learning intentions will go a long way toward helping students know what you expect them to be able to do. However, getting students to agree that learning objectives are relevant and worth pursuing may be another matter. Students become used to reading textbook chapters, doing math problems, writing compositions, bringing in newspaper articles, and so on, simply because that is what school requires. They often approach these learning chores with little enthusiasm because they fail to see how they connect with their present or future lives.

Some general strategies for helping students see the relevance of formal learning objectives are:

1. Take time to discuss with your students the objectives that will be the focus for

classroom learning. Rather than simply telling students that certain new learning is important, use an inductive approach in these discussions, one that in its ideal allows you and your students to derive learning objectives together.

2. When starting a new unit, begin with real-life applications of school learning and work backward to performance objectives. For example, make it a practice to confront students with realistic situations in their present or future lives where they will have occasions to use mathematical percentages or to communicate their ideas in writing. Take time here to develop a problem-solving frame of reference toward new learning before focusing on precise objectives and learning tasks.

3. Whenever possible, allow students to view new learning in wholes rather than in fragments. For example, students in a writing class are most likely to see the relevance of an objective stating ''the learner will demonstrate proper subject-verb agreement'' when this particular skill element is presented in context (e.g., after they have had opportunities to write compositions and to experience a need for better grammar). Basketball players are more apt to internalize an objective calling for a particular level of competence at freethrow shooting after they have played the game and found themselves lacking in this particular subskill.

4. Provide opportunities for students to immediately begin practicing new learning in their out-of-school lives. Have them bring in examples of applications they encounter in the mass media or in their physical and social environments. Have them keep journals documenting their efforts to practice new language skills, to recognize history in the making, or to make use of mathematics in their daily lives. By making such carryover activities an integral part of new learning, you help develop a perception that classroom learning objectives have relevance to something beyond school.

THE CONTROVERSY SURROUNDING BEHAVIORAL OBJECTIVES

Those who are strong advocates of behavioral objectives in teaching often present the following arguments in their favor:

1. Objectives provide a necessary focus for learning. They help teachers as well as students clarify learning goals. When teachers have written objectives, they know precisely what they want to teach and can spend their time concentrating on developing lesson plans and procedures aimed at the objectives. Students also know what is expected of them. They are likely to be more focused and businesslike when learning tasks are clearly spelled out for them.

2. Written objectives make evaluation easier. Teachers do not have to puzzle over what the next test should cover. Tests will cover defined objectives of the units presently being studied. Also, students are likely to be better prepared for written tests and other forms of evaluation when they have been told ahead of

time specifically what they are being held responsible for knowing. This reduces worry and anxiety on their part and allows them to concentrate on learning.

3. Learning objectives can help you as a teacher to assess students' entry-level skills. For example, if your prescription for student achievement requires that students be able to balance algebraic equations containing parentheses and multiple terms, you can do a task analysis of this objective to determine the necessary subskills required to solve equations of this sort (i.e., knowledge of the "distributive principle," ability to combine unlike terms on each side of the equation before proceeding further). You are now in a position to pretest students to determine whether they possess these necessary subskills.

4. Precise learning objectives give you necessary ammunition for dealing with parents and administrators when they are interested in knowing what you are attempting to accomplish in your classes. With the present emphasis on educational accountability, parents are concerned to know what their school taxes are buying and administrators want to be able to show that their schools are producing tangible learning in students. Teachers with precise objectives are able to give direct and confident answers to specific questions about learning achievement in their classes.

Other educators have been highly critical of the use of behavioral objectives as standard operating procedure for classroom teachers. Their criticisms are based on the following sorts of claims:

1. Behavioral objectives tend to promote trivial learning behaviors because these are the easiest to operationalize. If learning objectives must always be reducible to overt behavior, teachers will avoid classroom activities that promote less measurable learning. As a result, the really important outcomes of education will be underemphasized. (This objection has, in turn, been countered by the argument that explicit objectives actually make it much easier for educators to attend to significant instructional outcomes. Instead of encouraging shallow learning prescriptions, they in fact make it more possible to identify and reject those objectives that are unimportant.)

2. Specifying objectives in precise behavioral terms may be appropriate for certain kinds of learning, but it is inappropriate for many other types. Behavioral objectives may be suitable for simpler subject matter in the lower grades, but are too difficult to successfully prepare for complex courses and impossible to write for art and music classes and others where teachers' judgments must be subjective. (Although advocates of behavioral objectives would concur that it is indeed difficult to identify measurable student behaviors in areas like fine arts and the humanities, they believe that this should not allow subject specialists in these areas to avoid the responsibility for specifying in precise terms the learning outcomes they are attempting to promote. Promoters of behavioral objectives would point out that teachers in areas like English, art, and music are constantly making precise judgments about the acceptability of student performances. In the interests of good education and better communication, these teachers should be committed to making their criteria explicit.)

3. Teachers who devote themselves religiously to the achievement of stated behavioral objectives are likely to lose sight of what teaching is all about. As a result, their classroom manner will suffer. In order to reach their behavioral objectives, teachers are likely to become more impersonal and mechanical in their teaching approach. They may depart from their warm, friendly interpersonal tone and resort to force, threat, and intimidation. (Those in favor of behavioral objectives are quick to maintain that the use of specific objectives does in no way imply a need for threat or impersonality on the part of a teacher. There is simply no connection between the degree of specificity of one's goals and the particular methods one uses for achieving them. When teachers begin to stray from their educational missions, it is more likely the result of fuzzy and imprecise rather than highly specific goals.)

4. Adherence to behavioral objectives prevents teachers from seizing unforeseen opportunities for instruction. They will be less inclined to move spontaneously in new directions or to take opportunities for enthusiastic discussion of topics that arise unexpectedly during a lesson. Teachers will feel less free to depart from their lesson plans. (Proponents of behavioral objectives, on the other hand, would argue that any possible reduction in incidental learning is more than made up for by the greater mastery of important learnings that become highlighted through the use of specific objectives. They would also reiterate their contention that having precise objectives does not restrict the means a teacher uses to reach these ends. Although serendipity in the classroom is always welcome, the teacher should always be able to justify it in terms of its contribution to worthwhile learning goals.)

Deciding What Your Approach Shall Be

In attempting to decide how precisely you should specify the learning objectives for your own teaching, there are several things you should take into consideration: (1) the subjects you are teaching, (2) the grade level and ability levels of your students, (3) the expectations of the school administration where you are employed, and (4) your readiness as a beginning teacher to proceed without highly explicit objectives.

Some subject areas, like mathematics and physical education, lend themselves more readily to the specification of measurable criteria for student achievement. These are skill areas with relatively overt performance expectations. In other subjects, like English and social studies, where the indicators of achievement are often more nebulous, highly specific behavioral objectives may be appropriate for some learning tasks (e.g. spelling lessons, map-reading projects) and less appropriate for others (e.g., exploratory discussions, creative writing assignments).

Also, precise behavioral objectives are more difficult to write (and in some cases are less relevant) in the higher grades because of the increased complexity of the subject matter and because the teaching goals more frequently involve understanding and appreciation. Teachers in the lower grades are normally teaching more easily definable skills to more concrete functioning students. It is generally easier for elementary teachers to adopt a pattern of stipulating behavioral objectives, and with less doubt as to their appropriateness. Teachers at the senior high and college levels need to be careful not to trivialize learnings that call for the individual creativity or higher thought processes of students. They will ordinarily have more difficult decisions to make when it comes to applying performance criteria to student learning.

On taking a teaching position, you will want to determine what the district and school expectations are for teacher lesson planning. Some districts require teachers to periodically submit written objectives and/or lesson plans for the subject(s) they teach. They may or may not insist that these objectives be written in behavioral form. Regardless of how extensively you will apply them in your teaching, it is important for you to have knowledge of and be able to write behavioral objectives.

As a beginning teacher attempting to find your own way with lesson planning and objective writing, it is probably a good idea to give behavioral objectives a try. Although some investigators have argued that rigid adherence to objectives may result in mechanical learning and the loss of unexpected happenings, there is good reason to believe that the advantages of behavioral objectives far outweigh the disadvantages.[18] This is particularly the case when you are first learning to organize for teaching. You can better judge their appropriateness to your teaching after you have had experience with highly specific objectives. Allow one or two school years for you and your students to become comfortable with them. After a fair trial, you are in a better position to determine whether they are worth the effort.

It is important that your approach to learning objectives be as reasonable and flexible as possible. Here are some additional tips:

1. When teaching intellectually mature students, seek to avoid the trivialization of learning by working for a distribution of cognitive objectives across the six levels of learning and across the different domains. Some knowledge- and comprehension-level objectives are usually necessary, but a little planning on your part should lead to the development of application, analysis, synthesis, and evaluation objectives.

2. Do not be reluctant to specify in detail what you want your students to get out of a lesson for fear of discouraging incidental learning. Remember, you can always add objectives to describe any learning you want students to demonstrate in addition to what you had originally planned. You can also make allowances in your lesson plan for spontaneous exploration of topics that were not included in the objectives.

3. It is possible to write specific objectives for most any learning activity, if one deems it appropriate. However, it may not be necessary to develop long lists of objectives for each unit of instruction. Too many objectives may lead to a perception that the outcomes of learning will be trivial, just as too few may lead to vagueness and learner confusion. The correct number of objectives depends on many factors, but perhaps most importantly on the subject content and grade level of the learners. Usually, the more sophisticated the learners, the fewer the objectives required.

4. There may be times when you want to deliberately avoid projecting learning outcomes prior to exposing students to a new learning experience. Eisner, one of the critics of behavioral objectives, recommends the use of what he calls *expressive objectives* for some learning activities. According to Eisner, an expressive objective

identifies a situation in which pupils are to work, a problem in which they are to engage; but it does not specify what from that encounter, situation, problem, or task they are to learn. An expressive objective provides both the teacher and the student with an invitation to explore, defer, or focus on issues that are of particular interest or importance to the inquirer.[19]

A teacher who takes a class on a field trip to a local hospital for the purpose of allowing students to experience human activity in that setting realizes that each student will achieve different learning outcomes from the experience. In this case, the teacher may prefer to work from an expressive rather than a behavioral objective.

A SUMMARY OF GUIDELINES FOR DESIGNING TEACHING OBJECTIVES

1. Make an effort to "own" the objectives that govern your teaching and your relationships with students. Take time at the beginning of each new teaching module (i.e., year, semester, unit) to make explicit the learning objectives you wish to achieve. This will pay important dividends in terms of helping you to keep your teaching organized and focused.
2. Know the difference between *educational goals* and *behavioral objectives* and recognize where each is appropriate in your planning.
3. Be clear on your immediate objectives for each lesson, but do not lose sight of your *overriding objectives*. Make these reflect your most important priorities as an educator. Look to your overriding objectives as stabilizers for your teaching.
4. Know what your *enabling objectives* are and what enabling objectives are instrumental to the achievement of your immediate objectives.
5. Be capable of writing behavioral objectives that are learner-referenced, contain an action verb, and include conditions of performance.
6. Be able to write objectives in the three main learning domains (cognitive, affective, and psychomotor), and know how these domains relate. Realize that teaching goals in one domain may be reached through another domain.
7. Be able to write objectives that represent a progression from simpler to more complex levels of learning. In teaching areas where it is appropriate, work to include objectives that promote higher thought processes (cognitive domain) and those that foster the internalization of new learning (affective domain).
8. When trying to determine behavioral components of affective goals, think of people who exhibit these qualities (what do they *do?*).
9. Recognize the main strengths as well as some of the limitations of behavioral objectives. A decision to use or not use behavioral objectives is one you will have to make for yourself. Base your decision on experience. Try them and see how they work for you.
10. The following are some concluding generalizations to consider:
    a. The effort you devote to developing objectives can reduce the work and uncertainty involved in deciding what and how to teach. Teachers make decisions every day about what is and is not important. Your objectives communicate these decisions.

b. Sound evaluation of student learning requires the specification of objectives.

c. Outcomes of cognitive learning are usually inferred from verbal behavior.

d. Factual learning that never becomes manifest in skills or habits is learning in the weakest sense. Your overriding objectives are aimed at promoting behavioral habits and dispositions, or learning in the strong sense.

e. Behavioral objectives are means to certain ends, not ends in themselves. Most important, a good objective should describe an important learning outcome. Otherwise, a beautifully stated objective may be of little use.

f. Behavioral objectives become more difficult to write in the higher grades because of increased complexity of subject matter and because teaching goals more frequently involve understandings and appreciations.

g. Intentional learning is generally superior for students who are supplied with objectives, whereas incidental (unplanned) learning may be adversely affected (objectives may cause the loss of unexpected happenings).[20]

SUGGESTED ACTIVITIES AND QUESTIONS

1. Attempt to obtain a district-wide goal statement of a school system with which you are acquainted. Does it mention such things as democratic values, individual development, social adjustment, cultural traditions, or vocational preparation? What do you take to be its major emphasis?

2. Compose a statement of your present philosophy of education that takes into consideration some of the main developmental needs of today's young people as well as major requirements of life in a complex technological society.

3. Write a short critical appraisal of how instructional objectives will help or hinder you in your teaching.

4. In your own words describe an *experience objective*. Mention several possible learning activities in one of your teaching areas that could call for experience objectives rather than specific behavioral objectives.

NOTES AND REFERENCES

1. The process of goal development can be more manageable and rational if you have begun to formulate a workable philosophy of education and teaching for yourself. This should be an ongoing endeavor as you prepare for a teaching career. This handbook is designed to encourage you to reflect on the goals you carry with you into teaching.

2. Robert W. Travers and Jacqueline Dillon, *The Making of a Teacher: A Plan for Professional Self-Development.* New York: Macmillan, 1975, p. 30.

3. Hoover observes that "although evaluation of learning achievement has emphasized the can-do dimension, it is the does-do dimension that every teacher seeks. Thus, an individual who has internalized a specific value voluntarily behaves in a manner indicating that he or she holds that value" (Kenneth H. Hoover, *The Professional Teacher's Handbook,* 3rd ed. Boston: Allyn and Bacon, 1982, p. 16).

4. Searles argues that "ethical right demands that each individual be allowed to make up his [or her] own mind as to values and subsequent modes of conduct. Therefore the instruction system (of the school) has the right, and in a deep sense, the duty, to present the individual with the alternatives of behavior and leave him free to choose his [or her] own pattern" (John E. Searles, *A System for Instruction.* Scranton, Penn: International Textbook Company, 1968, p. 47). Searles suggests that the dilemma regarding the teaching of values might

be resolved if the school would agree to promote only "behavioral and procedural" values, and not "substantive" ones.

5. Childs, in a classic statement on the moral basis of deliberate education, maintains that "education is a value-conditioned activity. The school seeks to cultivate values in the young by means of both the subject-matters and the methods that it employs in its program. . . . The moral element is preeminently involved in all of those selections and rejections that are inescapable in the construction of the purposes and the curriculum of the school. . . . The fact that the outcomes we seek involve the lives of the immature deepens—it does not diminish—our responsibility to know what we are trying to accomplish when we undertake to educate" (John L. Childs, *Education and Morals*. New York: John Wiley, 1967, pp. 16–17).

6. For a pointed discussion, featuring two opposing views on the role of the schools in value development, see the articles by Lawrence Kohlberg and Edward A. Wynne in James W. Noll (ed.), *Taking Sides: Clashing Views on Controversial Educational Issues,* 5th ed. Guilford, Conn: Dushkin Publishing Group, 1989, pp. 44–63.

7. This set of requirements for writing nonambiguous behavioral objectives is adapted from Ronald T. Hyman, *Ways of Teaching,* 2nd ed. Philadelphia: J. P. Lippincott, 1974, p. 43.

8. It may not always be necessary to include these two performance criteria to be satisfied that you have a useful behavioral objective. For example, objectives like "Students will be able to describe the main causes of World War II" or "Students will write business letters utilizing three different types of salutations," may be sufficiently nonambiguous for your purposes. In the case of the first example, it would of course be more precise to stipulate that students will describe these causes "in writing on a teacher-made test," and that they will "accurately represent at least three of the four main causes." The particular subject matter, students, and context will no doubt have a bearing on the degree of specificity required.

9. David Krathwohl, Benjamin S. Bloom, and Bertram B. Masia, *Taxonomy of Educational Objectives, Handbook II: Affective Domain.* New York: David McKay, 1964, pp. 6–7.

10. Benjamin S. Bloom (Ed.), *Taxonomy of Educational Objectives: Handbook I: Cognitive Domain.* New York: David McKay, 1956, see Part Two, pp. 62–197.

11. Krathwohl, Bloom, and Masia, op. cit., pp. 6–7.

12. P. G. Kapfer and G. F. Ovard, *Preparing and Using Individualized Learning Packages.* Englewood Cliffs, N.J.: Educational Technology Publications, 1971.

13. Hoover, op. cit., p. 11.

14. Krathwohl, Bloom, and Masia, op. cit., pp. 45–62.

15. John A. Glover, Roger H. Bruning, and Robert W. Filbeck, *Educational Psychology: Principles and Applications.* Boston: Little, Brown, 1983, p. 333.

16. The widespread emphasis on less complex forms of cognitive learning has been documented by studies showing that more than 95 percent of the learning demanded by broad samples of teaching materials in an area like world history remains at the memory-recall and comprehension levels. See D. Trachtenburg, "Student Tasks in Text Material: What Cognitive Skills Do They Tap?" *Peabody Journal of Education,* 52 (1974), pp. 54–57.

17. Ardelle Llewellyn and David Cahoon, "Teaching for Affective Learning." *Educational Leadership,* 22 (April 1965), pp. 469–72.

18. Glover, Bruning, and Filbeck, op. cit., p. 339.

19. E. W. Eisner, "Instructional and Expressive Objectives: Their Formulation and Use in Curriculum." In W. J. Popham, E. W. Eisner, H. J. Sullivan, and L. L. Tyler (Eds.), *Instructional Objectives* (AERA Monograph Series on Curriculum Evaluation, 3). Chicago: Rand McNally, 1969, p. 31.

20. See J. R. Jenkins and J. T. Neisworth, "The Facilitative Influence of Instructional Objectives." *Journal of Educational Research,* 66 (1973), pp. 254–56; and E. D Gagne and E. Z. Rothkopf, "Text Organization and Learning Goals."*Journal of Educational Psychology,* 67 (1975), pp. 445–50.

CHAPTER 4

Organizing Subject Matter and Planning Lessons

GETTING A HANDLE ON THE PLANNING PROCESS

As you assume responsibility for your own classes, you will have a need to do both long- and short-range planning for your teaching. This will be an early test of your organizational skills and your ability to view your instructional role in large perspective. You may find yourself in somewhat of a muddle over where to start, how much planning is necessary, who the planning is for, where to find help, and so on. Instructional planning can in fact be a complex and confusing subject if it is not approached in the right manner. Before you plunge in and begin the task of organizing courses, units, and lessons, it is important to have a clear notion of capable planning.

It is rare for teachers to not feel some initial uncertainty about their readiness to organize courses of study and to prepare lessons for groups of students. One elementary student teacher expressed her early planning anxieties this way:

> I was hopeful I'd be able to use my cooperating teacher's lesson plans for a while, but she wants me to do all of my own planning. This is certainly a new experience for me. It's the first time in my life I've had to make decisions like this. It seems like quite a lot of responsibility. But I knew I was going to have to do my own planning sooner or later. I might as well get my feet wet.

Such apprehension mainly occurs because competent instructional planning assumes a relatively broad view of the teaching–learning process and some in-depth command of the subject matter one is preparing. The task of planning for teaching would be considerably simpler if our only concern was to identify the content to be presented to our students. The fact that we want to have some control over the learning that results from their contact with the subject, makes the planning process more involved.[1] It means we have important decisions to make regarding not only the basic content and general goals we will be working from (we can normally expect some of this to be provided by curriculum guides and textbooks), but the specific learning outcomes we will be attempting to achieve and the methods we will employ to reach these objectives.

64

When you begin identifying in precise terms the type of learning you wish to promote in your teaching, it becomes apparent that these learning objectives will not result from an arbitrary or haphazard presentation of content.[2] The subject matter must be organized and sequenced in a way that provides students the best chance of acquiring the specified learning behaviors. Capable planning, then, requires not only a reasonable grasp of learning goals, but an ability to predetermine major learning focuses, lesson sequences, class activities, and teaching approaches for the subjects you will be teaching. It draws on a teacher's abilities as a subject-matter specialist, a learning psychologist, a teaching strategist, and a designer and evaluator of learning outcomes. If it were not for the fact that organizing for instruction is something all teachers must give immediate attention to, the subject of planning for teaching might better follow rather than precede those sections of the handbook that deal with the conduct of classroom activity.

As it is, this chapter addresses a central aspect of preparing for teaching, and it also serves as an ''advance organizer'' for the skill-development chapters that follow. In addition to providing basic ideas for course, unit, and lesson planning, it discusses main types of lesson focuses and previews some fundamental teaching strategies and styles. The chapter is designed to help you overcome the initial disadvantage of having to organize subject matter and plan lessons before you have had substantial experience with teaching. By attempting to reduce instructional planning to its essentials, it seeks to make the planning phase of teaching more manageable.

Levels of Planning

Organizing for instruction normally takes place at three different levels: course or program planning, unit planning, and lesson planning. Each type of planning has a different purpose, a different level of generality, and covers a different time span.[3]

In its most fundamental sense, instructional planning means being involved in the design of the curriculums or courses you teach. It means developing your own teaching content from the beginning. However, new teachers are seldom in a position to author the courses they teach. Lack of experience in curriculum development is one factor making it unrealistic. Another is the fact that most entering teachers find themselves teaching in established subjects or programs where a good deal of curricular structure is already present. Also, in the case of elementary teachers, planning at the elementary school level often has unique constraints. When working in basic-skill areas with firmly implanted curricular guidelines, elementary teachers are more likely to be involved in intermediate and short-range planning than with program-level organization.[4]

One should not suppose, though, that course development is the only possible kind of course-level planning. Whether or not they have been involved in the original course design, all teachers should be involved in large-scale planning in which they consider subject-matter elements, learning goals, and teaching methods in terms of the whole course or program. They should become accustomed to planning segments of content or *learning units* in relationship with other learning units and making reasoned decisions about the order in which these units are taught. The sequence of teaching units should be deliberately planned, not allowed to happen arbitrarily or because suppliers of teaching materials have provided a particular sequence.

Beyond course-level planning, unit organization is an intermediate level of planning, normally involving two- to four-week blocks of teaching, and a point at which teachers often make their most important instructional decisions. Daily lesson planning is the third level and most immediate type of planning. It is important for you to be able to plan at each of these levels and to have your daily lessons become extensions of the initial organizing you have done at the course and unit levels.

COURSE-LEVEL PLANNING

As a professional teacher it is important that you be acquainted with the process involved in constructing a year- or semester-long course of study, including the determination of basic learning goals, course content, and instructional procedures. There may be occasions when you have an opportunity to apply large-scale planning skills in designing a new course or program, one that is of special interest to you, perhaps in an area that is new to your school. Also, understanding the process of course development allows you to better identify with the thinking that has gone into the preestablished courses you teach. It gives you a better context for the things you do in your classroom on a day-to-day basis, and makes it easier for you to feel ownership of the subject matter you teach.

Whether or not you are engaged in designing a course of study from the beginning, course-level planning usually involves the following steps:

1. Identifying (or reviewing) the central goals and purposes of the program or course you will be teaching.
2. Selecting course content, then organizing and sequencing it to make it as coherent and teachable as possible.
3. Determining the amount of time to be spent on the various topics in the sequence.

Identifying Course Goals

The process of course planning begins when you determine what students are to learn from this particular subject or course of study: What major understandings, skills, and attitudes are to be emphasized during the year? General goals are those that you want to focus on at this early stage in your planning, course aims that you can summarize in one written paragraph. As an example, a general statement of aims for a course in junior high school science might read as follows:

- The major purposes of this course are to help students develop (1) the rational thinking processes that underlie scientific method, (2) the basic terms and concepts that allow us to interpret, predict, and theorize about scientific events, (3) the fundamental skills involved in procuring and organizing scientific information, and (4) those scientific values, appreciations, and attitudes that allow us to investigate and better understand our lives and our environments.

In another instance, a possible goal statement for a course in basic mathematics (seventh- to ninth-grade level) could contain this kind of information:

- This class aims to promote useful life skills in basic mathematics for noncollege-bound students. It stresses being able to apply fundamental mathematical concepts and procedures in everyday-life situations such as counting one's change, comprehending and figuring simple percentages, and balancing one's checkbook. The class attempts to build student's confidence in their abilities to perform basic mathematical operations as situations require. It seeks to diagnose and help dissolve the main "sticking points" students encounter in performing mathematical calculations and procedures.

You will notice that each of these brief course descriptions touches on foundational skills and attitudes as well as basic understandings that are to be promoted. They are both balanced statements of intent that attempt to take into consideration not only the need to teach subject matter, but the learning needs of students, and the need for the subject to have carryover value in the student's life.

A statement of course aims can help you begin to conceptualize what you want to emphasize and what you want to avoid in your teaching. The previous description of course aims for basic math suggests that students in such classes often have a history of negative experiences with the subject. They desperately need to experience a reversal of this pattern. Based on this kind of awareness, a teacher may decide to adopt a set of overriding classroom objectives that center on promoting positive self-concepts and feature the need for all students to experience some successes in this class.

Well-conceived course goals can also serve to describe the kind of emphasis that is to be placed on student initiative, imagination, and higher thought processes in a particular class. The following summary of goals for a high school U.S. history course is an example:

- This course is designed to provide a basic understanding and appreciation of major events, ideas, and personalities that have had a central impact on our nation's development. Its subgoals are (1) to have students recognize distinctly important time periods in the history of this country and the prominent individuals and events that made these eras significant; (2) to make students aware of major crises in the nation's history and the patterns we have developed for meeting national problems; (3) to help students recognize the precarious nature of democratic institutions, and to appreciate the crucial investments of previous Americans in forming the foundations for our present way of life; and (4) to prepare students to perceive history in the making as they read newspapers, watch newscasts, and take part in events. Students will be encouraged and expected to perceive the history of their country as a dynamic rather than a static process. They will be called on to identify with historical personalities, to evaluate the decisions of former leaders, and to infer cause-and-effect relationships among historical events. An effort will be made to view factual knowledge in a broad context, to identify specific names, dates, places, events, and so forth within a timeline of larger happenings.

It obviously takes a certain amount of thought and effort, not to mention knowledge of subject and students, to summarize one's course goals in this concise manner. If you find it difficult to generate ideas, relevant course aims contained in curriculum guides and preestablished courses of study can be especially helpful. In fact, regardless of how self-reliant you may become in defining basic goals for your teaching area(s), it is important to remain aware of potentially binding district or state guidelines for the subjects you teach. In school districts and/or subject areas where curricular prescriptions are relatively firm, you should make an attempt to understand the thinking that has gone into these decisions in an effort to internalize the rationales. If you cannot identify with the course-level goals that have been provided, it may be difficult for you to become highly involved in what you are teaching. You should make an effort to change them if you find externally prescribed goals incompatible with your own rationally derived teaching aims.

Selecting and Organizing Course Content

The next step in course-level planning is deciding what course content will bring about the desired goals,[5] and organizing the central ideas in a way that will make them most interesting and understandable. You will want to determine the order in which these main components are to be taught.

Topic Selection.   Teachers with authorizations to teach a particular subject normally have some initial idea of the kinds of major topics or concepts that should be included in a course of study for that area. For further help in content selection, one can usually depend on assistance from textbooks, curriculum guides, and preestablished programs.

An appropriate list of topics for a course in general math, for example, might include:

> the set of whole numbers
> measurement
> the system of decimal fractions
> the metric system
> subtraction and division of whole numbers
> finite decimal operations
> addition and multiplication of whole numbers
> set theory
> whole numbers—bases other than ten
> the number line
> real numbers[6]

Or, as a group of master-topics for a course in junior high earth science, teachers might want their students to acquire some understanding of:

> astronomy
> ecology
> geology
> meteorology
> oceanography

    paleontology
    mineralogy
    physical geography

Having identified the major topics or concepts that are to form the superstructure of a particular course of study, you should be prepared to devote considerable thought to the internal organization of the course. To maximize course coherence and teachability, subject matter needs to be organized in a way that takes into consideration any necessary relationships among its various components (logical organization) as well as the learning needs of the students you will be teaching (psychological organization).

The Logical Organization of Subject Matter. With some subjects, it will be more critically important to give early attention to the logical requirements of course organization than is the case with certain other subjects. For instance, it becomes apparent that a fifth-grade reading program, featuring basic study skills, needs to be structured so that a unit on Reading for Main Ideas is allowed to serve as a foundation for a unit on Outlining. Or, to provide a more detailed illustration, the list of potential topics for the hypothetical math course in the previous example will need to be structured in a more cohesive and sequential fashion before further course organization can proceed in a meaningful way. These various topics should be grouped under appropriate major headings, for example:

Measuring
the metric system
measurement

Whole numbers
subtraction and division of whole numbers
the set of whole numbers

Decimals
finite decimal operations
real numbers
the system of decimal fractions

Sets
set theory
the number line
whole numbers—bases other than ten

The groups should then be sequenced to represent the order in which these major areas of concentration will be featured within the course:

    whole numbers
    sets

decimals
measuring

Within the individual groups the sequence of course topics should also be carefully determined. Once this is accomplished the master outline of course topics should be expected to look something like this:

Whole numbers
the set of whole numbers
addition and multiplication of whole numbers
subtraction and division of whole numbers

Sets
set theory
whole numbers—bases other than ten
the number line

Decimals
the system of decimal fractions
finite decimal operations
real numbers

Measuring
measurement
the metric system

These are examples of how the internal structure of the subject dictates the way in which course content is organized and presented. Generally, the planning for traditional academic courses and basic skill subjects, where program or course development proceeds from the simple to the complex, will require stricter attention to the logical requirements of course organization than subjects where the sequencing of basic units of study can afford to be more arbitrary. In areas like history, physical education, home economics, music, and art, internal relationships among course elements are often less crucial. Planning for these subjects may require less attention to logical organization of subject matter and more regard for the creative aspects of one's organization (not to suggest that sound planning in more highly structured subjects does not call for creative application).

Planning a U.S. history course, for example, provides opportunities for considerable variation in standard approaches to content organization. In contrast to skill subjects that build from simple to complex (e.g., math, reading) or theoretical subjects that proceed from concrete to abstract (e.g., government, economics, philosophy), history courses are typically organized to accommodate time sequences (chronology). This has probably led to overly simplistic notions of how history should be taught: The main topics in U.S. history courses are generally organized chronologically in terms of main time periods. This allows teachers to feature the progression of historical events and to emphasize cause-and-effect relationships within the subject matter. Yet it is possible to structure a U.S. history course quite differently. Instead of approaching main topics chronologically, by introducing first the Colonial Period, then the National Period, followed by a unit on Western Expansion, and so forth, the course might be organized to feature central concepts or themes (e.g., nationalism, wars), rather than major time periods. Though the more traditional approach may help students understand and appreciate causal factors or the timing of events in history, the alternative form of organization would seek to emphasize underlying issues, overriding themes, and the student's ability to think conceptually about history.[7]

The Psychological Organization of Subject Matter.   Whereas the logical ordering of course content focuses on necessary relationships within the subject matter itself, it does not take into consideration the learning needs and requirements of those who are expected to learn this material. Although logical organization helps to insure that common course threads get tied together and basic understandings and procedures are taught first, it is not designed to provide the type of course structure that will facilitate the interest and involvement of one's students. In other words, it is a *subject-centered* rather than a *learner-centered* form of organization.

The subject matter for a course of study can also be organized *psychologically,* or from the learner's standpoint, to take into account the learning tendencies and abilities of the students for whom the course is intended. This is the other dimension of course organization you will want to attend to as you do large-scale planning for your teaching. Here we are concerned with selecting and structuring course content so that it connects with student's present interests, experiences, perceptions, and knowledge backgrounds. There are some things you can do at this early stage in your planning to make a course of study as learner-centered as possible. You should

1. Select content that is appropriate to the developmental levels of students,
2. Make an effort to have main course topics suggest real-life applications, and
3. Design the course in a way that allows you to develop interests, perceptions, and frames of reference before you get to the more abstract and theoretical parts of the course.

Developmentally Appropriate Content.   This is clearly the first and most critical consideration in organizing course content that is psychologically appropriate for the students with whom you will be working. There is evidence to indicate that during their school years a young person's educational development proceeds in age-related stages, and that they will tend to make sense of the world and experience in significantly different ways at each successive stage.[8] For purposes of educational planning, consider some of the following basic developmental characteristics:

1. In some important ways young children's thinking and learning are very different from adults' thinking and learning. Children from approximately the beginning to the middle elementary school years make sense of the unknown world outside them in terms of the known world within. Egan tells us that their "major intellectual tools and categories are not rational and logical but emotional and moral. . . . True learning at this stage must involve their being able to absorb the world to the categories of their own vivid mental life and to use the world

to expand the intellectual categories they have available.''[9] Young children tend to learn best from stories and games that have clearly established meanings and contain basic concepts of good-bad, love-hate, fear-security.[10]

2. Students from approximately the middle elementary to the late high school years are fascinated by the world around them, by the extremes of what exists and what is known.[11] Part of this fascination stems from the sense of mystery and personal challenge they perceive in the external world. They are interested in exploring the limits of the practical reality with which they are now having to deal.[12] During this lengthy middle period in their schooling, students tend to be predominantly *concrete-thinkers:* They are able to readily form concepts of objects or situations for which they have immediate references, but they have trouble with hypotheticals and high-level abstractions.[13] At this stage in their mental development, young people tend to learn concepts and generalizations (a big part of school learning) best when the ideas are approached inductively, that is, from the particular to the general. However, their interest is largely in the particulars. For them to make sense of what is being learned, the story form is still important at this educational level. According to Egan, "History is best understood at this stage as a kind of mosaic of bright elements—anecdotes, facts, dramatic events—which are composed into a small story, which in turn is a segment of a larger story. It is important to realize that students' concepts of historical causality, and additional concepts of otherness, are still quite primitive."[14]

3. It is not until well into their senior high school years that most students develop a "craving for generality," a need to begin imposing order on the complex and fascinating world around them.[15] Up until this stage students are not inclined to think in terms of systems. Now they become interested in investigating the general laws by which the world works.[16] They are more likely at this level to become interested in general schemes that explain historical, psychological, social, or natural processes.[17] At this stage they are better able to connect abstract knowledge.

These developmental tendencies of school-age young people have some important implications for course and program planning at the elementary and secondary levels, including these suggestions:

1. Make a conscious effort to adapt subject matter to the developmental levels of your students. Be selective. Do not hesitate to leave out subject matter that is inappropriate for the age group.

2. When organizing subject matter for early elementary children, think about the subject to be presented through the categories used by a young child: basically emotional and moral categories, for example, opposing forces of good/bad, big/little, brave/cowardly.[18]

3. In preselecting course activities and materials for students through middle adolescence, plan to utilize the story form as often as possible to help convey meanings.

4. Unless working with groups of cognitively mature senior high students, avoid

teaching units that contain mostly abstract concepts and generalizations. Avoid putting pressure on children or early adolescents to size up external reality in large chunks.

5. Emphasize the experiential in designing new learning for adolescents. Expose them to many other realities (e.g., other customs), allowing as much firsthand exposure to "otherness" as possible (e.g., guest speakers, field-trips).

6. Plan course activities to allow adolescent students a great deal of opportunity for verbal and creative self-expression. In exploring external realities, they want to know how they relate, how they match up, how they are fitting into the scheme of things.

Real-life Themes. To make the various sections of your course more appealing to students, have the course topics suggest a reason for what the students will be learning. Each teaching unit should have an identifiable focus or major thrust that suggests a real-life application.[19] Here are some examples of major topics with thematic emphases from several different subject areas:

Mathematics. Formulas: How Mathematics Saves Time
Home Economics. Clothing: Improve Your Personal Appearance
Language Arts. Sentence Structure: Making Your Language Talk
Chemistry. Matter and Energy: Building Blocks of the World Around Us
History. The Roosevelt Era: A New Direction for the United States

Each subject area has its own specific requirements, of course. A teacher designing a program in literature might decide, in devoting a unit to the study of *Julius Caesar,* to have this unit focus on the theme of human ambition. *Julius Caesar* would provide the basic content for the unit, but the emphasis would be on the concept of ambition and the human qualities that it represents. In choosing relevant themes for the group of learners with whom you will be working, it is important to try to pick themes of current interest or relevance to that particular age group. In this high school literature class, other appropriate themes for a unit on *Julius Caesar* could include loneliness, frustration, or death.

Course-Planning to Facilitate Learning Readiness. In working with young learners, an essential part of the instructional task is to attempt to build student's interests and frames of reference before taking them into the more concentrated or abstract portions of a particular subject. So in organizing a sequence of major topics and activities for a course you plan to teach, it is generally advisable to structure learning events to move from the familiar to the unfamiliar, from the experiential to the conceptual, from the practical to the theoretical. There are several things you can do at the level of course organization to promote student readiness for the progression of learning activities they will encounter, including:

1. Provide sufficient time at the beginning of a new semester to lay a thorough groundwork for the course activity that is to follow. Deliberately plan introductions to the subject that will ease students into the course framework. This is

especially important when you are teaching a subject with a reputation among students as being difficult, uninteresting, or obscure. Be thinking of ''advance organizers'' you can use to help students perceive the essence and scope of the subject or the nature of the class activity (e.g., major course subdivisions, central questions to be answered, the student's role in the learning). In some cases you may want to use an initial unit to do ground-breaking or perception-building activities for the subject.

2. As you do course planning, try to lead off a new semester or school year with subject matter that is likely to be most familiar, manageable, and motivating for your students. Plan to use interesting and experientially accessible topics as a bridge to the unfamiliar and initially less interesting content. For example, in sequencing main topics for a secondary art class, an introductory unit on Looking at Old Artwork Through New Eyes is likely to be a better interest and confidence builder for students than an initial unit on Perspective, Structure, and Composition (although some art teachers might consider the latter unit a better choice). In a junior high English class, early units that plunge students into actual writing and self-expression will generally turn out to be better motivators and diagnostic points for further instruction than initial units on sentence structure and formal grammar.

3. In planning for a subject that involves abstract ideas, build-in activities that will serve to expand student's perceptions and experiential bases before they are required to conceptualize and generalize within your subject. Allow them to have encounters with new realities (through field trips, lab experiences, discussions, media reports, simulations, films, games, etc.) prior to focusing on verbal and textbook knowledge. Work first from *experience objectives* (see chapter 3) that allow students opportunities to explore, brainstorm, and free associate, as a means of setting the stage for precise cognitive learning.

4. As you are organizing a course of study, design it to unfold in a manner that will leave some sense of open-endedness in the minds of students. Provide early opportunities for students to plan activities and learning focuses with you. Make question raising and problem solving a foundational part of the learning experience regardless of the subject. Resist any inclination to make the class a canned learning experience. Attempt to promote student interest by building variety, inquiry, and serendipity into the course.

Deciding Time Frames

When you have completed the work of organizing and sequencing course content, the last major step in your large-scale planning is to decide the amount of time to be spent on the various topics in the sequence. This step is essential to ensure that the various portions of the course receive the attention they deserve. Failure to make firm time allotments often results in teachers spending disproportionate amounts of time on early topics, then having to rush through the last weeks of the course because of time limitations. A common mistake of U.S. history teachers, for instance, is to spend too much time on the earliest periods in the country's development and fail to give sufficient attention to crucial happenings within the last century.

Here is an example of unit divisions for a physical science course, indicating the number of weeks to be alloted to each unit:

1. Introduction to Physical Science—Air (four weeks)
2. Water (two weeks)
3. Fuels (three weeks)
4. Forces (four weeks)
5. Chemicals (six weeks)
6. Plastics (three weeks)
7. Sound (two weeks)
8. Light (three weeks)
9. Electricity (three weeks)
10. Earth Science (one week)
11. Astronomy (eight weeks)
    Review (two weeks)

For one beginning a career in teaching, externally prepared curriculum guides and courses of study can be helpful in suggesting not only course topics and sequences, but also the amount of time to be spent on individual units.

Application Exercises

1. Prepare a one-paragraph statement of general aims for a course (or program) you might teach at the secondary or elementary level. Identify the grade level for which this course would be designed. As you review this statement of course goals and intentions, does it appear to include affective as well as cognitive learning goals? Does it reflect a sensitivity to the learning needs and interests of the students for whom it is intended? Does your description of course aims indicate a concern to have this experience relate to student's lives beyond school? Rewrite as necessary to produce a more comprehensive or balanced statement.
2. Choose appropriate major topics (approximately seven to ten) to represent units of instruction for the course you have described in the previous exercise. Determine the best logical order for teaching these units. Does the sequence of topics you have arrived at take into consideration prerequisite skills or understandings that might need to be developed before it would be advisable to proceed to other learning topics? What are some other reasonable options for topic selection and unit sequencing as you begin organizing this course?
3. Consider the target group of students for whom you are designing the course in the previous exercises. Take time to sketch some main ideas for how you would like to see this course develop, taking into consideration the sorts of learning and developmental patterns to be anticipated in students at this age group. What particular kinds of course introductions, early experiences (e.g., exploratory opportunities, field trips), or unit sequences would help to promote interest and meaning for students at this level?

UNIT PLANNING

Beyond initial course-level organization, it is important for you to preplan each of the various units of instruction that make up a year or semester of teaching. A unit can be thought of as a series of interrelated lessons, placed in a certain order so individual lessons can build on one another. Unit planning helps you avoid the fragmentation of learning that often results when teachers get into a pattern of planning lessons a day at a time. Without the unit plan to aid in organizing ideas and approaches, teaching is likely to lack cohesiveness, continuity, and relevance. Regular unit planning will also ease the burden of having to prepare new lessons for each day of teaching. Having worked your way through the process of course planning, preparing a unit of instruction should be an extension of important foundational work you have already accomplished. To a large extent it will involve elaborating or "fleshing out" instructional ideas you began to develop during your initial course organization. It will allow you to convert generally stated learning activities and outcomes into specific objectives and lessons.

You should begin your unit planning with a consideration of the major purposes of the unit together with a listing of the content you will be teaching. Unit goals and content should actually be developed together because your stated objectives should have a bearing on what you teach, whereas unit subject matter is the context from which learning outcomes are to be achieved. You will likely find that the more closely you examine your teaching objectives, the more insight you will have for organizing subject matter. And by the same token, the more precisely you are able to specify the learning content you will be working from, the better sense you will have of appropriate learning objectives.

With these things in mind, the work of unit planning should consist of the following basic steps:

1. Identifying the main purposes of the unit
2. Producing a content outline for the unit
3. Determining types of learning outcomes to be promoted
4. Selecting teaching strategies and activities

Identifying Unit Purpose

As you begin planning a unit of instruction, you will want to identify the main goals and purposes of this particular segment of teaching: Essentially what is it you want the students to learn from the unit? It is important to take time here to identify the main thrust of this block of instruction within the larger course or program. Being able to summarize the major purposes of your unit in a brief paragraph or to list unit goals in a succinct manner gives you a foundation from which to organize the unit and helps you to establish its main boundaries. A teacher of eighth-grade U.S. history, planning a unit on Westward Expansion, might begin with a concise statement of aims like this:

- Students will develop a feel for the largely undeveloped nature of this country during the early nineteenth century. They will learn of the explorations, settlements, new forms of transportation, and land acquisitions that brought the United

States to its present boundaries. An effort will be made to have students identify with the adventure, hardship, and, in some cases, ruthlessness that accompanied westward expansion. They will also gain an appreciation for the native American cultures that came to be displaced during this expansionist movement.

Or, this teacher could directly list four or five major goals that will constitute the basis for the unit:

Students will:

1. Understand the various factors that allowed the American West to become opened to travel, fortune seeking, and new settlements.
2. Understand the motives that caused American leaders to want to extend the existing boundaries of the United States beyond the Mississippi river (e.g., "Manifest Destiny").
3. Become acquainted with some of the important personalities of the period— including native Americans—who demonstrated exceptional traits of leadership, bravery, or "rugged individualism."
4. Become acquainted with important details of pioneer life in the Western United States, including a feel for the excitement and adventure of frontier exploration, the California gold rush, and cross-country wagon trains.
5. Be made aware of the treaty violations and intrusions on Indian lands that took place during the westward expansion of the United States.

As another example, a sixth-grade language arts teacher, designing a unit on Thematic Writing, could decide to use the following statement of purpose as a basis for further planning:

*   This unit will focus on basic techniques for developing coherent written compositions around selected topics. Students will get practice in communicating their written ideas logically and persuasively. They will be encouraged to "brainstorm" manageable human interest topics, and to develop their ideas using techniques that will capture and hold the attention of the reader. While one main purpose of the unit is to help students achieve cohesiveness in their writing, it will also emphasize creative self-expression. Students will have opportunities to share their writing with classmates and to engage in "peer editing."

As an alternative, this teacher might have chosen to describe the instructional intent of this unit by summarizing main goals as follows:

Students will:

1. Generate original and manageable theme topics for their own writing.
2. Show a continuing interest in and potential for creative self-expression.
3. Demonstrate an ability to write thematic compositions that are both mechanically and logically coherent.
4. Demonstrate in their writing effective techniques for holding the interest of the reader.

5. Discern effective thematic techniques in the writing of others.

The important idea here is to establish *anchor points* for your unit, statements of purpose that are broad enough, yet sufficiently descriptive, to provide a solid basis for this series of lessons. The learning objectives you produce at this stage in your unit planning will normally be *intermediate level* objectives (see chapter 3), specific enough to help establish the boundaries of the unit, but not yet precise enough to serve as focuses for individual lessons.

Outlining Unit Content

In conjunction with your efforts to define the main purpose of the unit, you should take time to outline the concepts or ideas that are to form the superstructure of the unit. As an example, the U.S. history teacher planning a unit on Westward Expansion might produce a content outline that consists of the following topics and subtopics:

  I. Causes of expansion
    A. Adventure
    B. New land and new life
        1. "Rugged individualism"
    C. "Manifest Destiny"
 II. Land exploration and acquisition
    A. The wilderness road
        1. Daniel Boone
    B. The Land Ordinance of 1785
    C. The Louisiana Purchase
        1. Lewis and Clark Expedition
    D. The Northwest Ordinance
    E. Pinckney's Treaty
    F. "Manifest Destiny"
    G. Violations of treaties with native American inhabitants
        1. Jackson's Indian policies
            a. The Indian Removal Act
III. Early settlements
    A. Native American cultures
        1. Nomadic life-style of the Plains Indians
            a. No concept of private land ownership
    B. Fur trappers and traders
    C. Miners
        1. The California Gold Rush
            a. John Sutter
    D. Cattle ranchers
        1. Cowboys
    E. Pioneer farmers
        1. "Squatters"
            a. Squatter's rights
    F. Settlers

        1. Brigham Young
        2. John Bidwell
IV. Frontier life
    A. Pioneer homes
        1. Clearing the land
        2. Building the home
    B. Food
        1. Hunting and farming
        2. Food preservation
    C. Clothing
        1. Spinning and weaving
    D. Tools and supplies
    E. Health and illness
    F. Education
        1. Traveling teachers
        2. Rote learning
        3. Practical skills
    G. Law and order
        1. "Frontier justice"
    H. Social activities
        1. Corn-husking contests
        2. House-raisings
    I. The clash between native American and traditional European life-styles
        1. Divergent concepts of land rights
        2. Unstable coexistence
        3. Forced disintegration of native American culture
V. Transportation
    A. Wagon trains
    B. The Erie Canal
    C. The first transcontinental railroad

As is the case when preparing any outline, it becomes necessary to identify central concepts and to distinguish these from subordinate or supporting elements within your content outline. You will normally have important choices to make in determining what content gets emphasized and what is omitted or relegated to extensions of main ideas.

Determining Types of Learning Outcomes

Having identified main objectives and content boundaries for the unit, you should begin thinking in more precise terms about the specific kinds of learning outcomes you will want to feature in this unit. You will ordinarily have considerable leeway here. Although the content of a particular subject area may be standard, what you do with that content is not likely to be standard. The basic question you should ask yourself is: What is it that I want my students to know, feel, or be able to do as the result of this teaching unit? By taking time to focus on this question at this point in your planning, you help to insure that the teaching strategies and activities you select for this group of lessons will be consistent with the learning outcomes you hope to achieve.

In some subject areas it is to be expected that cognitive learning will be the primary focus, in other teaching areas the development of physical skills of one sort or another will be the normal emphasis, and in certain subjects and levels of teaching it will seem appropriate to give special attention to the development of student attitudes and appreciations. However, it will usually be necessary for you to specify learning focuses more precisely. Cognitive learning can mean simply the memorization of *facts* or it may involve the formation of *concepts* and *generalizations*. It can also involve the development of various kinds of *thinking skills* (e.g., analysis, evaluation). When we add the possibility of learning outcomes in the affective and psychomotor domains, we realize that teaching lessons might focus on one or more of at least five different varieties of learning: factual knowledge, ideas (concepts and generalizations), physical and manipulative skills, thought processes, or learner attitudes and appreciations.

In neglecting to identify appropriate learning focuses during your unit planning, you may end up teaching understandings when you ought to be teaching proficiencies, factual material when it should be concepts or thinking skills, or physical skills when the primary need is for perceptual and attitudinal development. Teachers may spend inordinate amounts of time promoting knowledge about certain topics when the student's ultimate need is to be able to perform certain behaviors (e.g., in writing classes or teacher training). Or in other instances the failure to properly conceptualize learning focuses may cause teachers to feature performance skills prematurely or at the expense of important cognitive understandings (e.g., in physical education or industrial arts). It is also quite common for teachers to attempt to force cognitive or skill learning in teaching situations where the initial focus should be on affective learning (e.g., in math, history, or physical education).

So, taking into consideration unit purposes, unit content, and student levels, the following are some of the kinds of things history teachers might want their students to know, feel, and be able to do in connection with the developing unit on Westward Expansion:

1. *Know facts*, for example,
   - Lewis and Clark explored the Oregon Territory in 1804
   - Native American inhabitants were the first true Americans
   - Pinckney's treaty settled a conflict with Spain in the Southwest
   - Farmers were granted title to land through "squatters rights"
2. *Form big ideas*, for example,
   - Rugged individualism, nationalism, Manifest Destiny (concepts)
   - The transcontinental railroad was a major factor in opening the U.S. West to travel from the east (generalization)
   - The life of the Western frontier helped form certain American character traits that continue to endure (generalization)
   - Events of the westward movement caught international attention and contributed to European immigration to the United States (generalization)
3. *Develop attitudes and appreciations*, for example,
   - This was a fascinating time in U.S. history
   - Many of those who helped settle the West were unusually brave and hardy people

- We owe a great deal to those early pioneers and explorers who helped extend our country to its present boundaries
- Along the way some of these early Americans did things to the native Americans and other countries that were less than honorable

4. *Practice higher thinking skills,* for example,
   - What kinds of people would have been interested in joining a wagon train to the West? (speculative analysis)
   - How did Jacksonian democracy contribute to the spirit of the westward movement? (cause-and-effect analysis)
   - What were the most favorable outcomes of the westward movement in U.S. history? Were there any negative effects connected with it? (evaluation)
   - How might U.S. history have been different if the Erie Canal and transcontinental railroad had not been developed? (synthesis or "divergent thinking")

It is apparent that the lessons in this unit center on one or more types of cognitive learning. Units in other areas may be aimed primarily at the development of skills or proficiencies of one sort or another (e.g., a unit on Preparing a Research Paper in English or language arts), although skill learning is usually always based on cognitive understanding. Sensitivity to such distinctions is important because these different types of learning require different teaching techniques and strategies in order to achieve the intended learning outcomes.

Selecting Teaching Methods and Activities

The topic of teaching methods and models is a potentially large and complex subject.[20] For your purposes as a beginning teacher, it is advisable for you to be acquainted with some basic alternative techniques and strategies that you can master early in your teaching career and continue to expand on as you gain further experience. As you set out to determine appropriate teaching methods for a series of lessons, there are two basic considerations that deserve primary attention, namely, (1) what techniques should I be using to promote specific types of learning, and (2) should I use a *direct* or *indirect* teaching approach?

Matching Teaching Techniques to Types of Learning.   It has been emphasized that the teaching of physical skills requires different teaching techniques than the teaching of factual understandings, that the fostering of student attitudes and values will call for a different teaching approach from that used to promote thinking and problem-solving skills, and so forth. The following are some concise and useful guidelines for goal-directed teaching in five main areas of learning:

Teaching Factual Information
1. Organize the material into a maximum of four or five chunks or learning units (e.g., spelling words, foreign language dialogues, historical events, lines of poetry or music) per learning encounter.

2. Help the students perceive relationships between the new information and what they already know.
3. Organize complex material into appropriate sequences of component parts.
4. Present information in the precise form it is to be remembered and help students achieve the correct response on the first trial.
5. Arrange for students to make use of new information in practical contexts over an extended period of time with provisions for immediate feedback.
6. Give students opportunities to independently evaluate the adequacy and accuracy of the new information they acquire.

Teaching Concepts and Generalizations
1. Determine the level at which students are able to attain the concept (i.e., concrete or formal levels).
2. Teach students a strategy for differentiating between examples and nonexamples of concepts (concrete functioning students will attend to perceptible properties, formal thinking students to defining attributes).
3. Provide for properly sequenced sets of examples and nonexamples in teaching and testing.
4. Emphasize the *defining attributes* to enable students to achieve cognitive understanding of the concept
5. Establish the correct terminology for the concept and its attributes.
6. Provide for feedback on student responses to these new ideas.
7. Provide opportunities for students to apply newly learned concepts in understanding principles and solving problems.

Teaching Thinking and Problem-solving Skills
1. Provide opportunities for students to engage in thinking operations like explaining, predicting, comparing, generalizing, hypothesizing, and evaluating within a typical teaching unit.
2. Stress student's abilities to be sensitive and discriminating observers as the foundation on which all other thinking skills are based.
3. Make regular use of sound questioning techniques to encourage reflective thinking in the classroom.
4. Develop a pattern of content learning that requires students to progress from factual, to analytical, to creative levels of thought.
5. Help students identify, state, and delimit solvable problems.
6. Give students initial help in analyzing and synthesizing information they would use in problem solving.
7. Promote basic forms of self-expression (figural, verbal, physical) as a means of fostering divergent and creative ideas.

Teaching Physical and Manipulative Skills
1. Analyze the skill in terms of the learner's abilities and developmental level.
2. Provide a good demonstration of the skill to be acquired.
3. Give a set of verbal instructions, or a plan, for carrying out the sequence of actions.

4. Arrange for students to practice tightly organized skills (e.g., diving) as a whole; loosely organized skills (e.g., football, baseball) as components.
5. Make the conditions of practice as close as possible to the conditions under which the skill will actually be used.
6. Make practice periods relatively brief, but distribute them over a good number of days at short intervals (except where fatigue is a factor).
7. Provide informational feedback and correct inadequate responses.

Teaching Attitudes and Values
1. State the attitudes to be taught as instructional objectives.
2. Provide exemplary models for students to emulate.
3. Provide for pleasant emotional experiences in connection with the school situations for which attitude changes are sought.
4. Arrange for students to receive accurate information about persons, objects, or situations toward which attitude changes are sought.
5. Use group techniques (e.g., role playing, group decision making) to facilitate commitment to group-held attitudes and values (particularly effective at the elementary level).
6. Arrange for appropriate practice opportunities within the classroom, school, and community environments.[21]

Direct and Indirect Teaching.   The question of whether you should employ direct or indirect teaching methods will be an underlying theme in all of your planning. It asks whether a particular learning outcome would be best achieved through a straightforward, information-transfer style of teaching, or whether a learner-centered, discovery-based method would be more appropriate. Direct instruction, sometimes referred to as expository or didactic teaching, is primarily a *teacher-centered* approach in which the teacher is the major source of information. It tends to be the easiest type of teaching to master at the beginning of a teaching career, and it allows teachers to transmit facts, rules, or procedures in the most direct way possible. Direct teaching features the logical organization of subject matter and a *lecture-explanation mode* of delivery. It emphasizes the *products* of learning more centrally than the *processes* by which students learn.

Indirect teaching, centered on an inquiry approach to learning, is normally the more difficult style of teaching to perfect. Inquiry learning, of which there are a number of established models, is based on the premise that questions and perceived problems should properly precede answers in the learning process.[22] Indirect teaching is a *learning-paced* style of instruction that is grounded in considerations of the internal processing students must do to achieve meaningful learning. It requires that the teacher be able to employ an *interactive mode* of classroom communication.

Each of these instructional approaches has its own unique advantages and disadvantages, areas of learning where it is appropriate and other areas where it is less applicable. Formal studies of teaching methods would indicate that direct instruction is most effective in the following teaching situations:

1. When the teacher's purpose is to disseminate information not readily available in written materials in easily digestible form.

2. When teachers wish to arouse or heighten student interest.
3. When the learning task calls for the mastery of facts, rules, or procedures that are foundational to later learning.
4. When students need to remember the material for only a short time.
5. When it is necessary to provide an introduction to a learning task or activity that is going to be taught by a more indirect method.
6. When control and efficiency are a high priority.

According to available research, indirect teaching strategies are most advantageous under these conditions:

1. When the teacher's objective is to teach concepts, patterns, and abstractions.
2. When higher-level thinking skills (analysis, synthesis, or evaluation) are the purposes of instruction.
3. When learner participation is essential to achievement of objectives.
4. When a learning objective calls for students to engage in problem solving.
5. When long-term retention of content is necessary.[23]

Your Developing Style.   You will no doubt find occasions in your teaching when direct instructional strategies will be both appropriate and efficient. In fact, while you are still working to achieve a base of confidence and security as a beginning teacher, you will likely find a direct style of teaching to be most suitable to your developing needs and abilities (see chapter 5 on getting established in the classroom).

However, as you think in long-range terms about where you would like to be in several years as a teacher (see chapter 12 on personal plans for professional growth), an ability to perform well in an indirect teaching mode is something to shoot for. As a general approach in teaching young learners, it is advisable to work from where they are to where you want them to be insofar as new learning is concerned. This means being able to use indirect or learner-centered techniques to advantage in many of the things you teach. Chapter 6, which discusses motivation, suggests ideas for getting students involved in new learning that utilize student's existing perceptions, interests, and experiences as starting points. Also, chapter 8 provides guidelines for communicating with students in an *interactive* mode, interactive communication being the basis for an indirect teaching style.

Even within lecture formats, it is quite possible to talk *with* students as opposed to talking *at* them about things you want them to know or do. Chapter 7 deals with strategies for providing students with sound and meaningful explanations, essentially a teacher-centered activity. It suggests ways of delivering learner-paced, understandable explanations as another foundational skill for classroom teachers.

Selecting Unit Activities.   The final phase of unit planning is to select and organize the learning activities that students will engage in during the course of the unit. What will you and your students be doing from the beginning to the end of the unit to bring about the desired learning? Depending on the subject, the students, and your own inclinations, there are ordinarily many kinds of activities you can utilize to promote student learning in your classes, ranging from more conventional activities like lectures, teacher–class discussions, films, lab exercises, and independent seatwork to less common activities like debates, field trips, small group discussions, simulations, guided imagery sessions, story form, invited speakers, creative writing assignments, and so forth.

In some teaching areas the pattern of learning activity will be fairly well established by tradition or by the nature of the subject. Industrial arts teachers at the high school level, for example, typically put students to work on individual projects that occupy the bulk of the learning time in these classes. Apart from introductory lectures or demonstrations, unit activities in skill-oriented subjects of this nature tend to become direct applications of well-defined performance objectives. Physical education units, mathematics units, and certain teaching units at the elementary level that draw heavily on programmed materials (e.g., reading) would also fall into this category. In most teaching areas, though, you can expect to have reasoned choices to make regarding appropriate activities for your classes.

Here are some general guidelines for selecting and sequencing learning activities within a typical teaching unit:

1. Have a deliberate progression of activities, a scheme for how the unit is to unfold, that is, a beginning stage, a developmental period, and a culminating phase. Either plan this with your students or help them understand the developmental plan of the unit from the beginning. Try to instill in the students a sense that they are working toward something. When possible, have them involved in ongoing projects or investigations related to the unit.

2. Allow ample time for an introductory or exploratory period at the beginning of the unit. Use these early sessions to arouse students' interests and to find out what present knowledge and abilities they may already possess related to the topic. This preliminary phase is especially important when teaching subjects that lack built-in motivators (e.g., most subjects that involve abstract learning). Whenever possible, give students opportunities at the beginning of the unit to suggest projects and activities for succeeding meetings.

3. Vary activities from lesson to lesson to maintain variety and stimulate different modes of learning. If you plan a teacher-centered activity for one session, arrange to have a small-group or independent-learning project for the next. Avoid falling into a pattern of sameness with your activities. Keep students interested by challenging them to suggest and attempt constructive new activities. Keep an active file of learning activities that you have used successfully, and others that have been recommended and you intend to try.

4. Give careful attention to how you want to end the unit and to the sorts of activities that will provide good closure. Plan culminating activities that will give students opportunities to size up what they have learned from the unit and to report on any special projects on which they have been working. Select evaluational activities that are good logical conclusions to the unit and that students will perceive as extensions of the unit activities.

5. In designing any learning activity, be sure to give careful thought to what the student is to do during that session. Try to have a minimum of activities where the students' role is to simply attend to someone else for long periods of time. Once you feel confident in your ability to control the class, find constructive

activities that will regularly get students out of their seats. In math classes, for example, where physical movement is often minimal, sending students to the board in rows can be an opportunity for needed stimulus variation, good-natured competition between the rows, and a convenient check on how students are progressing.

6. In designing activities for units that involve skill development, be mindful that skill learning of any sort requires sufficient practice. Whether the focus is physical skills, math skills, writing skills, or concept development skills, it is important to build ample practice periods (with feedback) into your lesson sequences. Remember also to provide adequate opportunities for students to conceptualize and visualize skill operations before they are expected to practice them.

To illustrate the kind of activity planning and sequencing that should constitute the final stage of unit organization, the following is a ten-day activity plan for the sample unit on Westward Expansion.

DAY 1 (Large-group discussion). Initiate the unit with a teacher-led discussion centered on a large wall map of the United States. Discussion will revolve around the drastically changed boundaries of the United States as we move from the late eighteenth to the middle nineteenth centuries. Invite students to speculate on how this large-scale national expansion could occur in such a short time historically. Ask students to share what they may already know about U.S expansion as an informal pretest of existing knowledge and interest. Ask students to begin thinking of a topic or question they might investigate on this subject. Provide some examples.

DAY 2 (Film discussion). Show an educational film depicting the exploration and territorial advances into the Western United States in the eighteenth and nineteenth centuries. Follow up with a teacher-led discussion of significant points from the film.

DAY 3 (Small-group activity). Have students work in groups of three or four to brainstorm reasons why there was so much sentiment for western expansion at this time in our history. Assign students textbook reading to compare their group inferences with the views of historians.

DAY 4 (Teacher-centered presentation). Prepare a teacher presentation that sketches as graphically as possible some of the landmark events of western expansion, for example, war with Mexico, the Gold Rush, the completion of the Transcontinental Railroad, and so forth. Assign textbook reading that asks students to acquire more pertinent detail about these events.

DAY 5 (Guided-imagery lesson). Conduct a large-group guided-imagery session in which students are led to project what it would be like to travel west on a wagon train, to live in a mining camp, to be involved in a battle with native Americans, and so forth. Demonstrate and assign students a simulation activity for the next day.

DAY 6 (Simulation activity). Have small groups of students simulate (or dramatize) some of the frontier events or situations that were the subject of yesterday's guided-imagery session.

DAY 7 (Videotape discussion). Use a documentary videotape to portray today's cowboy and life on the range in the modern West. In a follow-up discussion, have students compare conditions today with those of the nineteenth century.

DAY 8 (Large-group discussion). Conduct a large-group discussion that asks students to consider the moral standards of this period in U.S. history. Were some of these early Americans ruthless in the pursuit of their own passions and interests? How should we view our treatment of the native American during this period? What examples of noble and honorable behavior can be cited?

DAY 9 (Small-group and large-group reports). Have students give feedback on a topic or question they have been investigating. Have them share their findings in groups of three to four students, then have each group select one report to be shared with the whole class.

DAY 10 (Evaluation activity). Do an evaluation exercise that asks students to (1) identify noteworthy personalities of the period and to indicate what their main contributions were, (2) detail a progression of main events or accomplishments that contributed to the opening of the U.S. West to settlement, and (3) describe an event or life condition that struck them as particularly exciting, challenging, or unusual and have them discuss how they might have responded to that situation had they been living then.

Application Exercises

1. Select a suitable topic for an instructional unit within a program or course you expect to teach. Write a summary description of the unit, indicating the main goals and purposes of that particular block of teaching. As you examine this summary statement, are your goals descriptive enough to qualify as intermediate-level objectives? Does your statement provide for a range of learning outcomes, affective as well as cognitive? Rewrite if necessary to make your description more appropriate.

2. Produce a content outline for the unit of instruction you have described in the first exercise. Follow standard outline form in specifying main ideas in relation to subordinate or supporting ideas. Having completed this content outline, analyze it to determine whether it represents a proper logical sequence of learning topics. Rearrange as necessary to make the topical order more appropriate.

3. Reexamine the content outline you produced in exercise two in relation to your description of unit objectives from exercise one. What main types of learning outcomes would you be seeking to produce if you were to teach this unit to students at the level you expect to work (i.e., facts, concepts and generalizations, thinking skills, psychomotor skills, attitudes, and values)? What are some of the specific teaching strategies you would employ to promote these particular kinds of learning outcomes?

4. Describe a sequence of learning activities you might use to teach the unit under consideration in the previous exercises. As you attempt to specify activities and sequences for this series of lessons, make an effort to apply appropriate logical and psychological criteria for organizing learning experiences at the grade level you will be teaching.

LESSON PLANNING

Having done the initial work of preplanning at the course and unit levels, many necessary decisions and much of your basic lesson structure should already be in place by the time you get to the lesson planning stage. Lesson planning should be a practical, highly concentrated activity. Besides being an opportunity for you to pinpoint the specific objectives, activities, and teaching strategies you will employ, a lesson plan should include key reminders to help you stay organized and focused during a lesson. As a beginning teacher your lesson plans will probably need to be more highly structured than will be necessary after you have taught for several years. But, the actual format of written plans may vary depending on the subject, the nature of class activities, and the kinds of students you are working with (one general model is presented later in this section). Some school systems may require new teachers to use an adopted lesson plan form, particularly when being evaluated by supervisors. However, for your own purposes as a developing teacher, the format of the lesson plan is less critical than the quality of your planning and the practical value you derive from it.

One of the most important functions of lesson planning is to get you to think through a lesson before you actually teach it. On beginning a class period, most competent teachers have mental images of how the lesson should unfold. They have a *mental script* to follow. Creative teachers are flexible enough to be able to modify that script as situations might require, but their ability to do a simulated "walkthrough" prior to teaching a lesson helps to keep them on track once the class period begins. Some experienced teachers are able to rely on these internal plans to carry them through a lesson with a minimum of written reminders. Most early-career teachers, on the other hand, find it necessary to supplement their internal rehearsing with an explicit set of written plans.

Another practical reason for doing regular lesson planning is so you will be able to work effectively within the time constraints of a single lesson. By prefiguring the approximate amount of time to be devoted to various classroom events, you stand a better chance of being able to fit essential teaching activities and necessary classroom chores together into one short class period.

Some of the more important elements that should be included in a functional lesson plan are (1) a statement of the lesson focus and objective, (2) a concise description of lesson activities and teaching procedures in the sequences they will occur, and (3) reminders of things, external to the lesson itself, that need to be accomplished prior to or during the class period.

Pinpointing Lesson Focus

Your unit plan should have provided a solid foundation for the series of lessons with which you are presently involved. Now as you begin to concentrate on activities for a single class period, it is important to be able to identify as specifically as possible the learning focus for this particular lesson. There are good reasons for taking time to do this. For one, some lessons are designed to promote measurable understandings or performance skills. These lessons need to derive from behavioral objectives. Also, a common tendency of new teachers is to try to do too much in a single class period.

Their lesson concentration is often too broad. Having a precise lesson objective not only defines what you want students to get from the lesson, but it helps you to keep your learning topics manageable for both you and your students. As an example, if a unit-level objective for a U.S. government class is to have students "know the function of the administrative branch of our government," this intermediate objective will likely need to be reduced to a more pointed subobjective in order to be appropriate for a single lesson. A manageable extension of the larger objective, and one more suitable as a lesson objective, would be for students to "be able to enumerate the various powers of the presidency."

Although it is important to have an identifiable learning focus, it may not always be necessary to state your lesson objective in measurable behavioral terms. Of course that will depend on the subject matter and on your own teaching goals. For some lessons the learning focus may be deliberately broader than for others. As mentioned in chapter 3, there are learning situations where it will be counterproductive to prespecify intended learning outcomes in performance terms. When your intent is for students to have exploratory or perception-building experiences, these occasions may call for experience objectives rather than tight behavioral objectives.

Mapping Class Activities and Teaching Procedures

The heart of your lesson plan should be a concise description of lesson activities in the order they will occur. This progression of teaching events should be based on the same kinds of logical and psychological criteria that apply to course and unit organization. Generally, a well-organized lesson will proceed in three stages: a beginning or introduction, a main body, and a closing phase. Your effort should be to have the lesson unfold in a way that maximizes student interest and involvement.

In addition to being a time for attendance taking and other initial chores, the beginning stage of a lesson sets the tone for the teaching and learning that will take place during that class period. The way you begin a lesson often has a big effect on the success of that lesson. Your lesson introduction (or "set") should be designed to move students into an appropriate frame of mind for the learning that is to take place. This *introductory set* provides an appropriate focus for the lesson. It may consist of references to a previous lesson, a current event, or a relevant problem the lesson will address. An interesting object, photo, or story could also be an effective "grabber" at the beginning of a lesson. For a skill- or performance-based lesson, appropriate beginnings may entail efforts to motivate students to carefully attend to the skill items they will encounter. In contrast to conceptually oriented lesson introductions in science or history, effective lesson sets in music or physical education might involve getting learners charged to seek perfection in their performances or projects. See chapters 5, 6, and 9 for additional ideas on initiating learning in your classes.

The central activity of the lesson should constitute the main body of your lesson plan. In a content-based lesson where the approach is direct instruction, teacher presentations and explanations often dominate this portion of the lesson. If the class session is to be performance- or activity-centered, the middle part of the lesson will ordinarily be devoted to practice periods or student projects (following initial teacher explanations or demonstrations), where your main role will be to monitor student progress. In either case, it is important to preplan the succession of steps in the learning activity. With a teacher-centered lesson, aimed at presenting content, it will be necessary for you to give primary attention to the specifics of the content you are presenting and the route you will take to solidify student understanding. When there is subject matter to be processed or mastered, this portion of the lesson plan should contain not only a brief outline of content be covered, but locatable reminders of key teaching maneuvers you will want to employ. You will find it worthwhile to highlight points in the lesson where teacher *questions* or *internal summaries* are appropriate, other places where deliberate *transitions* or *stimulus variations* are in order. Chapters 7, 8, and 9 provide more detail on teaching strategies and tactics that have special relevance for lesson planning.

In planning daily lessons it is also highly advisable to give deliberate attention to the wrap-up activities that will close out a particular lesson segment. Instead of allowing the clock or the bell to end a lesson, it is important to conclude it with summary activities, plans and assignments for succeeding lessons, or some other form of deliberate closure. As the teacher you may have comments or summary remarks to make at the conclusion of a lesson, or you may decide to elicit pertinent comments or summaries from students. It is important that your planning allows for time at the end of a class period to achieve proper closure on lesson activities.

Incorporating Noninstructional Agendas

A final aspect of purposeful lesson planning is to be able to combine instructional activities with necessary support tasks and other attendant chores within a crowded classroom schedule. Normally there will be materials to be procured, announcements to be made, students to be contacted, paperwork to be completed, and so forth, in relation to individual classes. Or, there may be behavior management moves you want to make with a particular class (e.g., a new seating arrangement). It is important to be able to work these preliminary or extra-instructional agendas into your class sessions so they flow with rather than interfere with your teaching (see chapter 9 on classroom management). By preplanning how you will incorporate these noninstructional items into your classroom activities, you help to insure they get proper attention while remaining subordinate to your lesson.

Sample Lesson Plan

Introductory Algebra
Lesson Focus: Solving simple equations in one variable using four operations.
Behavioral Objective (if applicable): Students will be able to solve simple equations requiring the application of the subtraction, division, addition, and multiplication rules.

Content	Procedure
I. Comparing equations and balances	1. SET: Use a small weighing balance to

A. Weights (balance)
B. "Members" (equation)
II. Solving simple equations
  A. Performing four operations
    1. Subtracting
$$3x + 2 - 2 = 11 - 2$$
$$3x = 9$$
    2. Dividing
$$\frac{3x}{3} = \frac{9}{3}$$
$$x = 3$$
    3. Adding
$$x - 6 = 18$$
$$x - 6 + 6 = 18 + 6$$
$$x = 24$$
    4. Multiplying
$$\frac{1}{4}x = 5$$
$$4 \times \frac{1}{4}x = 4 \times 5$$
$$x = 20$$
  B. Combining the operations
    (use following exercise)
$$\frac{2}{3}x - 4 = \frac{1}{4}x + 6$$

1. represent the two equal sides of an equation—show an equation to be like two weights on a balance (five min.)
2. Using balance analogy, show how you can perform like operations (subtraction, division, etc.) to both sides of an equation without disrupting the balance (five min.)
3. Work several examples of each operation with student participation (ten min.)
4. Have students independently solve practice exercises involving all four operations (ten min.)
5. Send students to the board in rows to solve given examples using all four operations (fifteen min.)
6. CLOSURE: Select students to summarize the four rules (five min.)
7. Give homework assignment (two min.)
NOTE: *This lesson might be taught more indirectly by utilizing teacher questions at key points to promote a more inductive or guided-discovery route to this new learning.*

Evaluation: Observation of student progress during practice exercises and more formal check of tomorrow's homework.
Reminders:
1. Lesson Materials: weighing balance, overhead transparencies
2. Makeup tests: Cheryl, Philip
3. Send home notices for Back to School Night
4. See custodian about broken chairs

Application Exercises

1. Identify an appropriate topic for a one-day lesson in a subject you would be qualified to teach. Having selected the lesson topic, prepare a lesson plan featuring a direct mode of instruction and containing the following elements:
  a. A learning objective that describes the lesson focus in nonambiguous terms
  b. A description of an original learning "set" for initiating the lesson
  c. A brief outline of lesson content together with a sequential sketch of main procedures to be employed in teaching that content
  d. A description of the intended means for bringing the lesson to a close
  e. Miscellaneous reminders of evaluation plans, necessary materials, time allotments, or other pertinent items

2. Consider the changes that would be required in the aforementioned lesson plan if you decided to employ indirect or guided-discovery strategies rather than direct instructional techniques in teaching this lesson. What lesson elements would remain essentially the same? Which portions would require substantial changes or additions? What would be the role of teacher questions in the new lesson plan? Would time allotments for the various lesson segments need to be changed? Rework the lesson plan you developed in exercise one to make it a plan for indirect instruction.

PLANNING FOR INDIVIDUAL DIFFERENCES

As a classroom teacher, your instructional plans will ordinarily be group-based. Normally they are designed to accomodate the learning needs of the average student in a typical class. A problem arises, though, when you have a class of students with widely differing abilities, interests, and motivations. A common frustration for beginning teachers is the early realization that their well-designed lessons often fail to engage those students with learning needs that depart significantly from the norm. Some students will always seem to be ahead of the game when it comes to understanding lesson content and completing assignments. Other students will consistently appear disinterested or tend to lag behind the rest of the class in their abilities to cope with classroom agendas. This is not a new problem, of course. Teachers and school administrators have for some time been trying to find answers for the instructional problem caused by individual differences.

Some Basic Strategies

Although no procedure or device can actually solve the problem of individual student differences, there are some things you can do to somewhat reduce the scope of the problem, including:

1. Find opportunities to work separately with individual students. This will ordinarily take less of your classroom time than you might imagine. As you develop workable classroom routines, the ability to attend momentarily to individuals during the course of a lesson can become a well-integrated part of your total teaching pattern. Make these brief personal exchanges occasions for offering encouragement, criticism, correction, and inspiration. Taking time to look over students' papers, to compliment them on their progress, and to suggest possible avenues for improvement can be beneficial for both high achieving and slower students.

2. Allow students to work on various tasks individually or in small groups under your guidance. In such a setting, one group may be working in a corner of the room on a simulation. A second group might be working in another part of the room to prepare a report. At the same time, individual students may be involved at their desks on special projects. Others might be reading. Group students according to interests, abilities, or special needs. For example, allow students with similar interests and goals to work together to solve a particular problem or to pursue a certain type of research. Keep your grouping patterns flexible

to avoid creating a stratified social system. Allow grouping patterns to change in keeping with the evolving interests, problems, and needs of students.

3. Provide differentiated assignments. For example, in a mathematics class you may assign slower students fewer problems. Or, in history and literature classes you might provide differentiated reading materials, based on demonstrated reading levels of students.

4. Design instructional packages that allow students to work independently on course units. These are sometimes referred to as learning modules. Each module or instructional package should include (1) a behavioral objective (2) a set of directions and suggestions for proceeding through the unit, (3) materials for study, (4) frames of programmed material in which students proceed in small steps to apply what they have learned, thereafter receiving immediate feedback on their progress, and (5) a final mastery test. Students who meet the standard are then allowed to proceed to the next unit. Those who do not pass are given remedial assignments until they are able to meet the criterion.

5. Encourage students to help one another. Students often learn very effectively from their peers. Take advantage of this fact by having students who have mastered a concept or skill coach other students who are experiencing difficulty. This kind of assistance will free you to give your attention to other individuals. It also allows students to share their talents and to practice communicating their ideas to others. It helps them as well as the beneficiaries to learn the subject more thoroughly.

6. Use a variety of materials. Provide reading and other instructional materials that are suitable to the various interests and ability levels represented in the class. Make sure these materials are available when individual students need them.

Accommodating Handicapped Students

Federal law (P.L. 94–142) requires that whenever possible, physically handicapped youngsters should be taught in regular classrooms and, when suitable, in the same manner as other students. It will be necessary for you to make special provisions for their disabilities and to adjust your teaching to their individual educational needs. A plan for working with handicapped students is constructed by a joint team of specialists, regular teachers, and parents. A guiding rule accommodates handicapped students so that they are placed in the least restrictive environment where they can function effectively. This rule has resulted in the practice of mainstreaming, or the placement of handicappped students in regular classrooms with their nonhandicapped peers. In the event a handicapped student is unable to perform with reasonable competence in your classroom, it is expected that you will report this problem to a special education teacher, thereby initiating a referral process for the student.

A SUMMARY OF BASIC GUIDELINES
FOR INSTRUCTIONAL PLANNING

1. Your instructional planning should proceed from long-range to intermediate to short-range plans. The planning you do at each level should be an amplification of the next longer-range plan of which it is a part.

2. Course-level planning involves identifying course content and goals, then organizing and sequencing the content to make it most teachable.

3. In preparing subject matter for instruction, it should be organized logically to make it internally coherent and psychologically to take into account the learning tendencies and abilities of students.

4. Regular unit planning allows you to bridge the gap between course organization and daily lesson planning. It involves structuring groups of lessons around a central topic or project, thus providing system to your teaching.

5. Having determined the objectives and content boundaries for a particular unit, the remaining task of unit planning is to prescribe lesson focuses, learning activities, and teaching strategies for that series of lessons.

6. As an extension of previous unit planning, lesson planning should be a highly practical activity that allows you to structure the sequence of activities for single class periods. It should be an opportunity for you to define in precise terms the focus of particular lessons and to mentally rehearse a lesson prior to actually teaching it.

7. A main consideration in unit and lesson planning is the adoption of teaching methods that are instrumental to the achievement of specified learning outcomes in particular populations of students. Two central questions are important here: (1) What teaching strategies are most appropriate when promoting given categories of learnings (e.g., facts, concepts, mental and physical skills, attitudes), and (2) would it be best to use a direct or indirect approach in teaching a proposed lesson to a particular group of students?

8. Resolve to plan in detail as you start your teaching. Spontaneous ideas often come to the minds of experienced teachers as they are teaching a lesson that will not occur to a neophyte. Off-the-cuff teaching is best left until you have had some experience.

9. Make a consistent effort to be sensitive to individual differences in students as you do your instructional planning. Although there are no simple answers to the problem created by individual student differences, there are a number of strategies you can adopt that can help with this increasingly difficult challenge.

SUGGESTED ACTIVITIES AND QUESTIONS

1. What are some important things that all good lesson plans have in common?

2. Although it is generally held that sound planning is essential to effective teaching, some educators would maintain that lesson plans are made to be broken. Are these contradictory positions? Why or why not?

3. What are some of the most important decisions that a teacher makes in planning for instruction?

4. Discuss similarities in planning for teaching and planning for a vacation trip. What are some main differences?

5. What is the difference between the logical and the psychological organization of content for teaching? Discuss the main importance of each type of organization.

6. For what kinds of teaching situations are lesson plans most important? Are there times when formal planning may be less essential? Discuss.

NOTES AND REFERENCES

1. W. James Popham and Eva I. Baker, *Planning an Instructional Sequence.* Englewood Cliffs, N.J.: Prentice-Hall, 1970, p. 47.
2. Ibid., p. 45.
3. Richard Kindsvatter, William Wilen, and Margaret Ishler, *Dynamics of Effective Teaching.* White Plains, N.Y.: Longman, 1988, p. 60.
4. George J. Posner and Alan N. Rudnitsky, *Course Design: A Guide to Curriculum Development for Teachers.* White Plains, N.Y.: Longman, 1986, p. 2.
5. Some would recommend that large-scale planning start with the determination of central course topics, after which learning goals are derived from a consideration of main understandings, skills, and attitudes that are to result from the study of these major concepts or themes. As you will likely find in your own planning, learning content and learning goals tend to be two sides of the same coin. For conscientious planners, it is difficult to think of one's subject matter without thinking of what you want students to learn from it. And, vice versa, it is usually difficult to stipulate goals for teaching apart from considerations of the content that one will be teaching. As you gain experience in planning, you will be able to decide which approach works best for you.
6. This list of sample topics and the subsequent arrangement for "clustering" and sequencing them are from Posner and Rudnitsky, op. cit., pp. 113–14.
7. Posner and Rudnitsky, op. cit., p. 116.
8. Kieran Egan, *Educational Development.* New York: Oxford University Press, 1979, p. 7.
9. Ibid., p. 15.
10. Ibid., p. 18.
11. Ibid ., p. 31.
12. Ibid., p. 47.
13. See J. Adelson and R. O'Neil, "The Growth of Political Ideas in Adolescence: The Sense of Community." In Norman Adler and Charles Harrington (Eds.), *The Learning of Political Behavior.* Glenview, Ill.: Scott, Foresman, 1970, pp. 102–15; and E. A. Peel, "The Thinking and Education of the Adolescent." In V. P. Varma and P. Williams (Eds.), *Piaget, Psychology, and Education.* Itasca, Ill.: F. E. Peacock, 1976, pp. 172–81.
14. Egan, op. cit., p. 45.
15. Ibid., p. 52.
16. Ibid., p. 51.
17. Ibid., p. 56.
18. Ibid., p. 26.
19. The idea of providing basic themes when specifying course topics and several of the topic examples that follow are from Kenneth H. Hoover, *The Professional Teacher's Handbook,* 3rd ed. Boston: Allyn and Bacon, 1982, pp. 13–14.
20. For an in-depth treatment of various models of teaching, see Bruce Joyce and Marsha Weil, *Models of Teaching.* Englewood Cliffs, N.J.: Prentice-Hall, 1972. Also, for another comprehensive approach to the subject of alternative teaching strategies, see Paul D. Eggen and Donald P. Kauchak, *Strategies for Teachers: Teaching Content and Thinking Skills,* 2nd ed. Englewood Cliffs, N.J.: Prentice-Hall, 1988.
21. The groups of teaching guidelines in this section were adapted from Herbert J. Klausmeier, *Learning and Human Abilities,* 4th ed. New York: Harper and Row, 1975, chaps. 10–14.

22. John Dewey's, *How We Think* (Boston: D. C. Heath, 1933) is a classic description of inquiry learning. See also Jerome Bruner, *The Process of Education.* Cambridge: Harvard University Press, 1960; and Lee Shulman and Evan Kesslar, *Learning by Discovery.* Chicago: Rand McNally, 1966.
23. Richard C. Sprinthall and Norman A. Sprinthall, *Educational Psychology: A Developmental Approach,* 3rd ed. Reading, Mass.: Addison-Wesley, 1981, p. 362.

PART TWO

Conducting Classroom Activity

CHAPTER 5

Becoming Established with Student Groups

PLANNING FOR THE FIRST DAYS OF SCHOOL

As a new teacher you will no doubt approach the beginning of school with mixed feelings of anticipation and anxiety. You will want to make these first days and weeks on the job as successful as possible. In preparing to meet classes for the first time you are apt to find yourself musing over such questions as: How should I present myself to my students?; what is the best kind of relationship to develop with these young people?; will I be able to keep them interested and cooperative?; and what should I be doing at the beginning to build a solid foundation for the rest of the year? These are live concerns for most entering teachers. A good beginning generally depends on realistic images of the situation facing you as a classroom teacher (see chapter 1). It is important to have an initial perception of the leadership role you will assume with your classes and to begin firming up some of the group process strategies you will want to employ.

This chapter provides ideas and suggestions for developing an appropriate group climate in your classes, for establishing productive relationships with students, and for helping your students learn to work effectively together as a group. It offers tips for getting an early handle on classroom routines and for weathering the inevitable ups and downs of those first days on the job.

Setting an Appropriate Tone

In an occupation where personality and style are important, the things you do during the first days and weeks of school will set important precedents for what is to follow. The pattern of rules and expectations you instill, the kind of relationships you establish with your students, the prevailing learning atmosphere you foster—these are foundational to your classroom system, and are conditions that you actively structure in your early contacts with your students. Your ability to set an initial tone for your classes will go a long way toward determining the kind of year you will have with a particular group of students. The way you greet students as they enter your classroom, the interest you exhibit as you call the roll for the first time, the enthusiasm you convey toward opening activities, will all serve to create a class atmosphere.

Your role as a climate-setter is fundamental to everything you do as a classroom teacher. In most lasting groups of whatever size (including families), there will ordinarily be those who take responsibility for keeping the group energized and productive and others whose basic agendas do not include group-maintenance tasks. In the confines of your own classroom you are clearly in the former role. You are the single most important factor in determining whether students approach your class with interest and anticipation, whether they show initiative and enthusiasm toward class activities, or simply go through the motions while waiting for the class period to end. The group climate you foster at the beginning of the school year will be the one you and your students are destined to live with during the many hours you spend together.

Groups of school-age young people cannot be expected to settle into a harmonious and workmanlike classroom pattern without deliberate and sustained efforts on your part to bring it about. The younger the students, the more likely it is that minor distractions and preoccupations (e.g., an untied shoe) will militate against a productive group focus until skillful leadership intervenes to capture their interest and attention. At the high school level students will regularly enter your class carrying residues of hall conversations and preceding lessons, mental and emotional baggage that must be abruptly set aside if they are to effectively concentrate on the business at hand. A large part of your task as a group climate-setter is to work as a counterforce to those elements within the school environment that tend to compete with the learning atmosphere you are seeking to develop.

A key factor in your ability to engender student interest in your class will be the initial enthusiasm you demonstrate. Studies describe the enthusiastic teacher as "one who conveys a great sense of commitment, excitement, and involvement with the subject matter" and one whose students "seem responsive and appear to enjoy class activities."[1] The most in-depth research dealing with this seemingly elusive aspect of teacher behavior points to the following qualities as indicative of high teacher enthusiasm:

1. rapid, uplifting, varied vocal delivery
2. dancing, wide open eyes
3. frequent, demonstrative gestures
4. varied, dramatic body movements
5. varied, emotive facial expressions
6. selection of varied words, especially adjectives
7. ready, animated acceptance of ideas and feelings
8. exuberant overall energy level[2]

Starting with a Well-planned Routine

Students will enter your classroom on the first day of school with certain preconceived notions of what to expect. Regardless of how long they have been in school, they will bring an initial mindset—positive or negative, eager or apathetic—regarding school subjects and school classrooms. However, because teachers do vary widely in their approaches to instruction and class management, most students will be feeling some initial uncertainty and apprehension about what you might have in store for them. They will usually be extra attentive on the first day of school. Students want to know what your class will be like—whether it will be interesting or boring, comfortable or threatening, lenient or demanding. You should take advantage of this initial concern by immediately establishing the kinds of classroom patterns that will allow you to work effectively with these young people. Specifically, it is recommended that you:

1. Set aside time on the first day for a discussion of rules.
2. Take a systematic approach as with any other teaching objective.
3. Begin by involving students in easy tasks to promote early successes.
4. Use activities that have a whole-group focus for the first few days.
5. Do not assume students have learned class procedures after one trial.[3]

You need to be especially well organized for your first meeting with a new group of students. You will want to make a concentrated effort to foster a learning climate and expectation system that is businesslike and interesting. You can also expect the first day of school to be rather hectic. On opening day you can anticipate students will be nervous and highly social. Some will be hunting for classes and making last-minute schedule adjustments. These are all reasons to be particularly well-prepared for the first day of classes.

The following are practical suggestions for things you can do during the first few days of school to begin establishing a positive and productive learning climate in your classes:

1. Take time to *visualize* what you want to have happen in your classroom, the sorts of learning and behavioral patterns you would like to have in place after several weeks of school. Allow yourself to picture students carrying out assigned tasks. How will they respond as a group when asked to pass forward a homework assignment? How will they perform when you break them into smaller groups? Use these preliminary images as a basis for planning your introductory sessions with new groups of students.
2. Have a good first-day activity and an appropriate early assignment that you have carefully designed as *impression builders*. Be deliberate and emphatic in introducing classroom procedures. Plan early activities that require students to give careful attention to teacher directions. Find opportunities to walk them through simple procedures as a means of bringing the group into sync with you.
3. Show a sincere interest in your students as individuals—their names, their appearances, their personalities. Take the opportunity to greet students as they enter your class. Give the impression you are glad to have them with you. Students will be more likely to show an interest in your class and its activities if you demonstrate a sincere interest in them.
4. Begin on the first day of school to model genuine enthusiasm for the required activities. Nothing dampens the interest and initiative of students quicker than a teacher who appears to be simply going through the motions. Do not let your

enthusiasm appear contrived or wishful, but allow it to be based on curiosity, interests, and projects that students can share with you.

5. Take early opportunities to model the need for personal responsibility and individual choice. Work to convey the assumption that individuals in the class are responsible for their own behavior; for example, people speak only for themselves, people choose their attitudes toward the class and toward one another, people choose to represent themselves proudly or sloppily in the work they produce.

6. Take time to review your *overriding objectives* for your teaching (see chapter 3). When feeling confused, ask yourself what is most important to achieve during these first days with a new group; what are my most important priorities as a teacher?

Aiming for Managerial Efficiency

Classrooms are of necessity complex, busy places because of the number of people schools try to accomodate and the number of agendas they seek to accomplish. During a typical class period you will need to effectively manage administrative chores, learning activities, materials and equipment, student behavior, and clock time. Under the circumstances, a premium gets placed on managerial efficiency—the ability to keep things moving, to attend to several agendas at the same time, and to maintain a goal-directed emphasis in your approach.[4] This aspect of teaching usually has a profound impact on new teachers:

> Once class starts, it's definitely show time. You've got to be ready to perform. There's really a lot to do in a short space of time. In a way this makes teaching kind of exciting for me.

> I'm not quite sure how to describe the work of managing an elementary classroom. Someone compared it to the job of an air-traffic controller in a large airport. I can imagine how hectic that would be. But teaching can also overload your brain. You need to be able to move quickly in order to stay on top of all the activity.

> For me the most challenging part of teaching is managing time. During the first few weeks I never seemed to have enough class time for all I wanted to accomplish. I was always leaving out important things. Now I'm learning to use my time better. I still have a ways to go though.

It behooves you then to have an effective system for taking roll, for getting students quiet and attentive, for distributing and retrieving materials, for giving directions and monitoring compliance, for executing transitions, and for handling interruptions.

Competent teachers are able to maintain an instructional pace that reduces "dead time" and keeps students actively involved with learning activities.[5] You will want to develop a style of classroom management that moves students through activities with a minimum of fuss and wasted time (see chapter 9). Research on effective teaching has concluded that "teachers' ability to manage smooth transitions and maintain momentum is more important to work involvement and classroom control than any other behavior management technique."[6]

The following are some recommendations for streamlining your class routines to make them as efficient as possible in the interests of quality learning and fewer behavioral problems:

1. Make your directions and explanations crisp and succinct. When asking students to perform a task, tell them precisely what you want them to do and actively monitor compliance, for example, "Please pass your papers forward . . . quickly and quietly please.")

2. Learn to pace class activity appropriately. Generally, you should stress the economy and efficiency of movement in bringing groups to perform overt behavioral tasks, for example, giving undivided attention to the teacher, getting in and out of the room, passing materials, making transitions from large- to small-group activities. At the same time, it is important to alter the pace when promoting reflective thinking or other learning processes where concentration and deliberation are essential.

3. Work to avoid slowdowns that prevent or disrupt the momentum of a lesson. Slowdowns can be caused by spending too much time on a minor aspect of a topic or by fragmenting an activity by working with individuals one at a time when you ought to be concentrating on the whole group.[7]

4. Seek to maintain momentum in your teaching by learning to attend to two tasks simultaneously ("overlapping"), for example, admitting a latecomer without disrupting the flow of the lesson, directing the activity of a small group while monitoring the work of the larger group.

5. Make effective use of your class time by overlapping administrative duties with learning activities when possible. For example, start class by assigning students a short task while you are taking attendance. This is not only a good utilization of time, but a technique that gets students into an appropriate mental set at the beginning of class.

6. Work to achieve smooth transitions when moving from one activity to another. This is best accomplished through well-established routines, clear directions, and completing one task before beginning another.

7. Have prepared materials ready so you do not have to use class time to organize instructional material. Avoid taking class time to write extensively on the board with your backs to students. Substitute the overhead projector (and prepared transparencies) for the chalkboard whenever possible.

Chapter 9 is devoted to a more in-depth treatment of classroom management strategies and techniques from a behavior control standpoint.

ESTABLISHING SOUND TEACHER– STUDENT RELATIONSHIPS

As you look forward to spending your working hours in the classroom with groups of young people, it is important to know something about teacher–student relationships and the kinds of leadership and association patterns you want to develop with your students.

Should I be warm and friendly or should I remain somewhat distant from my students at the outset? Should I consult with students about classroom policies or should I be more dictatorial in the beginning? What type of teacher–student relationship will provide the best learning environment in my class? These sorts of questions are likely to be of special concern to you as you assume this new leadership position with student groups.

Autocratic Leadership

There are several main types of leadership patterns you could conceivably adopt as a classroom teacher. For one alternative, you may resolve to be as stern and businesslike as possible in your relations with students, emphasizing strict attention to subject matter and classroom ground rules. This approach is generally referred to as the *autocratic* or authoritarian leadership style. Its first priority is the establishment of teacher authority. As a beginning teacher, seeking to achieve control and predictability in your relations with students, you may find yourself gravitating to this no-nonsense style of classroom leadership. A main problem with autocratic leadership is its reliance on external pressure to motivate students. Autocratic teachers demonstrate control by imposing their will on the class.[8] Although they are usually able to force student compliance at a surface level, their methods often engender resentment and rebellion, resulting in bad morale and negative rapport.

Permissive Leadership

As a second option, you might decide to take a much less structured approach and start out loose and tolerant, allowing classroom rules and regulations to derive from group process as the need arises. This leadership style has been labeled the *permissive* or laissez-faire approach. It is based on the assumption that students will respond more genuinely and cooperatively to a teacher who gives them maximum freedom to make decisions and solve problems as situations require. If you are a new teacher with residual tendencies to identify with the student role, you may find yourself emotionally inclined toward permissive leadership. It may seem more natural to feature yourself as ''one of the group'' in your early encounters with students. However, the permissive style tends to leave students confused and frustrated because the free-for-all environment turns out to be as inhibiting as the autocratic classroom. Like the autocratic teacher, permissive teachers generally fail to develop facilitative relationships with students.[9]

Democratic Leadership

A third type of leadership style attempts to avoid the extremes by combining the best intentions of the autocratic and permissive approaches. This leadership pattern shares the assumption of the autocratic model that students need order, limits, and the firm hand of the teacher as a basis for productive class activity (the adult guidance function).[10] It also assumes, along with the permissive approach, that to develop personal initiative and responsibility, young people need a good amount of involvement in decisions that affect them (the decision-making function). This approach to teacher–student relationships is generally referred to as a *democratic* leadership model. Democratic teachers attempt to motivate students through intrinsic motivation techniques (see chapter 6).

They allow students freedom to choose their own behavior with the assumption that students will be responsible for the consequences. In contrast to authoritarian teachers, democratic teachers (those who gently guide the group, ask for suggestions, and allow for group decisions) are apt to have classes in which the members are more satisfied, more cooperative, less hostile, and better able to follow through on group projects when the teacher is not present.[11]

Whereas a democratic leadership pattern has important advantages over the autocratic and permissive approaches to teacher–student relations, it is a style that ordinarily takes time to perfect. It requires a high level of organization and interpersonal sophistication on the part of a teacher.[12] Nevertheless, the early investments you make in this more balanced and facilitative approach to class decisions and relationships will result in a better learning environment for teaching and learning.[13] The interactive teaching techniques presented in chapter 8 will be helpful in your efforts to develop a democratic leadership style with your classes.

Student Attitudes toward Teachers

The first few days of school will be a "feeling out" time for students, during which they will be trying to decide what kind of teacher you are going to be. They will ordinarily make every effort to like and accept you, in the hope that your class will turn out to be something special. In fact, you can usually expect to enjoy a short "honeymoon" period with your students for the first week or two. Students during this early stage may be unusually tolerant and cooperative, even inclined to give you the benefit of the doubt if your behavior should be somewhat puzzling or inconsistent. Depending on the grade level, the feelings of students toward teachers can be quite intense. Usually the younger the students, the more emotion they will invest in the relationship.

When in the beginning you encounter student attitudes that seem particularly positive or negative, you can usually anticipate an eventual leveling-off of these feelings. With older students especially, you can expect the honeymoon relationship to lose its edge once you have begun to give tests and grades or to correct misbehavior. As a matter of fact, it is not unusual for adolescent students to show a complete reversal of attitude toward a teacher or a particular class over a short span of time. For no apparent reason, students may go from honeymoon behavior to attitudes of disenchantment with class activities and/or teacher leadership patterns. Some students run hot and cold, one day ·amiable, the next day aloof.

Some of this changing behavior you will be able to attribute to student's environmental circumstances or to typical mood swings. Much of it, however, will be explainable in terms of advancing stages in group development, a topic considered in a later section of this chapter.

Some Practical Suggestions

In the final analysis, there are no simple formulas for arriving at the kind of teacher–student relationships that will be most appropriate for the conduct of your classes. Developing positive and productive human relationships is more of an art than a matter of prescription. Although a consideration of leadership styles provides an initial framework for looking at classroom relationships, there remains the need to devise practical strategies for one's early meetings with students. In this regard, there are some central premises that should guide your behavior as you begin interacting with the young people in your classes.

In the first place, you need to be mindful that you are an adult with groups of young people. You qualify by virtue of your superior knowledge and maturity to be in this leadership position. For you to have proper credibility with them, students need to perceive you this way. During the time you are becoming established in the classroom, it is essential for students to see you as an adult both mentally and emotionally.

Following from this requirement, it is also important for students to view you as being in control, as operating from an established set of guidelines for the conduct of classroom activity. Students will look to you for confident and consistent judgment. They will depend on you as the ultimate arbiter, and as the one responsible for keeping things together.

Finally, it is critical that students see you as a teacher who is there for the right reasons. They need to perceive you as a fair-minded person who is interested in them as individuals, as someone who will not sacrifice their best interests for the sake of the system or for your own personal advancement. Students must find you approachable, a person who is not so caught up in the formalities of teaching and learning that you ignore individual needs and differences.

From these basic guidelines we can proceed to offer a number of pointed suggestions for establishing solid working relationships with the students in your classes. They include:

1. Start with a few simple groundrules around which classroom procedures revolve. Work to be firm and consistent, but not rigid, in upholding these basic rules.

2. Be able to be relaxed and informal around students when it is appropriate, but firm and businesslike when the situation requires it. The more open and self-disclosing you are able to be with students, the less inhibited and guarded they are apt to be in your presence.[14] Attempt to earn student's respect through natural authority rather than through power or position.

3. Be able to draw the line between a friendly, relaxed teacher–student relationship and a peer-level relationship with your students. When searching for a way to address a class of students, "you people" is much preferable to "you guys." Also, allowing students to address you by your first name is taboo.

4. Do not allow yourself to overreact when things do not go exactly as you would like. Avoid projecting an image of yourself as a complainer or as one who is easily frustrated by minor problems and inconveniences.

5. Work to maintain predictability in behavior and temperament in your interactions with students. Try to avoid abrupt variations in your moods, policies, and responses to classroom situations.

6. Show understanding of and patience with the evolving feelings of students toward you and your class. Expect extremes of positive or negative affect to become more moderate once students are better acquainted with your system of operation. In the meantime, aim for moderation in your own feelings toward your students, being careful not to reciprocate when student sentiments toward you are unrealistic.

7. Make a consistent attempt to recognize students as individuals. Whenever possible, greet students as they enter class. Show appreciation for their idiosyncracies and special talents. Make efforts to acknowledge students in the halls, the lunchroom, and at extracurricular events.
8. Respect the inner life of your students. Let them know that their thoughts and feelings are important by demonstrating active listening techniques (see chapter 10). Whenever appropriate, consult with them in matters that affect them. Make the development of individual self-expression an overriding objective in your work with these young people.

THE DYNAMICS OF GROUP DEVELOPMENT: A MATURATION PROCESS

Beginning a school year with one or more classrooms of students is both an adventure and a challenge. The adventure part stems from the fact that all classroom groups are both unique and changeable. Veteran teachers will testify to the fact that each set of students is different from every other group of students and will tend to take on a distinct personality. Some groups will develop a collective warmth and will seem especially receptive to your influence. Others will appear distant and hard to reach. On balance, though, all student groups of whatever grade or ability levels will exhibit periodic changes in moods and tendencies. Some days they will be inclined to settle into a routine with a minimum of persuasion. The next day, for no apparent reason, the group mood will be abnormally restless or feisty. Beginning teachers are often dismayed by the unpredictable fluctuations in student temper:

> I've given up trying to predict the kind of mood my students will be in. One older teacher told me it had a lot to do with the weather. He said to watch out when the north wind is blowing. Students can be expected to be especially lightheaded on those days. I'm not sure how true that is, but I do know one thing: you've got to expect some wide variations in these kids' behavior patterns. I can't remember if I was that flighty when I was in school.

Making allowance for the changing dispositions of students is one of the things you must learn to do if you are to avoid being constantly unnerved.

Another part of the teaching challenge is to get this collection of individual students working together as a cooperative and productive group. Class cohesiveness and the skills and attitudes necessary for fruitful group interaction cannot be expected to develop by chance. They will generally be the result of a long-term effort on your part. The normal tendency is for classes to remain disjointed and inefficient at cooperative tasks until teachers take deliberate steps to transform them into coherent working groups. Although some students will have been together socially or in previous classes, they will still need to learn to work together on group activities in the context of your classroom.

Stanford has found that effective classroom groups share the following main characteristics:

1. The members understand and accept one another
2. Communication is open
3. Members take responsibility for their own learning and behavior
4. Members cooperate
5. Processes for making decisions have been established
6. Members are able to confront problems openly and resolve their conflicts constructively[15]

Group development has been likened to the progression from an infant into a mature adult. As with the human developmental process, groups must learn to cope with new problems and must generate new abilities in response to these problems.[16] Just as many human beings fail to grow up socially and emotionally, many classes also fail to develop into effective working units. You will feel a sense of genuine accomplishment when you have been able to take an assemblage of new students from a raw, entry level of group development to the place where they can work skillfully and trustfully together on group learning tasks. This process normally takes place in several identifiable stages.[17] It will help you to know what these stages are and to have some appropriate strategies for bringing classes to the mature level of group performance.

The Orientation Stage

As suggested earlier, you can expect the first few days of school to be a feeling-out period for the students in your classes. They will usually come into the class full of questions, wanting to know will there be a seating chart, how much homework will we have, what will we need to do for an A, and so on. The more precise information you can give them about what is going to happen to them in this class, the sooner you can quiet their anxieties and apprehensions.

Students will also be concerned to find out who else is in the class. They will typically scan the room to see if they have friends in the group, at the same time hoping there will be no one who might embarrass or intimidate them. This process of trying to determine what the class is going to be like and the nature of the social environment is likely to continue until students begin to feel comfortable with one another and with the situation. Some students will adapt very quickly. They will have no trouble finding friends in the group. At the same time, there will usually be students who feel strange and uncomfortable in the new class surroundings. These students will resist interaction with classmates, tending to wait for others to break the ice with them. Some groups of students will take little initiative to learn one another's names or to interact socially. The getting-acquainted process can be aided considerably by a teacher who recognizes the need for students to feel socially comfortable and acceptable as a necessary first step in group development.

Here are some things you can do to help students make a successful adaptation during the orientation stage in group development:

1. Start the first day with a brief sketch of what students can expect to be doing in this class. Give clear and precise information about the sorts of things they will be studying, the activities they will be involved with, the type of homework they can anticipate, and the approach you will take to evaluation and grading.

2.   Take the lead in encouraging social openness and self-disclosure by including a brief description of yourself in your course introduction. Give students insights into you as a person by mentioning significant things about your formative experiences: hobbies and interests, immediate family, and so forth.

3.   Use structured, low-threat get-acquainted exercises to help students get to know one another. Examples are: (1) Allow the whole group to mingle freely with the stipulation that each person take initiative to interact briefly with every other person and to share an interest, (2) have students wear name-tags for the first few days of school, and attempt to learn as many names as possible, (3) run a contest at the end of the week, offering prizes to those who learn the most names, and (4) pair students and have them share something significant about each other with the class.

4.   Make an early effort to model the interpersonal attitudes and behaviors you would like to have students acquire in your classes. In practice this could mean learning student's names, interests, and special qualities as quickly as possible, showing as much interest in poorly dressed as well-dressed students, giving the same amount of attention to slower students as to academically advanced students, and displaying as much concern and appreciation for minority students as for the ethnic majority.[18]

5.   Make the physical organization of the class reflect your interest in promoting fairness and equality. Use circular seating arrangements when appropriate to allow students to be face-to-face with one another. When breaking the class into subgroups, give students opportunities to work with different people each time.

6.   Allow reticent students time to adapt to the class environment. Be careful not to prejudge students who initially appear uninterested or distant, but be prepared to accept genuine expressions of fear and doubt in new students.

The Formative Stage

After the first few weeks together most groups of students begin to feel freer and less inhibited with one another. It is important at this stage for you to take note of these emerging patterns of influence and participation within the group. Friendship circles will start to become apparent, and you will start to notice "spheres of influence" within the classroom. Some students will establish themselves as more influential than others in helping the class with learning tasks, or in keeping the class functioning as a group. Other students may show signs of negative adjustment, perhaps as budding class clowns or teacher baiters. One of your main concerns during the pattern formation stage in group development should be to promote broad involvement in class activities, to discourage the dominance of a small minority of students, and to stimulate free-flowing and diffuse communication within the group.[19] Your ability to induce active two-way communication between teacher and students and among students will lead to more active involvement and interest within the class.[20] To facilitate genuine dialogue with and between students, the following basic communication techniques are especially useful:[21]

1.   *Paraphrasing.* Paraphrasing is restating what you think another person has said, but in your own words. It is a communication skill that shows a concern to

accurately understand the other person's message and to be corrected if you have misunderstood. A paraphrase usually begins with a lead-in such as, "I hear you saying that . . ." or "I understand you to say . . ."

2. *Behavior Description.* This technique involves depicting the overt actions of another person without attempting to attach motives or meanings to the behavior (a common cause of friction and miscommunication). The intent is to simply describe a behavior you have observed (perhaps a troublesome one) without attributing bad intentions or personal weaknesses. Some examples are: "I noticed you didn't have anything to say in class today," or "Several people are still talking while Debby is trying to make her point."

3. *Descriptions of Own Feelings.* The ability to directly communicate your own feelings about a situation promotes honesty and understanding within a group. By directly describing feelings and impressions, people can bring problems or likes and dislikes to a head in a precise way, and thus avoid misunderstandings. Members reflect openness and sincerity when they are able to say "I feel embarrassed" or "I feel angry." Similarly, it enhances interpersonal understanding when group members can describe feelings in language like, "I enjoy his sense of humor" or "I'm impressed with her abilities with language."

4. *Perception Checking.* Perception checking is similar to paraphrasing except that it involves interpreting feelings and internal processes rather than words and overt behavior of the other person. A perception check aims at getting the other person to talk directly about his feelings by describing in a tentative fashion what you think you are noticing. Examples of perception checking are: "I get the impression you're angry with me. Are you?," and "You appear disinterested in your work. Is that right?" When using this technique, you should avoid implying disapproval until some dialogue has occurred.

Another of your main agendas during this formative stage of group development should be to give students practice in group-centered as well as teacher-centered activities. Although the class will have made significant advances socially, they will still be relatively unsophisticated as a working group. They will lack the skills and attitudes necessary to carry out subject-matter tasks as a cooperative unit. For example, if you assign them subgroup projects, they will typically tend to stray from the task without close teacher monitoring. They will ordinarily be ineffective when it comes to establishing appropriate divisions of labor, allowing everyone to contribute, resolving differences of opinion, and getting proper closure on the group assignment. If you intend to have a class that does more than listen to the teacher and take notes, you will want to establish some fundamental group process goals during the first several weeks of school. The following five norms are considered foundational to productive group interaction:

1. Group responsibility—Everybody contributes to the work of the group; leaders emerge from the group itself.
2. Responsiveness to others—Members listen attentively to one another and attempt to combine their ideas to form a group product.
3. Interdependence—Members cooperate to achieve goals rather than competing with one another.

4. Decision making through consensus—The group aims to arrive at decisions acceptable to all, rather than imposing the will of the majority on the minority.
5. Confronting problems—Disagreements are faced rather than ignored, and solutions are actively sought.[22]

It is apparent, then, that there are a number of things you can do during the formative stage of group development to help students learn to function cooperatively and productively together, including:

1. Use indirect techniques to stimulate student participation. Besides employing *mirroring techniques* (paraphrasing, perception checking, behavior description), it is important at this stage to use questions that invite students to share thoughts and impressions and to be as accepting as possible of student's feelings and ideas. (See chapters 8 and 11 for further discussion of these communication skills.)
2. Work to stimulate effective two-way communication between members of the class. You can do this by modeling active attending and listening skills with your students (see chapter 8), by allowing only one person to talk at a time, and by giving students small-group tasks that require active listening and sharing.
3. Provide opportunities for the class to discuss and conceptualize group functions and processes. Help them to appreciate the kinds of communication skills necessary for effective decision making and problem solving in group situations.
4. Make a conscious effort to keep classroom communications as open and free-flowing as possible. Stress the importance of widespread contributions to the group process. Find ways to tone down members who threaten to dominate group interaction, without appearing to muzzle these students, for example, private talks, convenient ignoring.
5. Encourage group-based responsibilities. Shift more from teacher-centered to group-centered activities. Focus student attention on group tasks to be completed, defining explicit outcomes for these tasks and frequently grading the whole group rather than individuals.

The Conflict Stage

Student groups that spend extended periods of time together are bound to experience some conflict and disagreement. In fact, as group members become more open, responsive, and group-centered in their attitudes and behavior, the more likely it is that some interpersonal friction will occur.[23] It may be manifest in increased bickering and complaining among students or in a student challenging teacher authority. When it happens within a group that has begun to demonstrate cohesiveness and task-level competence, it should be considered a sign of growth rather than regression.

A period of intragroup discord is often a natural result of widespread participation and occurs when a broad spectrum of opinions, values, and personal styles are allowed expression. Also,when you have been successful in getting students to confront rather than ignore problems, this often increases their dispositions to be critical of one another and of the teacher. Another underlying reason for conflict in a developing group is a felt need for personal space and self-assertion on the part of students who are beginning to feel constrained by the group atmosphere. An expression of dissatisfaction, or even hostility, may reflect a temporary need for students to challenge teacher authority or peer influence in a group that has begun to come together as a working unit. When you sense that a classroom group is going through a normal conflict stage in its development, the following are some measures you can take to help students deal constructively with this period of instability:

1. Help students to understand that group conflict can be an indication that positive rather than negative things are happening to them. It is not something that should be avoided or suppressed, because it is usually a sign that group members care enough to be direct and honest with one another.
2. Provide support and reassurance for students who become nervous about the increased group friction or about perceived challenges to teacher authority. Give them time to understand you have the situation under control and that you see this as a normal phase in the group process.
3. Do not react defensively and become more authoritarian. The imposition of tighter limits at this point will not solve the problem students are experiencing. Instead, resolve in your own mind to help students learn constructive ways of coping with group conflict.
4. Use active listening techniques to assure students you are hearing and understanding their concerns (see chapter 11). It is important that you understand and accept the feelings that underlie the surface complaints or criticisms students are expressing.
5. Be able to conduct "airing-out" sessions with the class in which the topic is the group itself and its progress as a productive unit. Have a procedure for allowing students to express grievances in a reasonable and controlled manner. Use these sessions to practice the kinds of problem-solving skills you want the group to master.

The Productive Stage

As you take a classroom of students through the normal phases of group development you will often be amazed at the changes occurring in the group as the weeks and months go by. Once a group has reached a mature stage in their growth they can be especially enjoyable to work with. It will make the energy you have invested in group development well worth the effort. At the productive level students are not only able to interact effectively when involved in learning activities, but they can also deal with disagreement and intragroup conflict in constructive ways. One of the central characteristics of mature groups is their ability to effectively resolve their own problems.[24] At this level the students are ready to work effectively in subgroups or as a total body. Although such classes can at times be noisy places, and interpersonal tensions can arise unexpectedly, student interest is typically high and a good deal of learning normally takes place.[25]

When you are successful in reaching this level with a group of students, you will very likely notice increased intimacy among students and between yourself and the students.[26] The ability to effectively confront and clear the air on mutual problems tends to bring groups of people closer together. Stanford points to the deepening relationships that characterize the productive stage in group development. In this connection, he suggests teachers need to be prepared to deal with two types of common problems. First, students often have difficulty knowing how to deal with the stronger feelings that accompany closer relationships with their peers and their teacher. In addition, there is the frequent tendency for students at this advanced stage of group development to want to concentrate more on their intragroup relations than on subject-matter tasks. When this happens, teachers have to take steps to right the balance.[27]

As a teacher, it is good to have some strategies for helping students maintain their productive edge once they reach this level of group development. The following are some suggestions:

1. Be prepared for temporary regression (e.g., disorganization, lack of participation, conflict). This often happens when a short vacation or special event interrupts the normal routine. Regression to earlier group patterns can also occur after students have been working for extended periods of time in smaller groups or on individual projects.
2. Take measures to help the group maintain its skills. This may involve periodic class discussions aimed at getting students to see the need for skill maintenance. Often merely identifying and talking over the problems students are having is enough to get the group back on a productive track. If not, it may require structured practice sessions to reacquaint them with the group process skills they had begun to neglect.
3. Expect students to want to alternate between working on learning tasks and working on their interpersonal agendas. Try to arrive at an appropriate balance between subject-matter learning and the social-emotional learning that accompanies deepening peer relations. When possible try to devise learning activities that link student's personal concerns with content-related skills.
4. Maintain your prerogative to set boundaries around student power, but first give the group an opportunity to deal with its own problems.

COPING WITH THE NORMAL UPS AND DOWNS OF THE JOB

Teaching is the kind of occupation where the moods, abilities, and cooperative efforts of other people can have a large bearing on what you accomplish on any given day; thus it is realistic to expect there will be times when everything seems to fall in place and other days when nothing goes right. This tendency to experience a pattern of ups and downs, for example, several good days followed by a series of bad days, is a more acute problem for beginning teachers than for veterans. It is more likely to happen during the early days of a new job, before you have had an opportunity to establish a system and to become stabilized in your teaching pattern. The following samples from the diary of a first-year teacher of seventh-grade social studies dramatically illustrate the vacillating feelings and impressions that arise when a person is introduced to the rigors of full-time teaching:

September 7—I have the feeling that I am really going to enjoy teaching, and am very anxious to get at it! I'm surprisingly not nervous (yet!). None of the students seem particularly rowdy. There are a few dominant personalities and some very quiet individuals.

September 10—What a day this turned out to be! . . . Much of my former eagerness suddenly left me. . . . My main fear was that in going over the material after the test, I was going to seem unsure of myself. . . . The kids were testing me, for sure. Third period took a good five to seven minutes to quiet down. Lots of students getting up to sharpen pencils (for longer than necessary). Several boys in the back of the class found the whole thing hilarious and kept others from hearing.

September 16—A great day in classes today! . . . This was the most valuable experience I've had so far with the students. They asked for my help and I felt glad to give it to them. They showed obvious respect and appreciation, and the whole thing was very healthy for our mutual relationships. . . . Today I left school feeling like it was all O.K. and had a very optimistic attitude.

September 22—Today I gave the class a very short quiz on vocabulary and spelling. . . . Everyone moaned and groaned about how third grade it was, but not many scored all that well. . . . I've felt a lot of frustration in dealing with the class when they act this way. They don't see me as an authority figure, partly, I'm sure, because I don't see myself this way. I don't really know what I can do to change this. . . . I go home in the evenings and give myself little pep talks on how to deal more effectively with the students, then the next day it never seems to make a difference. I get awfully nervous when the class misbehaves.

October 3—Today we played a game that all the class seemed to like. . . . I really enjoyed the students in lots of ways. . . . I want to make next week a turning point in my teaching. I want it to be the best teaching job I've done, and I want each week after that to be even better. I'm feeling pretty good about teaching right now.

October 11—Well, considering that this was supposed to be the best week of the semester, it turned out to be right up there with one of the worst weeks of my life. Just when you think things might be looking up, there you are—face down again. . . . I am only glad that I didn't have a ton of lesson planning to do, because I was so emotionally distraught that I don't think I could have done it. . . . I spent a few days doing some serious thinking about whether or not I really should pursue this course in my life after all.

October 23—This week seemed to go fairly smoothly. . . . I am trusting the students to behave better and it seems that they are more comfortable also. . . . I'm finding I am enjoying the classroom experience much more. . . . I still have some high ideals that I'd like to see through to the end.

Understanding What Is Happening to You

Unless you have prepared yourself to deal with the normal succession of good and bad days that characterize early career teaching, you may experience initial reservations about your ability to accommodate to this feature of the work. It helps to have a good understanding of what you are going through and to recognize some of the main casual elements, in the event you should find yourself on an emotional roller coaster during those first days and weeks of the job. For one thing, you may have inadvertently set yourself up for disappointment. You could be hoping for more initial success than is reasonable to expect. Or some of your long-standing images of day-to-day teaching may need revising (see chapter 1).

Second, your emotions are likely to be running on high during your first few days of teaching. The profound enthusiasm and exhilaration you feel after a satisfying session with your students leaves you susceptible to a corresponding low when this experience is not repeated the next day. One of your personal projects during the first weeks of teaching will be to get your emotional equipment stabilized, to learn to adjust more effectively to the highly changeable circumstances of this kind of work.

You are also likely to experience alternating good and bad days as a beginning teacher because you have not yet settled into a teaching pattern that hinders such fluctuations. Once you have developed a stable and consistent set of classroom procedures, you are not as apt to allow externals, for example, student moods and inclinations, to negatively affect your teaching day.

In the meantime, here are some suggestions to help with the kinds of ups and downs you are likely to experience as an early career teacher:

1. Do not allow yourself to dwell on the negatives of the job. Find effective ways of clearing the slate after a bad day (e.g., meditation, exercise). Be able to put your mind to work on something more constructive and relaxing (e.g., hobbies, reading).

2. Try to be philosophical about the normal ups and downs of the job. Recognize that in a character-dependent activity, like teaching (see chapter 2), there are built-in obstacles to be overcome. The patience and confidence to deal with minor problems and setbacks is something every good teacher must cultivate.

3. When you are ready to view the situation rationally rather than emotionally, attempt to take an analytical approach to your teaching problems. Are there particular things you may or may not be doing that would help to account for these early problems. Take the initiative to review basic teaching strategies or management techniques that would relate to the problem you are experiencing.

4. Learn to reframe problems to get a look at them from a different perspective. What was it that actually happened in school today? Was it really all that serious? Is it possible I overreacted or misconstrued the situation to make it reflect on me and my competence, when in reality it was not something I created? Could my prevailing attitude or mood be the thing that is causing me the problem right now?

5. Find supportive people you can regularly talk to about your teaching. Keeping a personal journal (or diary) in which you note significant school happenings along with your subjective impressions can also have therapeutic value.

SUGGESTED ACTIVITIES AND QUESTIONS

1. Imagine yourself as a teacher about to begin a school year with a group of students in an area you are qualified to teach. Mention three or four orientational items you would want to be sure to discuss with your students on the first day. What are some things you would do to make this introductory session most effective?

2. How do you anticipate handling the matter of seating as you begin organizing for the first day of school? Discuss some of the pros and cons of each of these possible approaches: (1) allowing students to sit where they wish, (2) assigning seats alphabetically, or (3) seating students according to size or special problem, for example, short students or those with vision or hearing problems in front.

3. What is your attitude toward allowing students to be involved in the planning of classroom rules and procedures? Are there some areas of classroom life where joint policy planning would be appropriate? If so, what are some other areas where you believe it would not be advisable to give students a hand in developing group guidelines? How would the grade level affect your views on this issue? Elaborate.

4. What kinds of leadership roles have you had occasion to play at this juncture in your life? What previous situations have you been in where you were called on to be a prime organizer or climate-setter for other people, young or old (e.g., family, military, athletics)? How do you perform in situations where the task falls to you to bring energy, enthusiasm, and positive direction to a shared project or cause?

5. What degree of formality will seem most natural to you in relating to students at the grade level you intend to teach? What do you anticipate will be your preferred mode of addressing students in group settings (e.g., "boys and girls," "you kids," "you folks")? Will you feel comfortable calling students by their nicknames (e.g., Cal, Steph)? Would there ever be occasions where you would allow adolescent students to be on a first-name basis with you?

6. Imagine yourself as a beginning teacher faced with the following situation: You are in the first weeks of school with a class of early adolescent students who seem especially pleased to have you as their teacher. A number of students in the class are making it a practice to seek you out before and after school or during lunch, apparently just for the purpose of spending more time with you. During class you are noticing that some of these students regularly appear more interested in you and your personal mannerisms or clothes than they do in the lesson. What will be your attitude toward this special attention? In the event you wanted to discourage this preoccupation with you, how might you communicate this desire to the students without appearing insensitive to their feelings?

7. Consider each of the leadership styles discussed in this chapter: autocratic, permissive, and democratic. Analyze each approach in terms of its main advantages and disadvantages. Does one or another of these styles seem most suited to your own personality and/or philosophy of teaching? Should your amount of teaching experience have a bearing on the leadership approach you adopt at a particular point in your career? Discuss reasons why democratic classroom leadership requires more skill than the autocratic or permissive varieties.

8. Identify veteran teachers who are able to consistently bring positive energy and enthusiasm to their classes. Find opportunities to discuss with these teachers their strategies for remaining vital and upbeat on a day-to-day basis. Attempt to obtain insight into techniques they might employ to help them bounce back after a bad day on the job.

NOTES AND REFERENCES

1. Phi Delta Kappa, *Practical Applications of Research.* Bloomington, Ind.: Newsletter of PDK Center on Evaluation, Development, and Research, vol. 3 no. 4 (June 1981), p. 2.

2. Mary L. Collins, *The Effects of Training for Enthusiasm on the Enthusiasm Displayed by Preservice Elementary Teachers.* Doctoral Dissertation, Syracuse University, 1976, pp. 23–27.

3. Myron H. Dembo, *Applying Educational Psychology in the Classroom,* 3rd ed. New York: Longman, 1988, p. 259.

4. Jacob Kounin, *Discipline and Group Management in Classrooms.* New York: Holt, Rinehart and Winston, 1977, pp. 92–97.

5. Ibid., pp. 102–105.

6. C. M. Charles, *Building Classroom Discipline,* 3rd ed. New York: Longman, 1989, p. 33.

7. Kounin, op. cit., see chap. 5.

8. Charles, op. cit., p. 72.

9. Richard A. Schmuck and Patrick A. Schmuck, *Group Processes in the Classroom.* Dubuque, Iowa: Wm. C. Brown, 1971, p. 29.

10. Charles, op. cit., p. 73.

11. Richard C. Sprinthall and Norman A. Sprinthall, *Educational Psychology: A Developmental Approach,* 3rd ed. Reading, Mass.: Addison-Wesley, 1981, p. 549.

12. Charles, op. cit., p. 86.

13. Schmuck and Schmuck, op. cit., p. 29.

14. Joseph Morris, *Psychology and Teaching: A Humanistic View.* New York: Random House, 1978, p. 84.

15. Gene Stanford, *Developing Effective Classroom Groups.* New York: Hart, 1977, p. 26.

16. Ibid., p. 27.

17. The approach to group developmental stages presented here is adapted from the work of Gene Stanford, op. cit.

18. One study found that students in classes where they felt class members were treated equally and had little hostility toward one another had higher academic achievement (H. J. Walberg and G. J. Anderson, "Classroom Climate and Individual Learning." *Journal of Educational Psychology,* 59 (1968), pp. 414–19).

19 Schmuck and Schmuck, op. cit., p. 121.

20. Ibid., p. 121.

21. Ibid., p. 97.

22. Stanford, op. cit., pp. 77–78.

23. Ibid., p. 29.

24. Schmuck and Schmuck, op. cit., p. 122.

25. Ibid., p. 122.

26. Stanford, op. cit., p. 253.

27. Ibid.

CHAPTER 6

Drawing Students into Encounters with Learning

THE MOTIVATIONAL TASK

Before you can teach students subject matter, you must first be able to engage them productively in classroom learning. Yet, because of the formal nature of most school learning, students often fail to perceive its relevance to their own lives (see chapter 1). As a result, you can usually anticipate some initial apathy and resistance toward the content you are attempting to teach. This places a premium on your ability to approach new learning in ways that engender active interest and involvement on the part of your students. Veteran teachers often cite motivational skill as the main key to successful teaching:

> It all comes down to keeping them interested. On days when they happen to be jazzed on the lesson, my discipline problems are nonexistent. But when they're bored, they will always look for something extraneous to occupy them. That's when my problems start. If I had it to do over, I'd minor in psychology and make motivation my specialty.

> You've got to be able to motivate them in order to teach them. It's as simple as that. In fact, we should call the job motivation rather than teaching. Once you're able to get students really involved in a subject, they'll pretty much learn it on their own. But if they're not personally involved, you can talk about your subject until you're blue in the face and they won't hear you.

> Today's kids have too many other distractions. Most school learning bores them to death because it can't compete with what's going on around them. My main advice to anyone starting out in teaching would be to collect all of the techniques you can find for making your teaching stimulating.

Resourceful teachers are able to arouse student interest in their classes without having to rely on threats, grade anxieties, or strong social pressures to get them to learn. They are able to draw students into meaningful encounters with the subject by appealing to their present interests and curiosities, their previous experiences and understandings, and their innate tendencies to want to resolve problems. This requires some basic knowledge of learning psychology as well as appropriate strategies for introducing new knowledge and skills.

This chapter is designed to help you understand what it will take to involve students actively and meaningfully in classroom learning. It will offer a brief introduction to the psychology of productive learning, including a discussion of some of the obstacles that must be overcome if you are to foster in-depth learning in your classes. You will be offered motivational strategies that are both involving and growth facilitating for your students.

Avoiding the Path of Least Resistance

Formal or nonsituational learning tends to be inherently abstract, that is, removed from its normal life context, and therefore less meaningful than the learning that occurs through a person's give-and-take with the world outside of school. To compensate for this shortcoming of formal schooling, you will want to develop techniques to reduce its abstractness and to help students find meaning and purpose in school learning. In order to accomplish this you will need to overcome certain forces within the system itself that tend to foster superficial learning.

As discussed in chapter 2, the pressures and distractions of modern teaching can threaten to keep you preoccupied with organizational matters, causing you to seek short-cuts and routines that will make the job less burdensome. In the process of streamlining teaching to meet bureaucratic requirements, you run the risk of making learning more artificial and less meaningful to students. This has become a serious problem in U.S. schools at all levels.[1]

In many cases, teachers are attempting to cover more material in a shorter period of time. They are making less effort to ground new learning in the experiences, perceptions, and existing knowledge structures of students. And, particularly at the secondary level, teachers are attempting to carry more of the burden of instruction through verbalization, by talking about rather than getting students to interact with learning objects. On the whole, school learning has become more verbal, more subject-centered, and more remote from students' life experiences.[2] The resultant alienation many students feel toward school tends to increase discipline problems and to decrease the satisfaction teachers derive from their work.

To avoid taking the path of least resistance and falling into this overly mechanized pattern of teaching, your first imperative should be an unshakable commitment to meaningful learning. An appreciation for what it takes to facilitate student understanding and a firm resolve to promote this kind of substantive learning in your own classroom are necessary prerequisites to quality teaching and personal job satisfaction.

THE REQUIREMENTS OF MEANINGFUL LEARNING

A school's emphasis on verbal learning is particularly evident in academic subjects like science, math, English, and social studies where the subject matter is essentially language-based. Even performance classes like art, woodshop, physical education, and music normally depend on the student's ability to handle verbal information as a basis for skill learning. There are two basic ways in which students can deal with the verbal input they receive in school, whether it be in the form of teacher presentations, textbook readings, or the audio portions of instructional films. They may undertake to relate it to previously acquired knowledge, or in other words, to understand it; or they may attempt to store new information in the exact form it was received, which is to memorize it. When students are able to fit new knowledge into preexisting knowledge structures, it is appropriate to say that the learning has meaning. When they simply memorize it without relating it to knowledge that is already in place, we say they have learned it rote. The difference between meaningful and rote learning is crucial for both teachers and students. Meaningful and rote learning involve significantly different internal processes that appear to follow very different learning laws.[3]

Rote learning depends on the laws of verbal association, a mental conditioning process that establishes a bond between a certain stimulus and a desired learner response. It is inferred from the learner's ability to recite memorized content that learning has taken place. Rote learning theory deemphasizes the internal states and mental processes of students as they learn and attends exclusively to learned behaviors and the environmental conditions that cause them. Traditionally it has been the standard learning model used by teachers to get students to remember subject-matter elements such as vocabulary words, multiplication tables, and scientific symbols.[4]

Meaningful learning focuses on the inner processing that takes place when learners attempt to comprehend verbal material. In contrast to the rote learning model, this concept of learning places its main emphasis on the particular *mental structures* or frames of reference that students bring to new learning. It assumes that students need to be interacting with, rather than mechanically memorizing, the verbal input they are receiving if understanding is to occur. For a person to be able to retain and make use of new information, it must be assimilated or made to fit in with existing knowledge structures. "Learning is more efficient and complete to the degree that facts occur in networks or relationships."[5]

As suggested, meaningful learning has critical advantages over rote learning. Rote learning occurs without comprehension, thus the only performance supported by it is verbatim repetition. Information learned verbatim and not assimilated into a student's existing knowledge structures is quickly forgotten. Meaningful learning of information, on the other hand, makes possible the further learning of new related information and the retention of learned information.

What Does Understanding Involve?

Like the word *learning,* the term *understanding* is often used loosely in educational circles, without serious attention to its import. It is not uncommon for teachers to ask students, "Do you understand?", when they have not conceptualized what it means to understand something. Dictionary definitions include words like *comprehend, embrace, grasp,* and *seize* to convey the notion that understanding is a process of reaching out and gathering in individual items. As a learner is able to pull together items of information under an umbrella of existing knowledge, understanding begins to take shape.[6] Grounded understanding involves the establishment of *mental relationships.* When teachers ask students, "Do you understand this?", what they are really asking is, "Can you relate to this?", or "Are you able to connect this new information with what's already there?"

As learners, we begin to comprehend the meaning of a word like *fascism* when we are able to conceive of it as a type of government. It has more meaning still if we are familiar with a *totalitarian government.* Our understanding is further enhanced when we are able to compare and contrast it with communism, another kind of totalitarian system. If we have seen pictures of fascist dictators from the World War II era, we have yet another, more concrete, reference with which to connect the idea.

We have the potential to understand why heavy steel ships are able to float on the sea if we can relate this phenomenon to a general principle of flotation that is already anchored in our minds. The essence of understanding is the pulling together of particulars under one previously established generalization or "big idea" for which these particulars are an extension.[7]

A second requirement of grounded understanding is for a learner to be able to perceive an application of the new learning. Students take a big step toward understanding any object, process, or fact when they see how it can be used to fulfill some purpose or goal. As soon as they perceive what something is for, they understand it to some degree.[8] So learning that can be seen to have some practical use is more likely to be internalized than that which is encountered simply as academic exercise.

To have a solid understanding of a historical concept like imperialism, students need not only to comprehend it in the abstract as a particular variety of aggressive behavior of one country toward another, but to recognize how the concept is used in our present world. Students' understanding becomes firmer as they realize how the term is employed by the leaders of some countries to label and judge the activities of certain other countries.

For understanding to be functional, then, a learner's ability to see relationships among concepts, generalizations, and facts needs to be complemented by a perception of the purpose that is served by this formal knowledge. It turns out that understanding is best achieved when the learner can internalize a use for that which is to be learned. This is an important reason for teachers to consider motivation and understanding as integrally related.[9]

Featuring the Skills of Information Processing

The ability to process verbal information at an understanding level requires considerable skill on the part of a young learner. It is a skill that takes a good deal of practice to be able to do it well, even for students at the formal-operations level. It requires the ability to call up relevant background knowledge and to make appropriate connections between this existing knowledge and new information as it is being received. Within the school setting, learners must be able to process verbal input fast enough to keep pace with the incoming flow of new knowledge. If the informational input is fast-paced teacher talk, it is easy to see how a student may fall behind and give up trying to understand.

When students are consistently presented with abstract information that they are unable to assimilate because of inadequate knowledge backgrounds or lack of perceived relevance, they will be inclined to turn off their mental processors and resort to passive memorization. In other words, they will stop trying to understand and instead will devote their mental efforts to storing and recalling nonmeaningful material for purposes of the test. Although there is also a definite skill involved in the accurate memorization of arbitrarily associated bits of information, memorization learning is essentially a mechanical process with limited utility in helping students learn how to learn. It does not require nor provide practice in logical or reflective thinking, operations that are fundamental to independent learning.

Unfortunately, many students get more practice during their school careers in memorizing verbal material than they do in understanding it. Were it the case that these skills were complementary processes or that skill in memorizing information could lead to or serve as a prerequisite to skill in understanding, we might begin to justify this heavy emphasis on nonmeaningful learning in so many school subjects. For the most part, however, it is a dead end. Unassimilated learning is not only quickly forgotten, but it works counter to the development of understanding because it deprives students of much-needed practice in information processing. It also tends to foster negative motivation for learning.

When introducing new learning, there are a number of steps you can take to assist students in the meaningful processing of verbal information:

1. Provide "advance organizers" that preview the topic you will be exploring, showing logical relationships among the various elements of the learning content.
2. Attend carefully to the pacing of your informational input as you provide students with instructions or explanations. Allow adequate time for them to assimilate new information as it is being received.
3. Take an active interest in how students are processing the information you are teaching. Organize your lessons to accommodate the learning needs of students at their particular stages of conceptual development.
4. Have students attempt to talk through the mental operations they are using to process new information. Attempt to discover gaps or "sticking points" in their information-processing patterns.
5. Be clear in your own mind when it is important for students to understand new material and when it is appropriate for them to memorize information. Have rationales to support these decisions.
6. When introducing students to large segments of new knowledge, subdivide it into separate meaning units, each representing an assimilable idea or skill element (see chapter 7).
7. Offer students helpful strategies for approaching reading assignments, recognizing that it sometimes requires very different information-processing skills to assimilate different types of content (e.g., literature and history).

Application Exercises

1. Design a note-taking strategy that you might offer students to help them organize informational input in a subject you plan to teach. Make this note-taking procedure represent basic guidelines for the meaningful processing of new information.

2. Identify a cognitive process that could be the focus of a unit or lesson in your teaching area (e.g., dividing fractions, reading for main ideas). Analyze this cognitive operation from the standpoint of the component mental skills it would require (e.g., ability to multiply fractions, to recognize logical relationships between main ideas and supporting points). Based on your task analysis, outline a strategy for teaching this cognitive skill that takes into consideration the suboperations students would need to be able to perform.

3. Select a concept (expressible in a single word or two) that could be the focus of a unit or lesson in a subject you teach (e.g., animals). Brainstorm a number of related concepts that represent larger categories, uses, needs, and extensions of this main concept. For example, the concept of "animal" calls to mind the concepts of dog, mammal, reptile, living things, food, shelter, pet, and so on. Use your list of concepts to prepare a "concept map," showing relationships (links) among these various ideas, with the targeted concept at the center. Think of ways concept maps can be useful to you in your efforts to apply an information-processing model of learning. For a more extended treatment of the subject of concept mapping, a book by Novak and Gowin, entitled *Learning How To Learn,* is highly recommended.[10]

ACTIVATING INNER-SELF PROCESSES IN YOUNG LEARNERS

The human personality, like fruit, can be thought to have an outer layer and an inner core. The inner recesses of the personality contain the attributes that make a person distinctively human. Here lies our potential to think deeply, to love, to care, and to form values. It is the basis of our capacity to take initiative, to act as opposed to simply being acted on. This dynamic center of our personhood is our hub of self-expression, decision making, and creativity.[11]

We are able to depend on the external layer of our personalities to perform relatively mindless and perfunctory kinds of tasks. Our *mechanical-self* is usually the only part of us that is active when we are doing busy work, being superficially polite, or waiting in line to buy groceries. It is the part we are most likely to show strangers or to retreat to in situations where we do not feel comfortable enough to be "the real us." It is also the part of our self that is involved when we are inclined to simply go along with the crowd. Our mechanical-self does have some important functions. Besides its ability to serve as a protective shell for our more sensitive and vulnerable inner self, it allows us to "run on automatic" as we encounter tedium or routine in our daily lives, situations that do not require *dynamic-self* involvement.[12]

There is a serious problem, however, with allowing our mechanical-selves to take over life functions that properly belong to the dynamic-self. There is little chance for us to develop our potential to think, create, value and relate to others if we consistently allow this external layer of our personalities to represent our whole being.[13] In an increasingly impersonal society like our own, there is a distinct danger that a person's dynamic-center will remain inactive and underdeveloped. Unless we are regularly able to be in situations that stimulate dynamic-self involvement, this vital core of our personalities is likely to remain weak and inaccessible.

Young people in our schools are especially needful of learning encounters that challenge their inner selves if school is to be a true growth experience and not just a monotonous game. Genuine education must work to stimulate the dynamic-selves of young learners. To be effective, it has to activate and cultivate those inner qualities that make a person uniquely human.

Relying on Humanistic Appeal

As a teacher, you have an important role to play in the inner-self development of students. The way you begin lessons, the leadups you use in approaching assignments, and the rationales you offer for school learning will determine whether you encourage dynamic-self or simply mechanical-self involvement in learning activity.

When a history teacher opens a lesson by showing a picture of a famous historical personality and asks, "What do you see in the facial features of this person?" this teacher is appealing to the perceptions, imaginations, and human interests of the students. When a teacher of literature begins a new lesson segment with the question, "What would you have done had you been confronted with the same dilemma as the main character of this story?", that teacher is appealing to the students to identify with the inner life of another person and to apply their own experiences, values, and problem-solving abilities to the situation. And when a science teacher asks students to design through brainstorming techniques a lab experiment that would illustrate the process of oxidation, that teacher is presenting a challenge to the higher thought processes of these students.

In each instance, these teachers are summoning students to get in touch with a part of themselves that, at this stage in their lives, is likely to be largely undeveloped. They are asking students to think, to feel, and to care at deeper levels than they will ordinarily be accustomed to doing in their fast-paced interactions with the world around them. These teachers are seeking to activate inner processes that constitute the growing edge of the student's personal development.

When you as a teacher employ motivational and initiatory techniques that appeal to the dynamic-selves of students, the part of them that defines their evolving humanity, you are using what might be called *humanistic appeal*.

Unfortunately, there are forces at work in our schools that would tend to discourage teachers from employing humanistic appeal as a means of arousing students' interest in learning. An emphasis on getting through material and on learning products that can be measured and graded tends to be at cross-purposes with the inner-self development of students. Harried classroom teachers often find it more expedient to rely on *mechanistic appeal* as a motivational technique. Given the feeling of pressure to meet organizational demands, teachers will often begin lessons by invoking students' grade anxieties or competitive instincts rather than their dynamic-self processes. Openers, like "You people need to pay close attention here today because there will be a test over this material on Friday" or "We need to speed up the pace on this unit because the sixth-period class is already a day ahead of us on this," are popular forms of mechanistic appeal. They deemphasize the value of meaningful learning and instead call attention to the student's need to cope with the school system.

Mechanistic appeal focuses on the more instinctive and mechanical layer of the student's total personality. It attempts to provide incentive to learn by invoking students' fears, insecurities, and urges to conform. When widely used, it keeps students focused on perceived deficiencies rather than on their possibilities for growth beyond present levels. It conveys the notion that learning is something you do to avoid the stigma of failure or to be able to hold your own in a competitive society. It does not promote the realization that learning has value in and of itself. If we believe the school experience should enhance a young person's capacity for self-initiated learning, mechanistic appeal does a serious disservice to a student's potential as a lifetime learner.

As you seek to develop motivational techniques that will maximize the personal involvement of students in their own learning, the following general strategies are recommended:

1. Approach new learning by invoking student's intrinsic rather than external motivations to learn.
2. Avoid communicating to students a feeling of urgency to get through lessons.
3. Respect learning rythms by allowing sufficient time for "romance" before moving to the "precision" stage of learning.
4. Work to develop a learning atmosphere that promotes confidence, trust, and reflection on the part of students.

TAPPING INTRINSIC MOTIVATION TO LEARN

Humanistic appeal is directed toward students' internal motivation to learn, while mechanistic appeal attempts to gain student attention and cooperation by emphasizing external incentives for which learning becomes a means, for example, felt needs to avoid failure, to get into college, to be socially acceptable. Teachers sometimes give up rather quickly on efforts to stimulate intrinsic interest in subject matter, and fall back on external motivation because they feel it is more reliable. If students do not come to class feeling initial enthusiasm for the subject matter, a reminder of the need to pass or to please the teacher is normally a convenient motivator, as many teachers have found. When this happens, it is usually because teachers have not made a strong enough attempt to activate intrinsic interest.

Teacher investments in internal motivation are worth the effort for practical reasons as well as human development benefits. Learning that activates the inner-self processes of students is not only higher-quality learning, but it is also self-sustaining. Students do not need to be continually prodded to "stay on task" when they are engaged meaningfully in classroom learning projects. As a result, your need to be a disciplinarian is considerably reduced. Moreover, students who have developed an intrinsic interest in learning activities are more genuinely involved and more enjoyable to be around. It makes the long hours spent with student groups a great deal more satisfying.

The majority of students in our schools will respond to humanistic appeal if it is appropriately targeted to their interest and developmental levels. You will need to gain a sense of what will work as a "set" or a "hook" to draw students into active involvement with a particular lesson or project.

Student *curiosity* is one potential motivator to which you may appeal. As indicated in chapter 4, students at the concrete operations level will ordinarily have a live interest in nonabstract realities that strike them as extreme or extraordinary. Young people at this stage can be found to exhibit a sudden fascination with the extremes of what exists and what is known.[14] They are often attracted to knowledge sources like *The Guinness Book of World Records* with its accounts of the biggest, the smallest, the fastest, the highest, the furthest, and so on. You can take advantage of this developing interest in external reality when it comes to designing "grabbers" for initiating new learning.

Another internal stimulus to learn derives from the *mental challenge* involved in dealing with conflicts, discrepancies, and problems of one sort or another. Most people have an inborn desire to want to resolve incongruities and to get beyond sticking-points in their lives. When skillfully presented, students from middle elementary and on will usually respond to invitations to address challenging problems or dilemmas, whether their own or someone else's. Inattentive students will often sit up and take notice when a piece of new information conflicts with a personal belief or when the discussion turns to some interesting problem or predicament. Some exemplary teachers are able to employ a problem-solving frame of reference in approaching most any new learning activity, realizing its potential to arouse the intrinsic motivations of their students. Other highly successful teachers become known for their "devil's advocate" ploys to create mental dissonance. They feign disagreement or contrariness to give a sense of drama to classroom interaction, thereby helping to keep students interested.

Related to this internal motivation to resolve problems is a student's inner *desire for personal competence.* Most people have a felt need to be good at one or more things. It is an extension of the desire for personal adequacy. This inner disposition to achieve personal competence is thought to be self-initiating and unrelated to the drive for social approval or economic reward. Some students of human motivation have considered it a primary incentive for learning.[15] Skillful teachers are able to exploit this intrinsic desire for personal competence to draw students into encounters with learning, while taking pains to minimize potential social or competitive overtones.

Averting the Misplaced Challenge

You should take special care not to allow classroom learning to be equated with getting through a series of events. That is the attitude conveyed when a teacher says to students, "If you finish chapter 8 by Wednesday, I'll give you some free time on Friday." This sort of bargain reflects the high priority teachers place on meeting their own content coverage deadlines. It implies that the quality of the learning is a lesser consideration. From an educational standpoint it turns out to be a misplaced challenge because it appeals to students' desires to have a break from learning not to their motivations to learn.

It is also a mistake to tell students learning tasks will be either difficult or easy when giving assignments. To say to a student, "I'd like you to work on those problems—they're easy," is to represent the learning activity as relatively unchallenging, but something that needs to be done to satisfy the teacher. Similarly, to forewarn students that "this next assignment is an especially difficult one" is to suggest that they may be overmatched, but that the important thing is to complete the assignment. This turns out to be as poor a motivational technique for the teacher who believes in humanistic appeal as telling students something will be easy. You should attempt to find more sophisticated and intrinsically challenging methods for engaging students in school learning. Students who are stimulated to apply their best resources to a particular learning task will experience the kind of inner satisfaction that people generally feel when they are deeply engaged in a meaningful project. This is high-quality motivation for learning.

There may be occasions when your efforts to encourage intrinsic motivation simply fail to engage students. Particularly with younger students at the early elementary level, basic needs for security and belongingness will often override intrinsic interests in learning, requiring that you have some well-conceived forms of external motivation at your disposal.[16] Generally, however, humanistic appeal should be your first choice in motivational strategy. The following are some techniques you can use to promote students' intrinsic interests in your class and its activities:

1. Make individual self-expression a major priority in designing your teaching objectives. Consider self-expression to include initiative taking, caring, valuing, and problem solving as well as verbal and written performance. Provide ongoing opportunities for students to exhibit various forms of personal expression.
2. Design learning activities that are problem-based. By approaching learning from the standpoint of questions rather than answers, and projects rather than assignments, you help students recognize the practical value of organized knowledge in meeting human problems and needs.
3. Build a sense of drama into your teaching style. Use well-placed humor and "devil's advocate" ploys to maintain interest; and use indirect teaching strategies to produce unanticipated "learning payoffs."
4. Offer good-natured challenges to students' performance skills as a means of initiating and maintaining interest in class activities, for example, "Who would like to go to the board and try problem number six," "How many think they'll be able to finish their projects by next Friday?"
5. Use frequent small-group discussions in class. Shy or inhibited students will often find their voices and reveal their personalities in close encounters with peers. This can serve to "prime" reticent students for greater involvement in the class as a whole.
6. Regularly share with students details of interesting reading you are doing, unusual personalities you have met, exciting trips you have taken, or strange events you have witnessed. Arrange low-key group sharing sessions where students have opportunities to share something of their personal lives and experiences with one another. Use these occasions to promote respect and support for the individuality of students.
7. Attempt to liven the classroom with pictures and objects relating to the subject matter you are teaching. Make it a habit to bring in materials that have human interest appeal for students (e.g., old books and newspapers, costumes, artifacts).

RESPECTING LEARNING RHYTHMS

The Period of "Romance"

Those who are sensitive to their own learning patterns may have noticed that meaningful learning tends to develop in recognizable stages. Most of us learn best when we have first had an opportunity to "play with" ideas or objects for a period of time before narrowing our attentions to precise details or skills. During this early stage of learning we are allowing our intuitions, perceptions, and imaginations free expression. This is a time for exploration, free-association, and arousal of interest. Too much narrowly focused thinking at this stage can serve to abort the process. Whitehead refers to this period of first contact with new learning as the *stage of romance*. This initial stage in the learning process is the period of first apprehension:

> The subject matter has the vividness of novelty; it holds within itself unexplored connections with possibilities half-disclosed by glimpses and half-concealed by the wealth of material. In this stage knowledge is not dominated by systematic procedure.[17]

The Precision Stage

The second stage of learning is a period where romance gives way to the more controlled and concentrated study of facts and terms. This is the time for exactness and analysis of details. Whitehead calls this *the stage of precision*. He warns against the danger of introducing precision in learning prior to an extended period of romance:

> In this stage, width of relationship is subordinated to exactness of formulation. It is the stage of grammar, the grammar of language and the grammar of science. It proceeds by forcing on the student's acceptance a given way of analyzing the facts, bit by bit. . . . It is evident that a stage of precision is barren without a previous stage of romance: unless there are facts which have already been vaguely apprehended in their broad generality, the previous analysis is an analysis of nothing. It is simply a series of meaningless statements about bare facts, produced artificially and without any further relevance.[18]

The Generalization Stage

When learning proceeds in its proper cycle, the stage of precision is followed by a third phase that Whitehead labels the *stage of generalization*. Having had a chance to become acquainted with organized detail related to the subject under investigation, the learner attempts to frame the new learning from a wide-angle vantage once again. The third stage of the learning cycle is in a sense a return to the romance stage with the advantage of new information from the precision phase. It involves bringing the elements together in the form of new insights, and attempting to project relationships and applications.

With this learning cycle in mind, you should regard the introductory phase of learning as a time for building context. At this stage you are attempting to help students develop "mental sets" from which to assimilate the new information that is to follow. Your main objective here is to have students form enough curiosity, insight, and perspective to be able to see meaning in the forthcoming detail. Thus, in introducing a unit on the U.S. Civil War, the following types of statements and questions could be used to stimulate dispositions toward speculation and inquiry:

> More Americans lost their lives in the Civil War than in World Wars I and II combined.
> The Civil War threatened to leave us with two separate countries instead of one.
> Many soldiers in the Civil War were fighting against their own relatives.

How could such a destructive war have happened in this type of country?

Can you imagine something like this happening today, where neighboring states like California and Oregon would be fighting one another across state boundaries?

What would you imagine might have caused such an internal war of brother against brother?

It is important to dwell on the romance phase of learning long enough to allow students to form questions and viewpoints that will carry over to the precision stage. Then, following their exposure to pertinent details of the war, students should be assisted at the generalization stage to consolidate their learning through the formation of new insights and projections, based on questions such as these:

What factors do you think were most responsible for causing this war?

What would it have taken to prevent it?

Did the outcome justify the terrible suffering and loss of life? Is any war ever justified?

Did any real heroes emerge from this war? Who were they?

Had you been alive and eligible, would you have been willing to fight for one side or the other in the Civil War?

What was the main importance of this war in our national history?

Could a civil war ever happen in this country again? Why or why not?

An appreciation for learning rhythms causes us to realize that learning has its "propitious moments." There is a right time and a wrong time to introduce factual material or vocabulary words in a particular teaching unit. Good teachers know when students are in a favorable mental set to be able to meaningfully assimiltate factual information. There is also an appropriate time and an inappropriate time to summarize factual elements that have been encountered earlier. Competent teachers are keenly aware of readiness factors in their students. They sense when it is a fitting time to send students to the library for information or when the time is ripe for a field trip.

The most common violation of learning rhythms in formal education is the widespread practice of introducing precision at the beginning of a lesson or unit with no effort being made to develop learner readiness by allowing opportunities for romance. Consider the following key measures you can take in your own teaching to provide for sufficient romance in the learning process:

1. Take time at the beginning of new units to discuss with students their initial questions, interests, and perceptions relating to the area of study you are about to enter.
2. Always prepare good introductory sets for your teaching lessons.
3. Allow for a good number of expressive objectives as you design unit and lesson plans (see chapter 3).
4. When constructing performance-based teaching units (e.g., writing, basketball, painting), allow students to experience the whole activity before requiring the mastery of isolated skill elements.

5. Whenever possible, provide lab experiences, field trips, films, and other concrete experiences at the beginning rather than the end of teaching units.
6. Provide students ample opportunities for intuitive thinking and free association of ideas without the immediate compulsion to produce data or conclusions.
7. Place as much emphasis on learning processes as you do on learning products.
8. Resolve not to hurry learning.

PROVIDING A FACILITATIVE LEARNING CLIMATE

A main prerequisite for getting students to apply their best resources to classroom learning is to provide an atmosphere that is both encouraging and stimulating for these students. This means developing a learning climate that supports thought and exploration, where students feel secure and confident enough to throw themselves wholeheartedly into learning activities.

Making Learning Manageable

One way you can encourage students to become genuinely involved is to make learning tasks managable for them. Students are more likely to give their best efforts when they know what they are up against, when they feel a sense of personal control over their own learning. The attitudes you demonstrate toward the content you teach will go a long way toward determining the confidence with which students approach this new learning.

Too often the subject matter contained in textbooks and teacher presentations possesses an impenetrable mystique for young learners. They see the world of formal knowledge as representing a reality that fails to connect with their own experience. As a contributing factor, teachers are often inclined to treat formal knowledge as obscure and impersonal, something that demands unquestioned deference and ritualistic consumption. Students thus become passive receivers of preestablished truths that stand apart from their being and make them look small and insignificant in comparison.

When you are sensitive to the learning needs and perceptions of growing young people, you are less likely to take your subject matter so seriously that you promote a barrier between the student and the world of knowledge. You will be more inclined to emphasize the tentative nature of textbook knowledge, and to have students see that it represents the efforts of people like themselves to make sense of the world around them. This will help young people to view formal knowledge in its proper perspective, and to recognize that its status derives from its potential to enhance human lives.

In addition to the attitudes you exhibit toward the subject(s) you teach, there are a number of things you can do to give students a better sense of confidence and control in dealing with new learning. They include:

1. Make learning tasks as clear and explicit as possible.
2. Try to avoid technical language when introducing students to a new learning topic.

3. Work from where students are to where you want them to be (i.e., from a student-centered to a more subject-centered frame of reference).
4. Make new learning connect with the world outside of school.
5. Seek to provide early success experiences for each student.
6. Make use of objectives that are challenging but attainable.
7. Provide knowledge of learning results that emphasize the positive.
8. Permit and encourage students to direct their own learning whenever possible.

Establishing Trust and Support

When you employ humanistic appeal to stimulate learning you are asking students to invest a substantial part of themselves in school activity. In order for this to happen you must have established a solid bond of trust and respect with your students. This condition is enhanced when students perceive you as an autonomous person, one who is able to be personally responsible for your own decisions and your own behavior. The teachers who succeed in getting the most out of their students are those who have earned student respect and confidence out of natural authority. This means avoiding as much as possible the use of your official position as leverage to control students or to get them to learn. It means taking personal responsibility for what goes on in your classes. One of the things that helps to communicate a sense of natural authority is the use of *I-messages:* "I feel this is an important assignment and I'm going to ask everyone to do it" (as opposed to "All of the ninth-grade classes are doing this assignment. It's a departmental requirement"). Or "I'd like everyone to take a look at the problem I have here on the board" (as opposed to "Maybe we ought to get busy with our math so your parents don't think I'm wasting your time"). When you are able to use authentic I-messages to convey your intentions, you indicate a willingness to accept ownership for decisions that affect the behavior of students in your classes. You show a readiness to be personally accountable for your choices.

A student's willingness to become deeply involved in school learning usually involves some risk. When students show strong feelings over a poem or demonstrate serious concern about a particular social or environmental issue, they leave themselves vulnerable to the resentment or criticism of those who are less involved. There is the potential for being perceived as too intellectual or too sentimental. Some peers may regard such serious involvement as simply a ploy for a better grade. As a teacher, you must be prepared to support and reinforce students who respond positively to your efforts at humanistic appeal. Here are some ways you might do this:

1. Make it clear during the first meeting that this is a class where students need not be afraid to exhibit individuality, honesty, and a full range of personal expression.
2. Model genuineness and a willingness to share your own innermost thoughts and feelings with your students when it is appropriate.
3. Practice positive and supportive response patterns during class sessions. This entails listening attentively to students' ideas and providing feedback that encourages further participation.
4. Indicate privately to self-revealing students how much you value and appreciate their authenticity.

5. Make a conscious effort to avoid being judgmental when students are willing to share their deepest thoughts and feelings.

6. Be vigilant in protecting self-revealing students from the resentful behavior of students who are less open. Do this tactfully, so as not to alienate those who need to be encouraged to become better risktakers.

Encouraging Reflection

Reflective teaching techniques are those that use the learner's frame of reference to encourage questioning, imaging, and hypothesizing. The ability to produce a reflective atmosphere has been considered a key indicator of high-quality teaching.[19] There are some basic conditions that contribute to a reflective climate in a school classroom. One is a pervasive *spirit of inquiry*. The classroom where reflective thinking is promoted is one where inquiry and discovery are valued. Teachers in these classrooms are able to admit uncertainty: "We're not really sure how evolution works," or "I'm not sure about my interpretation of the poem—I continue to see other things in it." Such teachers welcome intellectual challenges: "You're right in raising that issue—I need to re-think the matter." Teachers repeatedly convey their own beliefs in the value of thinking and emphasize that education involves exploring the unknown as well as teaching what is known.

A spirit of inquiry is also fostered by teacher-questioning techniques that probe students' thoughts, imaginations, and prior experiences in a personal, yet nonthreatening way. Personalized questions that appeal to student's thoughts and feelings in the second person are highly recommended:

What do you anticipate would happen if . . . ?
What do you think the connection is between . . . and . . . ?
How would you account for . . . ?
Can you imagine a . . . ?
Suppose you were in a position where . . . ?
How would you feel if . . . ?
Have you ever seen a person who . . . ?
What do you think causes people to . . . ?

Another important attribute of a reflective classroom is an emphasis on *problem finding*. Normally, classrooms are places where answers are sought and solutions are valued. In a thinking-centered classroom, students are taught and encouraged to find problems, to wonder, and to speculate. The teacher nurtures the problem-finding attitude by encouraging students to ask questions, not just answer them: "Here are some data about voting patterns in the United States—what questions could we ask?", or "We'll be studying family life in the Soviet Union—what questions would you like to have answered?"

A third condition that serves to promote contemplative thinking in the classroom is a *deliberative pace*. Many classrooms seem to encourage impulsiveness—the teacher asks a question, expects an immediate answer, and calls on the first student who raises a hand. Although this practice may facilitate evaluation of student knowledge, rehearsal of facts, and student attentiveness, it is generally counterproductive when thinking is the focus. Teachers in a reflective classroom make it possible and comfortable for students to think about things without feeling hurried to produce answers. By allowing thoughtful pauses of several seconds at the end of teacher questions and at the end of student answers, teachers can help to promote this. Teachers who avoid bombarding students with rapid-fire questions, but instead give students time to construct ideas, are showing their respect for the internal processes that produce meaningful learning.

Application Exercises

1. Call to mind a lesson you have recently taught or one you expect to teach in the near future. Describe a problem-solving frame of reference from which you might structure this lesson (e.g., a need to accomplish a task, to clarify a misconception, to overcome a prejudice). Identify the general approach you would take in developing the lesson, including the set you would use, the central questions you would raise, and the main activity you would prescribe.
2. Devise a creative introduction (set) that you might use to initiate a junior high school science lesson on air polution. Compose a second opening for a third grade lesson on household pets. Also, compose an original set for a senior high school lesson on study skills. Design each of these lesson introductions to appeal to some form of intrinsic learning incentive. Identify the specific type of intrinsic motivation to which you are appealing in each case (e.g., competence, curiosity).

ADDRESSING INDIVIDUAL LEARNING NEEDS

As you continue to work closely with groups of young people, you will soon be aware of very significant differences in your students' interests, abilities, home backgrounds, social skills, and personal needs. Not only are students different, but they all have their own individual learning habits and patterns. Insofar as possible, you should attempt to adapt your teaching to the differing learning needs and styles of the students in your classes. It will frequently be necessary for you to vary your teaching approach as you encounter slow or gifted students, or students with different social class or ethnic backgrounds.

Differing Learning Styles

Some students will tend to learn readily through verbal exchanges with teachers and peers. These students are accomplished *auditory learners*. They are usually better than average speakers and listeners, with a facility for processing verbal information in a rapid manner. Such students are able to receive maximum benefit from teacher lectures, group discussions, tape recordings, and other forms of direct information transfer.

Other students will learn more effectively through a visual medium. People who are primarily *visual learners* depend on concrete props to activate cognitive processes. They often learn more from a reading assignment than from a teacher presentation covering the same material. This difference between auditory and visual learning dispositions in students implies that you should regularly attempt to supplement verbal teaching presentations with concrete aids, examples, and other visualization enhancers in order to meet the learning needs of students who are essentially visual learners.

A third category of students can be found to learn best through hands-on experiences. They need opportunities to interact physically and/or emotionally with learning materials or situations. In order to adequately comprehend new ideas or processes, *kinesthetic learners* usually need to go beyond hearing and visualizing and to become personally involved through feeling, touching, performing, and so forth. Kinesthetically oriented students need ample opportunities to manipulate, construct, interact, and experience if they are to profit from school learning.

Teaching Minority and Disadvantaged Students

It is important that you be able to adjust your teaching patterns to meet the special learning needs of minority students and disadvantaged or "at risk"[20] youngsters in your classroom. These students are frequently alienated by the prevailing school culture. Their educational aspirations, their learning styles, and their social patterns are often significantly different from those of the typical middle-class white student, sometimes giving the false impression that they lack the potential for learning.

The following are some basic measures you can take in your efforts to adapt your teaching to the learning needs of educationally disadvantaged or culturally alienated youngsters in your classes:

1. Do as much as possible to foster collaboration and working within groups (cooperative learning). These students need opportunities to practice critical thinking, to participate, and to work collectively. Minority and poor populations are often more group-oriented and interactive than students of the white, middle-class culture, which tends to stress and reward individualism.[21]
2. Build on the "unusual assets" these students display more than on narrowly defined academic skills. Recent, more broadly conceived notions of human intelligence suggest the need to recognize and cultivate student performances in areas other than verbal and logical-mathematical skill, for example, spacial relationships, physical coordination, music, interpersonal perceptiveness, and inner attunement.[22] Spend less time ranking students and more time helping them identify their natural competencies and gifts.
3. Attempt to provide some of the missing "social capital" in the lives of disadvantaged students. These youngsters are often lacking the kind of personal attention, intimacy, and assurance that has been available to their more fortunate peers. By making a deliberate effort to provide a reasonable and caring interpersonal environment for these students, you can help to foster the kind of confidence and positive outlook they will need to successfully cope with school.[23]
4. Work to gain the cooperation and collaboration of parents. Efforts to improve home–school relations do not have to be highly structured. "Almost anything that is systematic enough and done with great energy can bring about change."[24]
5. Take the attitude that all students can learn. When you have high expectations for all of your students, you foster an atmosphere that allows success to become

the norm; that is, your expectation becomes a self-fulfilling prophecy. Conversely, when you have low expectations, you tend to create a condition that promotes failure.[25]

SUGGESTED ACTIVITIES AND QUESTIONS

1. Discuss the main differences between rote and meaningful learning in human beings. What has to take place inside a learner before one can claim understanding has occurred?

2. Name several school learning tasks where you believe rote learning is appropriate. Why is it not necessary for learners to achieve grounded understanding in these areas? Mention other kinds of school learning where you believe meaning and understanding are crucial. What are some of the central advantages of meaningful learning?

3. Take the opportunity to learn more about the laws of associative learning as you encounter them in other contexts (e.g., educational psychology texts). What are some of the different varieties of conditioning or stimulus–response learning that have been identified by behavioral psychologists?

4. Make an effort to extend your knowledge of human learning by becoming acquainted with areas of human study such as cognitive learning theory, humanistic psychology, and existential philosophy. What common assumptions regarding human nature and human learning are shared by the aforementioned schools of thought?

5. What kind of inner-self development do you believe U.S. schools should be promoting in young people? What types of thinking skills will you be attempting to promote in your teaching?

6. What does it mean to have "learned how to learn"?

7. Will you be teaching subjects where the perceived usefulness of the learning will be relatively apparent to students, or will you have to make special efforts to build this into learning activities? Elaborate.

8. Discuss some of the main techniques teachers can use to draw on students' internal motivations to learn. On what kinds of theories and assumptions regarding human motivation are these methods based?

9. What are some of the motivational techniques that good teachers should avoid if they are to depend on humanistic rather than mechanistic appeal as their primary form of classroom motivation?

10. What are the differences between *romance* and *precision* in human learning? Mention general strategies you might use to build sufficient romance into the learning you will be promoting.

11. What are some of the important ways teachers can produce an atmosphere of thoughtfulness and deliberation in their classrooms? Which of these methods have you seen used effectively by teachers in your own school career? Which do you feel confident you will be able to put into practice in your own teaching?

12. How does a natural-authority relationship with students help teachers to better facilitate the inner-self development of these young people?

NOTES AND REFERENCES

1. See John I. Goodlad, *A Place Called School*. New York: McGraw-Hill, 1984, and see chaps. 6 and 7; Stuart B. Palonsky, *900 Shows a Year: A Look at Teaching from a Teacher's Side of the Desk*. New York: Random House, 1986, and see chaps. 3 and 7; and Theodore R.

Sizer, *Horace's Compromise: The Dilemma of the American High School.* Boston: Houghton Mifflin, 1984, and see Part Two.

2. Goodlad, op. cit., pp. 229–31.
3. Morris L. Bigge and Maurice P. Hunt, *Psychological Foundations of Education.* New York: Harper and Row, 1980, p. 81.
4. For a concise discussion of techniques for improving rote learning, see Myron H. Dembo, *Applying Educational Psychology in the Classroom.* New York: Longman, 1988, pp. 334–36.
5. Joseph Morris, *Psychology and Teaching: A Humanistic View.* New York: Random House, 1978, p. 158.
6. Bigge and Hunt, op. cit., p. 454.
7. Ibid.
8. Ibid., p. 455.
9. Ibid., p. 456.
10. Joseph D. Novak and D. Bob Gowin, *Learning How to Learn.* New York: Cambridge University Press, 1984.
11. Gordon W. Allport, *Becoming: Basic Considerations for a Psychology of Personality.* New Haven, Conn.: Yale University Press, 1969, p. 48.
12. Ibid., p. 63.
13. Ibid., p. 51.
14. Kieran Egan, *Educational Development.* New York: Oxford University Press, 1979, p. 31.
15. Robert White, "Motivation Reconsidered: The Concept of Competence." *Psychological Review,* 66 (1959), pp. 297–333.
16. For a useful treatment of strategies for external motivation, see N. L. Gage and David C. Berliner, *Educational Psychology,* 4th ed. Boston: Houghton Mifflin, 1988, chap. 15.
17. Alfred North Whitehead, *The Aims of Education.* New York: Macmillan, 1929, p. 28.
18. Ibid., p. 29.
19. Bruce R. Joyce and David E. Hunt, "Teacher Trainee Personality and Initial Teaching Style." *American Educational Research Journal,* 4, no. 3 (May 1967) p. 254.
20. The term *at risk* has become a popular expression for describing students who are in danger of dropping out of school or otherwise failing to achieve their educational potential due to their disadvantaged status, persistent underachievement, drug involvement, or other such serious problems.
21. M. Sandra Reeves, "Self-interest and the Common Weal: Focusing on the Bottom Half." *Education Week,* April 27, 1988, p. 18.
22. Ibid.
23. Ibid., p. 19.
24. Ibid.
25. Ibid., p. 21.

CHAPTER 7

Explaining Things So Students Will Understand

A UNIVERSAL TEACHING BEHAVIOR

The ability to provide clear and concise explanations is essential to a teacher's effectiveness in promoting student learning.[1] Explanation is teacher talk designed to clarify any idea, process, or procedure that students have a need to understand. This means you are furnishing explanations any time you set forth procedures for fire drills, discuss reasons for a particular assignment, or describe details of your grading system. More fundamental yet are the instructionally related explanations you will provide when you attempt to show the meanings of terms, the steps involved in certain processes, or the causes of particular events.

Whether the approach to new learning is primarily teacher-centered or more activity-based, teacher explanations usually constitute the starting point if not the main thrust of classroom instruction. You will also be called on to provide explanations when students raise questions during group lessons or when they need help with seatwork or independent projects. Given the central importance of verbal understanding in the learning of most school subjects, you will likely be delivering explanations in all phases of your teaching. Explanation giving is as basic to the work of a teacher as the ability to use a hammer is to a carpenter.

To achieve a sense of mastery as a classroom teacher, you will need the confidence and skill to be able to generate preplanned as well as spontaneous explanations for your students. It is a skill to which you will want to give some concentrated attention.

This chapter focuses on basic requirements for sound and understandable classroom explanations. It presents main criteria for recognizing good explanations as well as guidelines for making your own teacher explanations meaningful to your students.

Explaining Ability Seldom Comes Naturally

If you are like most entering teachers, you have had considerable experience attempting to explain things to others before coming to teaching. You have had numerous opportunities to give directions, to clarify the meaning of language, and to offer reasons for behaviors or events. Unfortunately, this is no guarantee of proficiency.

In the normal give and take of life, there is a tendency for a person's explanations to be hastily formulated and delivered in a rather hit-or-miss fashion. Chances are you have been the recipient of off-the-cuff directions to some location while you were traveling, only to find yourself more confused by the explanation than you were beforehand:

> **YOU:** Excuse me sir, but could you direct me to the nearest gas station?
>
> **STRANGER:** Sure. There are two of them in this area. One is about a half-mile from here. The other is a little further away, but I like their gas better because their tanks are cleaner. I used to work there. But if you want cheaper gas, you might try the other one. I'll tell you how to get there first. I can't remember the name of the street, but you go north for about five blocks until you come to an intersection with a white building on the southeast corner. Make a right turn, and you'll go over a set of railroad tracks. Be sure to stay in the left lane. . . .

Out-of-school explanations are frequently delivered on the run or in situations where feedback on the adequacy of these explanations is seldom available. Consequently, few people have had occasion to become good explainers prior to teaching.

The ability to deliver clear and accurate explanations, and especially impromptu ones, does not come naturally for the majority of teachers. It is a skill that needs to be deliberately cultivated if one is to become competent. Before entering the classroom, most teachers have received very little constructive feedback on their explaining behavior, so it is easy for new teachers to assume greater natural proficiency than is the case. Thus, when teachers allow their classroom explanations to become simply extensions of long-term, previously unexamined language patterns, these explanations can be expected to lack professional quality.

This points up the need for you to begin perfecting your explanation techniques as you prepare yourself for the classroom.

DESIGNING LOGICALLY SOUND EXPLANATIONS

To qualify as a good explanation there are two main requirements. First, the explanation should meet certain standards of appropriateness and accuracy—Is it technically sound and does it explain what it is supposed to? Second, the explanation should be organized and presented in a fashion that makes it understandable to the students, which is especially important for teachers of young learners.

Types of Explanations

In order to give explanations that are technically well-constructed and be able to judge those presented by students, you should be familiar with the main varieties of explanations,[2] be able to recognize where they are applicable, and know what they require to be considered sound.

When teachers attempt to specify the meanings of terms like *metaphor, percentage, propaganda,* or *aerobic exercise,* they are presenting what are referred to as *interpretive explanations* because the explanation seeks to interpret or clarify. A sound interpretive explanation amounts to a good analytical definition of the concept. The task is to establish both the meaning and the boundaries of the concept. This requires identifying the class of things to which the term belongs and then showing its differentiating characteristics within that class. For example: A tariff is a form of tax imposed by a government on imports or exports for the purpose of raising revenue, protecting home industries, or coercing other countries into mutual trade agreements. A meter is a unit of length equal to 39.37 inches.

A second class of explanation describes a process or procedure such as how to extract a square root, how a bill becomes a law, how sulphuric acid is made, or how a computer works. This type of explanation, or a *descriptive explanation,* will usually involve showing the series of steps, events, parts, or functions that come together to achieve some goal or end state. Although an interpretive explanation can be thought of as clarifying what something is, a descriptive explanation is aimed at delineating how something occurs or is constructed.

A third main type of explanation relates some happening to a general rule, law, or human purpose. A *reason-giving explanation* attempts to explain why it is cold in winter and warm in summer in the northern hemisphere, why the United States entered the Vietnam War, why we use quotation marks in written English, and why Hamlet waited so long to kill Claudius. Reason-giving explanations are employed to answer why questions.

Lecture as Explanation.   Whenever you have occasion to be involved in direct instruction, you will likely be providing one or another (or a combination) of these three types of explanations. In fact, a teacher lecture is best thought of as an extended explanation, or series of explanations, in which the intent is to have students understand a particular concept (interpretive), process (descriptive), or causal relationship (reason-giving). Although there are other purposes for direct teaching (e.g., motivating, story telling), most of your teacher-centered input should be aimed at explaining ideas or procedures of one sort or another. By construing direct instruction as explaining rather than simply information giving, you accomplish several important things.

In the first place, when your conscious effort is to provide a descriptive or interpretive explanation, this gives you a precise task focus. It becomes easier to draw deliberate boundaries around your teaching, and thus keep it from wandering.

An explanation approach to lecture also keeps you mindful of the need to make your input understandable. When you are explaining, you are always explaining something to someone. You are more likely to set comprehension as your goal when the task you have set for yourself is to clarify an idea or a procedure rather than to just pass on information.

Finally, an explanatory frame of reference carries some well-established guidelines for making your verbal presentations logically sound as well as meaningful for your students. These prescriptions for good teacher explanations provide the focus for the rest of this chapter.

Guidelines for Logically Sound Explanations

When judging the logical soundness of an explanation we are concerned with the suitability of the explanation to the situation, and with its thoroughness, coherence, and accuracy. The following are basic recommendations for designing classroom explanations that are technically and structurally appropriate:

1. *Have a clear conception of purpose before launching into an explanation.* Does it ask for an illustration of a process or procedure (like illustrating how to prepare an outline for an essay)? Does it involve showing a direct cause-and-effect relationship (like the effect of heat in changing a liquid to a gas)? Does it entail showing the intent of an action or process (like explaining the role of primaries in the election process)? Does it require showing that a particular action is governed by a general rule or law (like explaining the need for protective glasses when using power tools)? Or does it involve classifying and showing the boundaries of a concept (like identifying a mammal as an animal that is warm-blooded, suckles its young, etc.)?

It is possible to combine the three kinds of explanations in one explanation sequence. When explaining *how* a bill becomes a law, one might well give reasons *why* certain steps rather than others take place, and one might well explain the *meaning* of some of the terms involved. However, because each of the different kinds of explanations considered separately raises different problems, for purposes of analysis there is good reason to treat them as distinct.

2. *Recognize the potential ambiguity of the word* explain. Attempt to clarify what is being asked when a student makes an unclear request like "Explain the invasion of Normandy." It could be taken as an appeal for a descriptive explanation or for a reason-giving explanation. That is, it could be a request for an account of the major events of the invasion, or it could be a request to clarify the reasons for the invasion. Sensitivity to the ambiguity allows you to probe further to find out specifically what kind of explanation the student is asking for.

A clear way to indicate that an interpretive definition is sought is to make explicit reference to meaning, as in "Please explain the meaning of sovereignty." The most common way to ask for a descriptive explanation is "Explain how . . ." The most dependable cue for a reason-giving explanation is the word *why:* "Explain why the fuse blew," or "Explain why 'compelled' is spelled with two *l* 's." However, reason-giving explanations can also be requested in other ways, such as "How do you know that angle HEF is equal to angle EFD?" or "What accounts for the blowing of the fuse?"

3. *Do not allow synonyms and examples to become easy substitutes for interpretive explanations.* When we turn to a dictionary for the meaning of an unfamiliar word, we ordinarily find three kinds of definitions: synonyms, examples, and analyses of meanings. Each of these may help us to better understand the new term. However, the most conceptually useful type of definition is the analytical or classification definition. Synonyms and examples are helpful when all we desire is a reference to the sort of thing for which a word stands. For example, a synonym for automobile is "car" and an example is "Ford Escort." But although synonyms and examples provide us with familiar references for the word *automobile,* neither of these brings us closer to a conceptual understanding of what constitutes an automobile. We need to look to a classification definition for that; that is, an automobile is a self-propelled land vehicle usually having four wheels, designed primarily to carry passengers, and driven by an internal-combus-

tion engine. A conceptual understanding allows us to distinguish automobiles from other motorized vehicles.

4. *Try to avoid "circularity" when offering interpretive and reason-giving explanations.* One of the main problems with relying on synonyms to define terms is their tendency toward circularity: "A morally good man is one who acts virtuously." "Morally good" and "virtuous" are synonymous in this context, so the definition merely repeats the word that is being defined. Whereas synonyms may help to advance concrete understanding, they do not have the explaining power to be considered interpretive explanations.

Circularity can also be a problem with reason-giving explanations. When in response to the question, "Why did she commit suicide?", someone gives the answer, "Because she had a death wish," we have a case of circular reasoning. The introduction of the term *death wish* has little explanatory value beyond that already implied in the original question.

5. *Take care to clarify and simplify the elements of a descriptive explanation.* The thing to be explained should be broken up into parts, which should be presented in a carefully chosen order depending on their relationship to one another. In explaining processes like long division or the making of sulphuric acid this would ordinarily be chronological. In some explanations a choice must be made between presenting the parts in order of increasing generality or decreasing generality. In explaining the structure of the United Nations, for example, one must decide between starting at the top and starting at the bottom to show lines of authority.

6. *Make an effort to complete reason-giving explanations and encourage students to do the same.* It is quite common for students to offer incomplete explanations, as in the following examples:

> TEACHER: Why are the two sides of the triangle equal?
> STUDENT: Because the two base angles are equal.

> TEACHER: Why is the penguin a fast runner?
> STUDENT: Because it is unable to fly.

In each of these examples the student has made progress toward a satisfactory explanation, but has neglected to complete it. In the first case the student has left out the general rule regarding isosceles triangles that allows her to make this claim ("In any isosceles triangle—a triangle with equal base angles—the two sides other than the base are equal"). In the second example, the student could have completed the explanation by indicating that the penguin's ability to run reflects a natural survival provision that often gives animals with physical liabilities in one area compensating abilities in another.

Application Exercises

1. Identify the type of explanation—interpretive, descriptive, or reason-giving—that is called for in each of the following explanation requests. In cases where more than

one kind of explanation could be appropriate, rephrase the question to make clear that one or another type of explanation is being sought.

  a. What must a person do to get a driver's license?
  b. What makes a person's muscles twitch?
  c. What are animals?
  d. What were the circumstances of President Kennedy's death?
  e. What causes a thunderstorm?
  f. What are the effects of pollutants in the air?
  g. What is the process of preparing vegetables for a salad?
  h. Explain how to diagram a sentence.
  i. Explain the arrangement of material in a dictionary.
  j. Explain the purpose of firing pottery.
  k. Explain the need for protective glasses in the shop.
  l. Explain the meaning of the word *classical* in literature.
  m. Explain the entrance of the United States into World War I.
  n. Explain the structure of the court system in the United States.

2. Determine the adequacy of the following as logically complete explanations. Suggest any revisions or additions that would make them more sound.

  a. Physical fitness is a term used to describe people who are in good shape physically.
  b. The reason wool is worn in the winter is because it is warm.
  c. A democratic form of government is the type you find in the United States and Great Britain.
  d. A home is a place of residence.
  e. The reason for the president's inability to bring about social change was a Congress dominated by the opposite party.
  f. The reason why the classroom is well-lighted is because it has light-colored walls.
  g. The reason no true believers were condemned is because true believers were not heretics.
  h. The reason you can screw a nut on a bolt tighter with a wrench than you can with your fingers is because there is more mechanical advantage with a wrench.

3. Outline appropriately sequenced explanations to describe:

  a. The process we use in the United States to elect a president.
  b. A procedure for students to follow in preparing a special report or research project in a class you would teach. Give reasons for the particular sequence of steps you have adopted in each case.

4. Plan logically appropriate explanations to meet the following teaching situations:

  a. You wish to explain the concept of capitalism to a junior high social studies class.
  b. You need to explain the use of an exclamation mark in written English to a group of elementary school children.
  c. You are preparing to explain to a general science class the conditions that cause water to boil.
  d. You have undertaken to explain the concept of percentage to an elementary school math class prior to helping them learn to calculate percentages.
  e. You must explain to a group of high school juniors the general procedure for being admitted to college.

MAKING EXPLANATIONS
MEANINGFUL TO STUDENTS

It is possible to produce logically well-constructed explanations that students fail to understand. Your teacher explanations must be *psychologically* as a well as logically appropriate if they are to be comprehensible to your students.[3] In other words, they must be *meaningful* in addition to being sound.

There are some important general guidelines to be followed in making explanations understandable for young learners: (1) center on the learner's frame of reference, (2) do not provide more information than can be meaningfully assimilated, and (3) use techniques to enhance clarity and emphasis.

Working from the Students'
Frame of Reference

To make classroom explanations understandable to students, you must learn to work simultaneously from two different frames of references. You will need to maintain a focus on the object to be explained, while remaining attuned to the learning needs and dispositions of the students. Teachers who are especially well-acquainted with a particular domain of knowledge are often preoccupied with the first area of reference, to the neglect of the latter. Their knowledge becomes second nature to them and they lose sight of the route they took to achieve understanding. Thus, it is sometimes the case that highly knowledgeable people lack the initial predispositions to be good explainers in their own areas of competence.

As a teacher, it is essential to remain mindful of what understanding requires for a learner. As discussed in chapter 6, understanding involves (1) making a connection between new information and existing knowledge structures, and (2) internalizing a use for new knowledge. These two basic requirements must be met in order for explanations to be meaningful to students.[4]

Building on Existing Knowledge.   Skillful teachers are able to use explanation, not to simply *give* students new information, but to *rearrange* and *extend* what is already there.[5] Students' existing knowledge and experience can be valuable resources for developing new knowledge. A major part of the teacher's task is to draw on this present knowledge by helping students see it in a different light and with some new labels. The following teacher–student exchange illustrates how a teacher can use a student's past experience to help explain a new idea:

> STUDENT: (on encountering an unfamiliar term in the reading) Can you tell me what "military punishment" means?
>
> TEACHER: Have you ever been in a situation where everyone in the class had to stay after school because of the wrong behavior of several students?
>
> STUDENT: Yes, and I thought it was unfair. I didn't think the teacher should have held everyone responsible for the problem. I thought the teacher should have picked only those who were disrupting class.
>
> TEACHER: This is an example of what is sometimes referred to as military punishment. It's

a case where a whole group is punished for the behavior of a few of its members. They sometimes do this purposely in the army to help develop group responsibility by showing that everyone is affected when one or two people make mistakes.

This teacher resisted any temptation to simply tell the student what military punishment is and be done with it. In this brief exchange the teacher was able to get the student to contribute some personal thoughts, feelings, and values toward understanding the new term. This teacher wanted the student to do more than just memorize a formal definition. An appeal to students' present understandings or past experiences, sometimes in the form of a well-placed question, can help establish reference points for what is to follow.

In attempting to foster insight into the process of multiplication with a group of elementary school students, a teacher undertakes to show that multiplication is actually a streamlined form of addition:

TEACHER: Can you think of a practical use for multiplication that all of us are familiar with?

STUDENT: Yes. It helps you to count your change more quickly.

TEACHER: O.K. That's one good example. What special advantage does multiplication give you here?

STUDENT: Well, if you had six quarters, seven dimes, and four nickels you could do some quick multiplication and a little adding in your head and come up with the total.

TEACHER: Otherwise, if you didn't know how to multiply, you'd have to do what?

STUDENT: You'd have to add each separate coin. That would take longer and you might need paper and pencil.

TEACHER: So multiplication is really a shortened way to do what?

STUDENT: To do addition.

TEACHER: Exactly. Let's take a closer look at this . . .

Again, this is an example of a teacher explanation that begins with what students already know and attempts to build on that existing knowledge to form a new understanding. It proceeds from the assumption that meaningful learning involves seeing new relationships rather than simply acquiring new pieces of information.

Centering on Ideas Rather than Terms.   The teachers in the previous examples avoided the use of formal language and monologue as the basis for their explanations, appealing instead to students' present levels of understanding in a language that was mostly conversational and familiar.

Often teacher explanations introduce too many abstract terms too soon; for example, "Today we're going to talk about photosynthesis. Photosynthesis is the process by which complex carbon compounds are manufactured in green plants with the help of light energy. The light energy needed for the process is absorbed by a geen pigment called chlorophyll."

To begin an explanation with formal terms, using abstract definitions to try to explain complex ideas, will cause students to lapse into a mechanical mode of verbal processing (see chapter 6). Their mental energies will be directed toward memorizing nonmeaningful material. Too many unassimilated ideas will overload their short-term memory, and clog students' thought channels.

Students need to confront new ideas in their own language and at their own levels of understanding before they are ready to "own" textbook-level concepts. If you fail to allow this initial "romance" stage in learning, your explanations are likely to be processed in a nonmeaningful way. The best strategy is to seek to solidify the ideas before attaching the labels. Although it may not always be possible to do this without using some formal language, it is important to deemphasize the mastery of terminology as an end in itself and to give priority to meaning and understanding.

Stressing the Function of New Learning.   It is important to stress the functional aspects of new learning so that students can internalize a use for new information or skills. Students will best understand explanations that have a direct bearing on something they are trying to do or do better. A good time then for a teacher explanation is following an activity that has caused students to realize a need for new knowledge. Students are likely to benefit more from explanations relating to subject–verb agreement when they have had previous opportunities to do meaningful writing. Basketball players can be expected to be more attentive to a coach's demonstration of good defensive play following a scrimmage that showed inadequacies in this aspect of their games. Taking advantage of these propitious moments for new learning will make explanations simpler and more meaningful because the functionality requirement will have been satisfied.

When a sense of perceived usefulness is lacking, you should work to build it into your explanations. The younger the students, the more need there is to make explicit the functional and operational dimensions of all new learning. Teacher explanations should describe: "This is how it works," "This is what you do with it," "This is the need it helps us to satisfy." An important assumption to work from is the premise that whether it is something found in nature or something people have contrived, it has an identifiable use.

Using Analogies to Bridge the Understanding Gap.   Teacher explanations in some subject areas may involve the introduction of new ideas or realms of study that require a "mental leap" on the part of the student. As an example, it is possible for students to talk meaningfully about plant life from a concrete and experiential point of view, yet find a biologist's conception of "plant" to be obscure and incomprehensible; for example, "A plant is an organism of the vegetable kingdom which characteristically has cellulose cell walls, grows by synthesis of organic substances, and lacks the power of locomotion."

Analogies are an effective and often essential technique for bridging the understanding gap and helping students gain insight into complex ideas or processes. The inner nature of a plant becomes more transparent to biology students when they can relate it to a concept with which they are already familiar:

> Think of a plant as a factory that needs raw materials. To make a ship a shipyard needs steel plates, rivets, wood for decks, etc. It also requires a supply of energy in the form of fuel or electricity for working cranes and other machinery. Well plants are nature's factory, and they also require energy and raw materials. . . . The sun provides the

energy needed by plants in the form of light. . . . And what are the raw materials that make up a plant? . . . Suppose we took a plant, weighed it and then dried it in a warm oven. . . . So you can see that a large part of a plant is water.[6]

Appropriate analogies can be very helpful in shedding light on complex new ideas. Understanding always involves comparisons of one sort or another, so good analogies are capable of advancing understanding quite rapidly because they offer large-scale comparisons to which students can immediately relate.

Another illustration of the creative use of analogies to help explain concepts is the following set of definitions of some twentieth-century governments (author unknown):

Socialism: You have two cows and you give one to your neighbor.

Communism: You have two cows. The government takes both of them and gives you the milk.

Fascism: You have two cows. The government takes both of them and sells you the milk.

Capitalism: You have two cows. You sell one and buy a bull.

Although teacher explanations can be helped considerably through good analogies, it is important to insure your comparisons are appropriate. Poor analogies can oversimplify and trivialize explanations as can the misuse of synonyms and other forms of concrete reference. However, this should not discourage you from seeking good analogies to promote student understanding of complex ideas.

Focusing on Individual Units of Meaning

There is a limit to the amount of new knowledge students can meaningfully assimilate in a short teaching session. Particularly when dealing with abstract content, your explanations should be organized and paced to allow students to process one idea at a time (individual concepts can generally be thought of as constituting distinct ideas, or single units of meaning, e.g., energy, government, metaphor).

It is important for you to avoid a textbook mode of presentation as a model for your explanations. Textbooks often present too much information per paragraph and at an abstraction level that makes understanding difficult. The following passage from a junior high school world history text is an illustration:

Like all other Greek city-states, Athens started out as a monarchy. However, about 750 B.C. some Athenian nobles, merchants, and manufacturers took over the government. After a time, fighting broke out between them and the farmers and artisans over land ownership and debt. Since upperclass Athenians did not want the fighting to turn into revolution, they agreed to make reforms. To do this, they had to reorganize the government.[7]

This portion of content represents an attempt at descriptive explanation of events leading to democracy in ancient Greece. To meaningfully process this sort of tightly compacted information, students would need time to focus on individual units of meaning before having to deal with succeeding points. The initial statement of the paragraph is a condensation of a lot of information about the Greeks. To appreciate its import, students would need to have a grounded understanding of concepts like "city-state," "monarchy," "revolution," and "government reform."

It would take considerable elaboration for them to grasp the significance of the political transition from a single ruler to the unsettled state of affairs and eventual revolutionary conditions that followed. For example, what does "took over the government" mean in terms of activities and events to which junior high students could relate? Was the takeover violent? How did the citizens get control? Did they use the army? Is there significance to the fact that the revolutionaries were nobles, merchants, and manufacturers rather than farmers, artisans, and military leaders? What were the human factors involved? Were the Athenian monarchs hateful and selfish? Were they involved in scandals like some present-day political leaders?

Lifeless, highly concentrated information presented in this fashion has little potential for meaningful assimilation by most precollege students. It fails to make contact with realities to which they can identify. The purpose of an explanation should be to unpack ideas for students, not to compress them so tightly that their inner contents are never revealed.

When you have occasion to expose students to abstract knowledge through teacher-centered presentations or assigned reading, you should take measures to facilitate their ability to process this information at an understanding level. There are several things you can do to accomplish this:

1. Be certain of what it is you want students to understand, that is, a concept, a process or procedure, or a series of events with causal connections. This will normally point to the need for some kind of extended explanation. When, at any point in your teaching, you are simply exposing students to information with no clear focus on a what, how, or why question, you are in all probability giving students knowledge they will have difficulty assimilating in a meaningful way.

2. Provide students with "advance organizers" to help them anticipate the logical flow of the information they will receive. This should amount to a brief introduction that tells how information is to be structured. Advance organizers make it easier for students to learn and retrieve new material.[8]

3. Organize your explanations to allow students to deal with one idea at a time. Make an effort to help students separate complex ideas into separate meaning units (individual concepts or principles). This will frequently involve providing explanations within explanations.

4. Identify points within the explanation that will deserve special attention. Then determine the kind of elaboration these internal ideas are to receive in terms of illustrations, previous references, or human interest anecdotes.

5. In building explanations on abstract concepts to which students have previously been exposed, do not assume familiarity. When new learning depends on students' abilities to handle concepts like "monarchy," "government," "revolution," and "reform" in the abstract, you cannot take for granted they possess a functional understanding simply because they have encountered these terms in earlier lessons. At the very least, you should take time to do some "reaching back" to previous learning: Who can remind us of the differences between a

monarchy and an oligarchy? Can you recall why the Greek city-states were all monarchies at this time?

Achieving Clarity and Emphasis

Making Explanations Graphic.   Most precollege students are still developing abstract thinking capabilities in the school subjects they are studying. To achieve grounded understanding of complex ideas in these subjects they will need as many concrete references and hands-on experiences as you can provide. The more graphic you can make your explanations, the more meaningful they are likely to be for your students.

Certain kinds of teacher explanations are virtually impossible to perform in the absence of visual aids or demonstrations. Other types of explanations are difficult to enrich through concrete props. For example, the most skillful teachers of beginning auto mechanics would have trouble explaining how a four-cycle engine operates if they had to rely exclusively on language. They would need at least a two-dimensional diagram to facilitate the required perceptual understanding. Ideally, they would make use of an actual engine or instructional model as a reference. Demonstration is the most graphic form of representation teachers can provide when giving an explanation. It is often a necessary extension of descriptive explanations of processes and procedures in performance-based subjects and in science labs.

At the same time, there are teaching situations that depend primarily on a teacher's verbal skill to explain abstract concepts that resist concrete illustration. Interpretive explanations of concepts like ''justice,'' ''democracy,'' ''culture,'' and ''mental health'' are not easily enhanced by visual or physical devices because they refer to intangibles such as forms of government, human behavioral tendencies, and patterns of human relationship. Skillful teachers may use techniques such as role playing to simulate the social behaviors that exemplify abstract ideas like democracy and justice, but understanding of these complex ideas ultimately depends on symbolic rather than concrete representation.

As a general rule, however, you should avoid trying to carry the burden of explanations through verbal means alone. Your explanations should be supplemented whenever possible by visual or physical representation. You have a number of options in addition to the traditional chalkboard—overhead transparencies, posters, pictures, physical objects, slides, and films.

Besides using concrete props to support your instructional input, you can make your explanations more graphic by learning to provide lucid verbal descriptions of objects, events, processes, and personalities in your teaching. For teachers in areas like social studies, history, and English it is especially desirable to be able to enhance explanations with appropriate verbal descriptions. Explanations in these teaching areas need to have a dynamic quality in order to capture student interest. The captivating force here is the human element: What happened to them? Why did they do what they did? What kinds of people and what kinds of lives are we talking about? How can we identify with these life situations?

Providing Verbal Emphasis.   Part of your instructional task is to help students to focus on individual units of meaning, to appreciate significances, and to sort the important from the less important. You can provide emphasis to particular points you want to make through voice modulation, verbal highlighting, and probing for below-surface meanings. Through deliberate voice adjustments—such as periodically raising or lowering, slowing or speeding-up your voice—you can alter the pace of your verbal input as a means of providing emphasis. To pause over or purposely give vocal stress to a particular point conveys to students that something is worth special attention.

You can use *verbal highlighting* to tell students directly, "This is important," or "This is a key point," or "I'd like you to think for a moment about what this means." When you have occasion to add information that is less important or tangential to the explanation, it is helpful for you to advise students, "This is just an aside," "These remarks are parenthetical," or "This is unrelated to what we've just been talking about."

Taking the opportunity to dwell momentarily on particular ideas allows you to emphasize meanings and implications; for example, "Now, we've been told that the upper-class Athenians did not want the fighting to turn into a revolution. What did they stand to lose if a full-scale revolution were to happen? Before we answer that, maybe we ought to consider some of the typical happenings in a country during a revolution."

Application Exercises

1. Organize brief interpretive, descriptive, and reason-giving explanations in subjects you are able to teach. Brainstorm ways of anchoring these explanations in the imagined frames of reference of a particular target group of students. Avoid grounding your explanations in formal or abstract terminology. Concentrate on communicating your ideas in as conversational and nontechnical a language as possible.
2. Examine the explanations you have constructed in exercise one to determine which have made clear the function of the new learning. Add necessary elements to any that do not meet the functionality requirement.
3. Referring to the explanations you have developed in exercise one, decide what visual aids or props you would want to use to make these explanations as graphic as possible. Would any of your explanations call for demonstrations? Which would be enhanced the least by physical props?
4. Analyze the explanations you have constructed in exercise one to determine key points or understandings that should receive verbal highlighting. Underline these key ideas.
5. Examine a textbook currently being used in an area you are qualified to teach to determine the way it presents ideas in a typical paragraph. Do the paragraphs generally represent single units of meaning or do they present meaning units in multiples? (Reminder: A meaning unit is ordinarily represented by a single proposition, e.g., "The early government of the United States was formed by men with an aversion to monarchies.")
6. Think of analogies you might use in your teaching to offer insights into concepts or realms of understanding that would otherwise be difficult to explain without using highly abstract terms and definitions (e.g., in introducing the list of atomic elements in a chemistry class, a teacher might show their functional similarity to the letters of the alphabet in the English language).

A SUMMARY OF GUIDELINES
FOR EFFECTIVE EXPLANATIONS

The following list of "Do's and "Don't's" constitutes a summary of guidelines for developing sound and meaningful classroom explanations:

Do
1. Know what a sound explanation entails and be sure of the purpose before starting an explanation.
2. Make the learner's frame of reference an integral part of teacher explanations.
3. Be as conversational and informal as possible when explaining new ideas or skills.
4. Strive for clarity and simplicity when describing processes, procedures, and structures.
5. Make explanations as graphic as possible through the use of visuals and other teaching aids.
6. Cultivate the language skills to provide vivid descriptions and effective emphases during explanations.
7. Use analogies to help students understand abstract ideas and processes.
8. Structure explanations so as to focus on one unit of meaning at a time.

Don't
1. Give students more information than they can meaningfully assimilate at one time.
2. Trade on formal or abstract language to shed light on complex ideas.
3. Use a textbook form of organization as a model for teacher explanations.
4. Allow synonyms and examples to substitute for conceptual understanding when giving interpretive explanations.
5. Allow circular definitions or circular reasoning to weaken explanations.
6. Allow reason-giving explanations to remain incomplete.
7. Get in the habit of attempting to carry explanations through verbal ability alone.

SUGGESTED ACTIVITIES AND QUESTIONS

1. It could be argued that a major part of a teacher's job is to function as a professional explainer. Discuss the basis for and some of the implications of this claim.
2. Define explaining behavior and the underlying purpose it serves as a teaching skill.
3. Summarize your understanding of this chapter by enumerating eight to ten considerations you would want to keep in mind when formulating explanations for your students.
4. In reflecting on your career as a student, have you had teachers you would regard as highly proficient explainers? Were they some of your favorite teachers? What particular techniques did they employ to make their explanations effective? Would you ordinarily expect school counselors to be good explainers? Why or why not?
5. Pay special attention to the explanations you encounter in your everyday life. Do you find many people who take pains to insure they are being properly understood when they explain things to others? Can you think of particular areas outside of school where it is especially

important for people to be able to deliver clear and concise verbal explanations? Would you favor a course in explaining behavior for doctors? For merchants? For parents?

6. What are the most common violations of good explaining technique you encounter in your interactions with other people? How do these poor habits develop? One of the premises of this chapter has been that good explanation technique is an unnatural behavior for most people in this fast-paced society. Discuss reasons why this might be true. What are the implications for teacher education?

7. Make an effort to attend to the explaining behavior you encounter in schools where you are involved. Do the teachers you observe place a high priority on being able to provide students with good explanations? Do the administrators and office staff generally provide clear and precise information, instructions, and so forth? Take the opportunity to study the techniques of teachers you would consider competent explainers. Ask them to share their strategies? Compare their ideas with the explanation strategies developed in this chapter.

8. Take deliberate steps to perfect your own explaining behavior as a developing teacher. Make an effort to practice good explaining techniques both in and out of school (e.g., in giving someone directions, in describing events, ideas, or processes). Learn to monitor and assess your own explanatory skills as you progress through teacher training, for example, as you provide explanations in microteaching sessions and during student teaching. Arrange to obtain periodic tape-recorded and/or videotaped samples of your explaining technique in formal teaching situations. Ask students to provide you with feedback on the clarity and meaningfulness of your explanations. Make use of these indicators to monitor your own development as a professional explainer.

NOTES AND REFERENCES

1. Robert J. Miltz, *Development and Evaluation of a Manual for Improving Teacher's Explanations.* Stanford, Calif.: Stanford Center for Research and Development in Teaching, Stanford University, 1972.

2. The discussion in this section is adapted from Robert H. Ennis, *Logic in Teaching.* Englewood Cliffs, N.J.: Prentice-Hall, 1969, chap. 14.

3. Jonas F. Soltis, *An Introduction to the Analysis of Educational Concepts.* Reading, Mass.: Addison-Wesley, 1968, p. 59.

4. Adapted from Morris L. Bigge and Maurice P. Hunt, *Psychological Foundations of Education,* 3rd ed. New York: Harper and Row, 1980, pp. 454–56.

5. Frank Smith, *Comprehension and Learning.* New York: Holt, Rinehart and Winston, 1975, p. 159.

6. From John R. Hall, *Biology.* New York: David McKay, 1974, pp. 13–14.

7. William Cox, Arthur Greenblatt, and John Seaberg, *Human Heritage: A World History.* Columbus, Ohio: Charles E. Merrill, 1981, p. 147.

8. N. L. Gage and David C. Berliner, *Educational Psychology,* 4th ed. Boston: Houghton Mifflin, 1988, p. 291.

CHAPTER 8

Mastering the Art of Interactive Teaching

DIRECTIVE AND INTERACTIVE TEACHING STYLES

An important key to quality teaching is the ability to talk *with* rather than *at* students when conducting classroom business. Skilled teachers are able to depart from a predominantly teacher-centered or directive style of teaching and to interact with their classes in a manner that is learner-paced, conversational, and personally engaging for young learners. Once perfected, an interactive teaching pattern not only promotes student participation in the learning process, but it allows teachers to be more spontaneous and natural when working with student groups.[1]

Teachers are often inclined to regard teaching as simply "telling," and adopt an overly direct, information-giving approach to classroom instruction. This style of teaching tends to be impersonal and keeps student's attentions focused primarily on externals. An information-centered mode of teaching is useful in getting students to focus on learning tasks and to master basic information, but it has limited utility when it comes to actively involving students in their own learning. Students will tend to learn more and to develop more positive attitudes toward the learning when you are able to employ a less direct, interactive mode of instruction.[2]

Also, when you rely on the directive approach as your primary means of communicating with students you will find yourself handicapped when it comes to discussing matters involving feelings and emotions. To be able to provide instruction that actively engages students in their own learning and to effectively share thoughts, feelings, and personal concerns with students, you will need to develop dialogue rather than monologue.

Interactive teaching ability requires considerable interpersonal skill, but takes some of the burden off you by allowing you to deviate from a presentational manner of teaching. Proficiency in interactive communication gives you a capability for conducting discussions, talking to students about feelings and problems, and performing more leisurely and creatively in stand-up teaching. Its high versatility will allow you to more easily generate good impromptu lessons, explore new areas of learning with students, and function without having all of the answers. Interactive teaching emphasizes the shared communication process in learning and de-emphasizes the need to rely on pre-packaged materials and tightly structured programs. When mastered, it will allow you to take a more relaxed and artful approach to the demands of classroom instruction.

This chapter introduces you to basic elements of interactive teaching and will detail the specific maneuvers that will allow you to apply interactive communication in your teaching.

The Essence of Interactive Teaching

A competent teacher's group communication skills are manifest when the teacher, acting as an adept catalyst, is able to orchestrate productive interaction without having to dominate the proceedings. Exemplary discussion leaders have developed a series of skillful maneuvers that allow them to direct lively and stimulating flows of exchanges with and between students, while keeping the discussion organized, focused, and respectful of individual needs and sensitivities.

These teacher behaviors include verbal tactics and nonverbal mannerisms that promote positive and productive classroom interaction. They fall within four general categories, including (1) *structuring* techniques, (2) *questioning* techniques, (3) *attending* behaviors, and (4) *responding* behaviors.[3]

STRUCTURING TECHNIQUES

You use structuring moves in a class discussion to establish the nature and context of the interaction, regulate student participation, provide continuity and emphasis, and help foster an appropriate group atmosphere. These tactics include focusing, gatekeeping, climate-setting, redirecting, transitioning, informing, and summarizing.

Focusing

Your first task is to draw student's attentions to the problem, issue, or inquiry being discussed. To get students into an appropriate mental frame for discussion, you should ordinarily begin by providing a context for learning. This is commonly referred to as building a *set*. You may seek to develop a learning set by citing a recent newspaper article, by reading a passage of poetry, or by giving a brief history of a social problem. Pictures, posters, physical objects, and short films also make good starting points for discussion. You will want to establish a well-defined focus before launching into discussion. This initial focus becomes the point of reference for keeping the discussion on track.

Gatekeeping

Competent gatekeeping involves keeping tabs on who has or has not participated, recognizing students who are next in line to contribute, and making sure only one person speaks at a time. You may find it necessary to ignore high frequency participants in order to give less vocal students an opportunity. To avoid becoming overly mechanical, you should attempt to vary your techniques for bringing students into a discussion. On one occasion you may give a student the green light by simply saying "Yes, Chandra," in another instance it could be "Let's hear Enrico's opinion on this," and in some situations you may use a simple nod or hand gesture in the direction of the student.

Climate-setting

Climate-setting strategies are usually subtle verbal or nonverbal behaviors that teachers employ to create positive affect and direction in group interaction. In showing genuine interest and enthusiasm, for example, you are seeking to set a constructive tone for discussion. By demonstrating a balanced, carefully reasoned approach to human problems, you are setting a precedent for students to also be reasonable in expressing opinions on sensitive issues. Well-placed humor can be used to help reduce group tensions.

Redirecting and Transitioning

To keep a discussion moving and avoid belaboring irrelevant or sufficiently established points, you may need to deliberately and tactfully redirect student thought to the original focus or in a new direction, for example, "I think we've had an opportunity to hear a number of different views on that idea. I'd like to raise a somewhat different question now," or "I believe we're beginning to stray from the main issue. Let's remind ourselves what the original disagreement was."

You should insure that new focuses are accompanied by clear and smooth transitions. Transitioning moves call student's attentions to changes in the direction of a discussion, for example, "Now that we're clear on what happened, I'd like us to consider the cause," or "We've been discussing the role of primaries in a presidential election; let's shift gears now and talk about the campaigns that follow."

Informing

Skilled discussion leaders are able to provide information that has a structuring effect on group interaction without directly manipulating the discussion. You may give reminders of the time limits of the discussion: "Please keep in mind we have twenty minutes left. You may want to keep your comments short." Or you might offer information that has to do with principles of sound reasoning: "Remember the rule of logic that says you can't go directly from factual statements to value conclusions in your reasoning." A teacher may also give factual information that moves a discussion beyond impasse: "For the record, I did notice in this morning's paper that the new land-fill project you're debating about does not include environmental impact provisions."

When entering a class discussion as an information-giver, you should avoid telling all you know about a subject. Otherwise you may needlessly turn the discussion into a lecture, and thereby defeat its purpose.

Summarizing

Resourceful discussion leaders will use *internal summaries* at main junctures in a discussion to pull loose ends together or to remind students of what has transpired to that point, for example, "O.K., before we go on, let's summarize the arguments, pro and con, that we've heard so far,'' or "We've talked about many things that contribute to poor driving records. Let's see if we can reduce all of these to several main causes.''

It is also important to provide a final summary at the close of a discussion. You may ask students to assist in providing internal and/or final summaries.

Application Exercises

1. Label the particular structuring move represented by each of the following teacher statements:
   a. "You people have been doing a good job of researching these topics. I'm anxious to see what you've found.''
   b. "O.K., now that you understand the idea, let's look at a few practical examples.''
   c. "Remember, I'm asking for hands when you have something to say. I believe Bill had his hand up first, then Nancy is next.''
   d. "All right, it's important for us to recognize the point that's being made here. What I'm hearing many of you say is . . .''
   e. "Now for openers, I'd like to ask this question: What do you think you'd do if faced with a situation where . . . ?''
   f. "This is a topic we've discussed before in some detail. I'm going to ask that we table it for now and consider a more basic issue.''
   g. "Let me give you a hint. There's one piece of information that you seem to be overlooking. Will you look at the word in italics in the first paragraph of this chapter.''
   h. "O.K., let's stop for a moment and see if we can retrace the steps we've taken to solve this problem.''
2. Compose a verbal structuring move for each of the following teaching situations, identifying each tactic with an appropriate label:
   a. You wish to tighten the groundrules for turning in late homework and have decided to initiate a class discussion of the problem as a means of getting student input and cooperation.
   b. You feel a need to call a group's attention to the fact that people are repeating comments that have previously been made, perhaps indicating insufficient attention to one another's contributions.
   c. A number of students are wanting to join a discussion. Two, in particular, have kept their hands waving while others have had the floor.
   d. A class of capable students has been taking a somewhat matter-of-fact approach to group interaction. You want to set a more spirited tone for today's classwork with a few well-chosen comments at the beginning of class.
   e. You have been working with a class on the basic procedure for multiplying fractions. You want to reiterate the essential steps they should be mindful of before beginning to work problems.
   f. A class discussion has moved from a consideration of why South Americans experience summer during our winter months to an argument over who produces the better soccer players, North or South America. You wish to reestablish the original focus.

QUESTIONING TECHNIQUES

A teacher's questioning strategies and techniques play a central role in interactive teaching. Skillful questioners set the stage for discussion, draw students into the dialogue, and evoke higher thought processes.[4]

Some guidelines for the use of teacher questions are: (1) approach questions strategically, using a variety of questions to promote different levels of thought, (2) ask questions in clear and succinct language, using only one question at a time, (3) give students ample time to answer, and (4) use follow-up questions when appropriate to elicit more information.

Using Questions to Promote Thought

Different types of questions foster different thinking processes. The most commonly used type of teacher question is the *memory-recall question* that requires students to recollect names, dates, events, and other factual items they have memorized: for example, "When did Columbus arrive in the New World?"; "Who was the author of *Great Expectations*?"; "What does *effervescent* mean?"

A second type of question aims at comprehension rather than the recall of facts. *Comprehension questions* call for relational thinking because they require students to demonstrate understanding of information by generalizing, comparing-contrasting, or relating it to some larger principle or process: for example, "Why do you think the leaves have shriveled on this plant?"; "What is the main idea of this story?"; or "Contrast today's life-style with that of your grandparents."

A third variety of educational question invites students to go beyond understanding information and make projections that require reflective thought. *Reflection questions* ask students to form hypotheses, to create new forms, or to evaluate situations: for example, "How can we get the community to support our beautification project?"; "Suggest a new way to heat your home"; or "Do you agree that honesty is the best policy?"

Whether discussing a short story in English, a famous battle in history, or a laboratory experiment in science, it is advisable to use a questioning scheme that entails a progression from lower to higher levels of thought.[5] With this in mind, an English teacher may decide to open discussion of a short story by focusing on factual level questions about the story: "Where did the story take place? Who were the main characters? What did they do for a living? What problem did they encounter at the beginning of the story?"

Having developed a factual base to work from, the stage is set for comprehension-level questions. These questions serve to advance beyond factual detail and engage the conceptual understanding of the student: "During what time of year did the story take place? (An inference question—assuming the story did not give this information directly) Would you consider the people in the story to be a close-knit family? Why? How would you describe the standard of living of this family? (Another inference question) Compare the personalities of the two main characters in the story."

At this point you might move to some reflective thought questions. These call on students to do divergent thinking that goes beyond a conceptual understanding of the story itself: "Could you see a family like this adapting to life in the United States today? Would you consider the father in the story to be a good parent? What might be a way to reorganize the welfare system to alleviate problems such as this family encountered? If you could change one thing about this story, what would it be?"

Clarity in Questions

Clarity in questioning is essential because students have little time during a discussion to contemplate the meaning of a question. Questions should be clear and brief. You should ask the exact question in explicit and unambiguous language, avoiding unnecessary words, parenthetical expressions, and multiple questions.

The following are examples of questions that should be rephrased for greater simplicity and clarity:

"Tell us, if you can, what contribution police officers make to our society. (Better: "Why do we need police officers?")

"Explain, in as much detail as possible, how rising temperatures can effect the humidity of a particular area of the country." (Better: "Explain the effect of rising temperatures on humidity.")

"How do the basketball, football, and baseball players you see on TV keep themselves in good condition day after day?" (Better: "How do professional athletes stay in shape?")

"Considering the amount of traffic on our freeways, the lack of effective devices for controlling pollution, and the apathy of the average person, is there any answer to the smog problem in our metropolitan areas?" (Better: "What can we do about smog in our large cities?")

Pausing to Allow "Think-time"

When you use pauses to allow students sufficient time to formulate answers, you can expect more adequate responses, involving more complex thinking.[6] Students will be more confident in their responses and more inclined to participate in discussions. You should make a habit of asking the question first before calling on a student to answer. After asking the question, you should pause for approximately three seconds before calling on a student. You should allow another pause of three to five seconds after calling on the student to give time for an answer, then another three- to five-second pause after the student answers before commenting or asking for additional input.

Probing for More Information

Your students will give more serious thought to questions when you encourage them to think beyond their first answers.[7] You can use follow-up questions or *probes* to elicit further thought when you feel students' ideas could be more complete or imaginative. These probing questions may come from any of the three questioning modes: "Do you remember anything else about it?" (memory-recall); "Can you explain in more detail?" (comprehension); "Can you think of any other way to accomplish that?" (reflection); "Do you regard that as a positive step?" (reflection).

Probing questions are always to be used for the purpose of stimulating more comprehensive and creative thought, never to grill students or to punish them for lack of preparation.

Application Exercises

1. Design a twelve- to fifteen-minute interactive teaching segment in an area you are qualified to teach, using teacher questions to determine the direction of the lesson. Attempt first to establish a factual base with descriptive questions, then work to encourage higher conceptual thought through a series of comprehension questions, and, finally, introduce several reflection questions as a means of stimulating divergent thinking in your target group of students.
2. Prepare yourself to practice the previous lesson on a group of your peers in a simulated teaching situation. Using the questioning guidelines presented in this chapter, take the opportunity to practice clarity, proper wait-time, and probing techniques as main emphases in your questioning pattern.

ATTENDING BEHAVIORS

Teachers who listen thoughtfully and attentively to student contributions are conveying their respect for students and what they have to say. By modeling interest and attention, you are also encouraging students to take group discussion seriously and to use their best listening skills when others are speaking. Active, attentive listening is demonstrated primarily through body language and involves such things as eye contact, leaning slightly toward the speaker, showing evidence of contemplation, and offering subtle encouragement.

Eye Contact

One of the first essentials of authentic listening is direct eye contact.[8] Failing to make eye contact with a speaker may reflect nervousness or disinterest. Similarly, darting eyes may indicate that the listener's thoughts are not with the speaker. On the other hand, compulsive eye contact on the part of a listener, if not broken periodically with pensive glances away from a speaker, can also be disconcerting. Comfortable, nonmechanical eye contact is sometimes difficult for people and may require deliberate cultivation.

Leaning

When you lean away from a speaker you tend to show less interest and attention than when you lean slightly in that person's direction. Leaning toward students when they are talking communicates a concern to hear what is being said. Your posture, however, must appear natural and unexaggerated to be effective.

Contemplating

Good listeners usually show indications they are thinking about what is being said. Face and eyes directed upward with a thoughtful expression generally signal listener involvement; eyes looking down at the floor or out the window tend to communicate preoccupation with other thoughts. An index finger poised under the chin or folded hands are other signs of concentrated attention. As with other attending behaviors, indicators of contemplation should not be allowed to become merely tokens. When you feel internal motivation to be an attentive listener, these nonverbal manifestations will have less tendency to appear artificial. For effective attending skill it is necessary that your verbal and nonverbal behaviors are congruent.

Encouraging

It is important as a teacher to be able to offer tactful encouragement to students who speak in class. This is especially beneficial when students are shy or lacking in confidence. One of the most effective "encouragers" is the empathetic listener who nods appreciatively as a speaker offers ideas. Sometimes a soft verbal nudge like "keep going, you're doing fine" can be invaluable support. More than anything else, such mannerisms convey your sincere involvement in students' efforts to contribute.

Application Exercises

1. Working in groups of three (triads) on a designated discussion topic, practice effective attending behaviors when you are the recipient of input from the other group members. Design a pattern for providing one another with constructive feedback on the nature and effectiveness of demonstrated attending skills.
2. Consciously practice facilitative attending behavior in your interpersonal encounters, formal and informal, both in and out of school. Make an effort to reach the place where good attending skills are second nature to you, where they become an integral part of your interpersonal style.

RESPONDING BEHAVIORS

The manner in which you respond to student contributions is critical to a free and harmonious interchange of ideas in your classes. It will usually have an important bearing on the confidence and enthusiasm students show toward class discussions.[9]

Your repertoire of responding behaviors should include techniques for (1) acknowledging and reinforcing students for their contributions, (2) clarifying to insure messages are being properly understood, (3) evaluating both right and wrong answers, and (4) mediating between individual contributors and the group at large.

Acknowledging and Reinforcing

Classroom participation should be a positive experience for students. Class members who feel ignored or put down when they contribute will be reluctant participants. You can avoid some potential negative reinforcers by insisting that students show respect and sensitivity toward one another as they attempt to communicate their ideas to the class.

Realizing how easy it is for some input to be lost in the course of a lively discussion, it is important for you to attempt to acknowledge all student contributions regardless of quality or length. Recognizing contributions does not require that you evaluate them, but that you simply allow students to know they have been heard and their input is appreciated: for example; "O.K. Thank you," "Alex agrees with the minority on this," "I hear you," or "That's one way of looking at it." With some students, simply a visible nod or other nonverbal gesture may be enough to convey recognition and appreciation for their efforts. Reinforcement is also provided when teachers use student ideas to make a point or to compare points of view:[10] for example, "Mary also took that position a few minutes ago," or "Jules had a good answer to the question you're asking."

Whereas the most effective reinforcers are often the words of praise teachers provide students following right answers, a student's willingness to participate in class discussion should not hinge on the ability to supply correct answers.

Clarifying

Besides providing reinforcement to students for their contributions, you should take responsibility to insure that these messages are properly understood. By reflecting back to students the substance and import of their messages, you demonstrate interest and a concern to understand. This can be accomplished by a simple *paraphrase* of the idea or feeling just communicated: for example, "So you believe we'd be better off with fewer automobiles on the road," or "You think the war was unnecessary."

A paraphrase should be a brief restatement (not a question) of the message delivered in as neutral a manner as possible, and implying no obligation for the student to respond. It should avoid repeating the student's message word for word.

It is important that the clarifying paraphrase merely reflect, not question or confront. Simply letting the student know you have heard correctly may be all that is needed to encourage further dialogue.

Evaluating

In discussion situations where evaluation of student knowledge or thought is appropriate, a major part of your response to student contributions will be your reply to correct and incorrect answers. As a general rule, it is good practice to respond to correct answers with praise of some sort. Short answers should ordinarily receive brief praise: for example, "Good," "Good point," Right," "Fine," "Exactly," "That's correct," or "You've got the idea." You should try to vary these words of praise so responses do not become monotonous and superficial. It is necessary that your praise sound genuine to the student.

With longer answers, praise should be lengthier, though simple and specific to the answer: for example, "Yes, you've done a good job of separating the main cause of the war from the contributing causes," or "Very good, I think you've managed to identify each step of the process."

To be most effective, praise should be tailored to fit individual situations and individual students. As a general rule, the older and more mature the student, the less the need for direct or extensive praise and the more likely that indirect, subtle praise will be appropriate: for example, "Yes, that's an interesting point," or "O.K., I hadn't thought of that before."

In responding to incorrect answers, it is generally advisable to avoid giving a direct

"No, that's not right."[11] Instead, your first effort should be to remain noncommittal, to avoid making a ruling until other students have had an opportunity to be involved. When you place a high priority on student thought processes you should be less inclined to feature right answers as the focal point of evaluation. Rather than immediately passing judgment on an answer, you will be more interested in working with students on the process for arriving at answers. This may entail giving hints, probing to locate "sticking-points" and confusions, and so forth.

During value-based discussions, you will at times find yourself in disagreement with student's opinions. On these occasions, responses that begin with "I disagree" or "Yes . . . But" have a tendency to put students on the defensive. Learning then becomes less important than defending oneself. To maintain your supporting role in a discussion, your should be able to "disagree with finesse," without being confrontational. This is best accomplished when you can present your differing view in language that downplays the disagreement while acknowledging the student's right to an opinion: for example, "Those are some good arguments against a curfew. I'm inclined to favor the curfew because studies indicate that students in towns with curfews get better grades," or "A lot of people feel like you do in opposing gun control. On the other hand, I'm aware that law enforcement officers feel helpless without it."

Mediating

Another of your main functions during discussion is to insure that individual contributions are being properly understood and utilized by the group. You are in effect a mediator between individual students and the larger group, which means you must alternate between talking to individual contributors and addressing the group as a whole. It will sometimes be necessary to rephrase or amplify particular ideas so they are usable in the discussion: "Have we heard Marna's point? She thinks that . . ." On other occasions you will need to play advocate for the group at large to prevent individuals from monopolizing or diverting the discussion: "We may need to put that idea aside for the time being. I'm afraid it's going to get us sidetracked."

You may need to stop the discussion periodically to ask for definitions or to inquire where a particular line of thought is leading. As an illustration, in a discussion on teenage crime it may become apparent that some students are using the term *juvenile delinquent* uncritically. Rather than allow key arguments to be built on ambiguous language, you as discussion leader have a responsibility to call attention to the need for definition. Later in the same discussion a student may be succeeding in advancing an argument based on a premise that you know lacks factual support: for example, the notion that jailing juvenile delinquents would teach them not to break the law. By requesting evidence for this assumption, you are not only teaching principles of sound reasoning, but are protecting the group from a potentially blind alley.

Application Exercises

1. Working in groups of three (triads) on a designated discussion topic, practice reflecting back (paraphrasing) the message of the previous speaker each time you offer input of your own. The groundrules for this exercise are: (1) Each speaker provides

a brief paraphrase of the preceding speaker's message as a precondition for entering the discussion, (2) the previous speaker must verify the accuracy of the paraphrase before the discussion is allowed to proceed, and (3) the third person in the group plays the role of monitor when not the paraphraser or the person receiving it.

2. Make an effort to practice your reflective listening skills in your day-to-day conversations, both in and out of school. Attempt to make this an integral part of your communication style. As such, it will be a more natural behavior for you in the classroom.

3. Being mindful of the desirability of varying teacher response patterns, specify a number of different responses you might use to convey acceptance and approval of student contributions in your classes.

DEALING WITH COMMON PROBLEMS IN GROUP INTERACTION

When you encourage high levels of interaction and involvement in your classes, you should anticipate and be prepared to deal with some of the possible problems student-centered activities engender. Classroom discussions, in particular, can be a special challenge to your managerial skills. The following are some of the potential difficulties you should be aware of, along with suggestions for confronting these problems.

Nonparticipation

There may be times during a planned discussion when you have trouble getting students to say anything. It is important that you not convey immediate displeasure with the students for their apparent reluctance to become involved. Periods of silence in the classroom should not cause you to become nervous. Patience is usually the answer here.

Do not be afraid to ask students what the silence means. Sometimes lack of response means reflection rather than apathy. Or it could be a case of students not understanding a question. You may need to regroup and come at the topic or issue from a different direction. If you sense that the silence simply reflects difficulties getting started, let students know you are able to empathize with shyness or reluctance to be the first one to talk.

One good way to prime students for class discussion is to allow them to work in small groups of three or four as a warmup (an idea-generating session) for large-group discussion.

Overstimulation

It is also possible to have the other extreme, namely, discussions that get out of hand. Group discussion should afford students opportunities to express thoughts and opinions on subjects of particular interest to them. As such, the best discussions are often those in which students demonstrate the most exuberance and animation. However, interest and excitement can turn out to be counterproductive when it leads to shouting matches or displays of uncontrollable emotion. It can also be disturbing to adjoining classes or disconcerting to more reserved students. Skillful interaction leaders usually have a knack for bringing discussions to the boiling point without allowing them to boil over. Here are several things you can do to avoid the problem of overstimulation during class discussions:

1. Select topics that are appropriate to the maturity levels of students.
2. Attempt to keep the discussion balanced by maintaining appropriate tension between opposing points of view. This discourages students from vociferously celebrating one-sided victories in debate.
3. Avoid emotionally charged language when providing your own input. Temper your own enthusiasm with demonstrations of rationality and personal control.
4. Attempt to redirect discussions that seem to be heading toward verbal confrontations or strong emotional displays.
5. Help your students to recognize that productive discussion is possible only when participants agree to be rational.

Conformity

One of your efforts in group interaction should be to encourage the interplay of differing ideas and personal styles. Class discussions should be opportunities for some students to express minority opinions as well as occasions for majorities to exercise their influence. The peer influence in a typical classroom often militates against this objective. Conformity is an especially prevalent phenomenon among groups of school-age young people. It usually takes a particularly self-confident and strong-willed youngster to avoid acquiescing to the wishes and opinions of the majority or the most popular students in the group.

One of the things you can do to discourage majority attitudes and patterns from holding sway over the entire class is to make concerted attempts to elicit diverse viewpoints and to insure they are allowed thoughtful consideration. Another is to foster alliances among those who hold minority opinions. Students who feel they are supported by at least one other member of the group are less likely to yield to the views of the majority.[12]

Teacher Influence

It is no less a problem when the honest exchange of thoughts and opinions is hampered by students' felt needs to conform to the teacher's views. With this in mind, you should be careful to avoid letting your own opinions and personal agendas influence the direction of students' thinking during a discussion. Unless you are conducting a recitation session, open discussion should not be allowed to degenerate into a situation where students are feeding you the ideas they believe you want to hear. There are several things you can do to insure that your presence does not affect the authenticity of student contributions:

1. Tell students directly that you are interested in hearing their thinking, not simply a reflection of your own.
2. Attempt to keep students guessing as to what your views are on questions that

allow for more than one conclusion. Frequently play the devil's advocate to demonstrate your versatility.

3. Do not take your own opinions so seriously that students are afraid to have different views. Take opportunities to poke fun at your own lack of certainty in some areas: "I'm still not sure what I believe about this. One of these days I'll figure it out."

4. Provide positive feedback to students who express honestly held views different from your own. Show that you are supportive of their attempts to think for themselves: "I'll have to admit, you may have something there. I hadn't thought of it that way."

Controversial Issues

Teachers are sometimes reluctant to engage students in discussions of controversial topics for fear they will be entering forbidden territory.[13] At the other extreme, some teachers have no reluctance to lead students into sensitive areas, often giving little thought to the biases they encourage through one-sided approaches to disputable issues.

Generally it is possible to engage students in fruitful discussions of controversial issues without stepping on toes or prejudicing students' thinking. This will require that you have an approprate objective as you lead students into the discussion of controversial subjects. Perhaps the most educationally justifiable purpose is to have students appreciate the basis for controversy, usually involving the clash of significant human values. Your ultimate objective here should be to get students to understand what makes an issue an issue rather than simply a problem (i.e., issues persist because they represent strong tension between competing social values). One good way to foster a balanced approach to controversial topics is to have students role play arguments for both sides of difficult issues. When one of your goals is to encourage social empathy and understanding rather than simply the taking of sides, you have a sound basis for approaching the discussion of controversial issues in your classes.

SIMULATED DIALOGUE

Teachers who are effective two-way communicators are able to use *simulated dialogue* to bring an interactive quality to most of their classroom communication. Simulated dialogue is learner-paced teacher input that features the liberal use of rhetorical questions, personalized references, and "pregnant pauses." It attempts to engage student's interests, imaginations, values, and experiences. Although you may not be engaged in live discussion, you are anticipating and appealing to the frames of reference of the students.

Simulated dialogue has the effect of being a great deal more involving than impersonal teacher monologue. In opening a unit on the colonizing period in U.S. history a teacher using simulated dialogue would begin,

> NOT BY SAYING: Today we start reading about the colonies, first Jamestown, then Plymouth, and so on. You will want to get the dates fixed first and then find out about which people colonized which section and why.

BUT BY SAYING: Let's go back about 300 years and think about who was around here and what the countryside must have looked like. Were your ancestors around here then or did they come later? What brought them here? If we could talk about the questions for a while maybe we could get some ideas about what a colony was.

Although the teacher in the second case was still doing all of the talking, this simulated dialogue was a more indirect and conversational way of approaching the learning activity. This personally involving style of teaching gave students the feeling this teacher was discussing the topic with them rather than simply talking at them.

In another teaching sample, a woodshop teacher in a brief, relatively teacher-dominated portion of instruction uses the interactive mode, with some simulated dialogue, to provide a short introduction to the final stages of a student project:

- Let's all gather around this bench right here. That's right, bring your projects over with you. . . . Let's hold up our projects so we can see how the sanding work is coming. . . . All right, fine. I'm seeing some good efforts here on this one. . . . What grade of sandpaper are you going to be using next, Sarah? . . . O.K., that's a good choice. . . . Will you all pull in a little closer so we can see one another's work . . . . How many of you are getting ready for the next step? What is the next step? . . . The finish coat. That's right. . . . What are some things we'll want to do to prepare for this? . . . Evan do you have an idea . . . Yes, you've apparently been thinking ahead. . . . Where will we want to look for the keys to the finish cabinets? Who remembers? . . . Now most of you were probably planning to use the same approach with this one as you did the last. . . . I want to suggest a minor change.

The use of questions and second-person references gives this teaching episode an interactive character that might easily have been missing had the teacher decided to take the simpler and shorter route and merely tell students what he wanted them to know. In examining this dialogue we recognize the skillful weaving of elements of structuring, questioning, attending, and responding into one concise segment of interactive teaching.

Application Exercise

1. Design (on paper) a segment of simulated dialogue that you might use to introduce a lesson, to present a concept, or to provide instructions of one sort or another to students in a subject area you are qualified to teach.

NONACADEMIC INTERACTION

Some of the attending and responding behaviors that are fundamental to interactive teaching will also be highly useful to you in talking with students about matters that do not relate directly to instruction. Here the concern is to be able to discuss with students such things as their attitudes toward the class, difficulties they are having with peers, or out-of-school problems that are affecting their school performance. Although you will not actually carry the title, there will be many opportunities for you to take the role of counselor, in addition to that of teacher, in your work with these young people.

The communication skills that will allow you to be effective in these situations are sometimes referred to as "helping skills." They include the ability to listen nonjudgmentally as students express personal feelings and agendas, techniques for offering constructive and supportive feedback, and positive strategies for helping students resolve school-related problems.

Often the tendency is for teachers to insist on being supreme authorities, even in casual conversations with students. For the student, such conversation typically becomes another endurance test, another example of the kind of monologue they are used to receiving from the adults in their lives. One of the keys to positive relationships with students will be your willingness to hear and understand the student's concerns without rushing to impose your own agendas on the conversation. It will be a big plus for you in your teaching if you are able to employ fundamental helping skills in the counseling and personal conferencing you do with students. This topic is treated in considerably more detail in chapter 11.

SUGGESTED ACTIVITIES AND QUESTIONS

1. Identify teaching tasks that you believe can be accomplished most effectively through interactive teaching. What do you see to be the main advantages of interactive teaching? Does it have any significant limitations? What are the main shortcomings of a directive style of teaching?

2. Summarize your understanding of this chapter by identifying what you take to be the main components of an interactive teaching pattern. Describe in your own words what each of these elements entails.

3. Discuss the theory of learning that supports an interactive approach to teaching. Compare this with the conception of learning that underlies a directive style of teaching.

4. Do you see yourself as an accomplished interactive communicator? What would you consider to be your main strengths and weaknesses when it comes to engaging in genuine interpersonal dialogue? Will it be necessary for you to make substantial changes in your interpersonal style in order for you to perform well in an interactive teaching mode?

5. Find occasions to observe the interactive techniques of teachers in schools where you are involved. Make note of the specific interactive maneuvers used by these teachers. As you observe classroom interaction, make an effort to identify points in these lessons where you might employ specific interactive maneuvers were you the teacher, for example, places in the lesson where you would use a teacher paraphrase, where you would insert an internal summary, a probing question, and so forth.

6. Make it a point to focus on the questioning techniques being used in the classrooms you are able to observe. Take it on yourself to do an informal survey of (1) the frequency and types of teacher questions you encounter, (2) the relative clarity of teacher questions, and (3) the amount of think-time teachers are allowing when using questions.

7. Take the opportunity to study the attending and responding patterns of teachers you have occasion to observe. Do you find many teachers who are modeling highly effective skills in these areas? Do you encounter teachers who demonstrate poor attending and responding behaviors in their interactions with students?

8. To what extent are the attending and responding behaviors of teachers a reflection of teacher attitudes as well as skills? How high a priority are you presently willing to place on this kind of skill development?

9. Some teacher educators recommend that teachers adapt their response patterns according to the self-concepts and ability levels of their students. Does this seem like a reasonable idea to you? For example, would you favor using a different, perhaps briefer and more businesslike, technique when responding to the contributions of more confident, intellectually mature students than the approach you employ with less assertive, less academically talented students?

NOTES AND REFERENCES

1. Mary Lynn Crow, "Teaching as an Interactive Process." In Kenneth E. Eble (Ed.), *New Directions for Teaching and Learning.* San Francisco: Jossey-Bass, 1980, p. 42.

2. Ned A. Flanders, *Analyzing Teaching Behavior.* Reading, Mass.: Addison-Wesley, 1970, p. 401.

3. Arno A. Bellack and Joel R. Davitz, "The Language of the Classroom." In Ronald T. Hyman (Ed.), *Teaching: Vantage Points for Study,* 2nd ed. Philadelphia: J.B. Lippincott, 1974, p. 168.

4. Deborah B. Strother, "Developing Thinking Skills Through Questioning." *Phi Delta Kappan,* December 1989, p. 324.

5. Ibid., p. 325.

6. Francis Hunkins, *Teaching Thinking Through Effective Questioning.* Needham Heights, Mass.: Christopher-Gordon, 1989, p. 64.

7. N.L. Gage and David C. Berliner, *Educational Psychology,* 4th ed. Boston: Houghton Mifflin, 1988, p. 551.

8. Sandra Sololove Garrett, Myra Sadker, and David Sadker, "Interpersonal Communication Skills." In James M. Cooper (Ed.), *Classroom Teaching Skills,* 2nd ed. Lexington, Mass.: D. C. Heath, 1982, p. 240.

9. Flanders, op. cit., p. 415.

10. Gage and Berliner, op. cit., p. 555.

11. Ibid., p. 556.

12. Ibid., p. 445.

13. Ibid., p. 435.

CHAPTER 9

Staying on Top
of Classroom Management

MAKING THE NECESSARY INVESTMENTS

The job of teaching in today's schools can be considerably less burdensome when you are able to manage a classroom assertively, smoothly, and humanely. Competent classroom management is essentially a human relations skill. It will reflect your ability to purposefully direct group learning activities with a minimum of confusion and distraction. You will need to possess the leadership skills to draw students into orderly encounters with activities toward which they may initially be indifferent or resistant. This usually requires a firm presence and a strong sense of purpose, qualities that need to be balanced with considerable patience and good humor.

There are no simple formulas for developing and maintaining an appropriate learning atmosphere in a school classroom. You should avoid thinking of classroom management as a set of prescriptions to be applied when behavior problems arise. Instead, your ability to keep students constructively involved in school learning will be the result of an ongoing condition you manage to create, a group climate you cause to prevail in support of the learning activities you are promoting.[1] To become a skillful director of group learning, you should make a determined effort to plan for class management and to regard it as an integral part of your interactive teaching pattern.

This chapter provides management strategies to help you develop a smooth flow of classroom activity. It emphasizes behavior control and the preservation of teaching energy through voice conservation, artful response tactics, and preventive maintenance measures.

Three Main Requirements

In general, there are three conditions that contribute to effective classroom management. First, approach it with an appropriate *frame of mind*. Class control is facilitated by a commitment to something you are attempting to accomplish with a class and the determination to have a supportive environment. The second requirement is *perceptual sensitivity*. Effective group management involves an ability to recognize when the classroom climate is appropriate to the developing activity and to immediately sense when it needs adjustment. The third essential is an appropriate set of *management strategies.* To maintain a productive class atmosphere you will need to have at your disposal a repertoire of behavioral management tactics that you can skillfully apply to a variety of classroom situations.

THE PSYCHOLOGY OF CLASSROOM MANAGEMENT

First of all, sound classroom management requires something personally and educationally important that you want to achieve with the class, ideally something that is maximally involving for the students.[2] When you come to class feeling confident you have done your homework and that you have a lesson worth your student's attention and cooperation, you will be more mentally prepared to insist on a favorable learning climate than when your primary concern is to get through a class period. You will feel more of a personal stake in the outcome of the lesson. The management task is less likely to loom in your mind as something extraneous to the act of teaching, as something you do out of self-defense or because it is expected of you. Your class management behaviors will tend to emerge more naturally and intuitively out of your resolve to carry out an agenda for which student attention and cooperation are instrumental.[3] This is a discovery that conscientious teachers often make at some early point in their careers:

> I guess I should have figured this out before, but I know I teach differently when I have a lesson I feel real confident about, one that I have a special interest in teaching. I think I'm more focused and in a way I'm more demanding. I expect students' attention when I'm well-prepared myself. And I think they can sense when I've done the job with my own homework. It's almost as though they feel they owe me something in return.

> We were told in methods classes that we would have less discipline problems if we planned well for our classes. Although I admit it didn't mean much to me at the time, I'm finding it to be true now that I'm teaching everyday. I seem to teach more naturally when I have a definite objective and a lesson that I've thought a lot about. And my students seem to have less trouble staying with me.

Conversely, when you allow yourself to approach a class with less personal commitment to a learning agenda, you lack a strong pretext for promoting student involvement. You are less able to generate the kind of teaching momentum that will, at its best, allow classroom management to become an integrated part of the lesson itself. In other words, you put yourself at a psychological disadvantage when you fail to construe the control function as a means to an objective you are committed to accomplish. Under the circumstances, your endeavors to keep the class quiet and orderly are likely to appear artificial. In the students' minds, your attempts to control the class will tend to be perceived as a game. Students get used to having teachers insist on their attention and cooperation without realizing a learning payoff. Their responses can be expected to range from apathy to resentment, thus creating the potential for control problems of one sort or another.

It does of course take a special effort to always have the kinds of lessons that will help to make the management task more intrinsic and less artificial. Yet, teachers who are consistently good classroom managers succeed somehow in keeping themselves mentally prepared to meet their students. Although at times they may agonize over the long hours they spend captive with student groups, they find ways to generate new enthusiasm and to avoid becoming stale (see chapters 1 and 2). Your endeavors to stay vital as a teacher will be helped considerably by your ability to have personally meaningful teaching agendas and an abiding sense of purpose.

Application Exercises

1. What is your own tolerance for inattention or distraction when you are attempting to communicate important thoughts to others in either formal or informal situations? Do you generally keep talking, even when there are indications others are not listening? How insistent on attention are you likely to be when addressing groups of students in a classroom?

2. It has been maintained that a teacher's frame of mind has an important bearing on their effectiveness as a classroom manager. Speculate on the kinds of class management patterns that are likely to be associated with each of the following teacher attitudes: (1) feelings of need to get through a series of activities, (2) feelings of minor irritation over student inattention or poor effort, (3) feelings of quiet confidence and determination, (4) feelings of basic insecurity and indecision, and (5) feelings of passivity or boredom—a "let's see what happens" attitude. Which of these mental sets would you consider most functional for a competent classroom manager? Which are least functional? Why?

SENSITIVITY TO THE LEARNING ENVIRONMENT

To be an effective class manager you must become a skillful orchestrator of group activity. You will need to recognize when students are in sync with you and with one another, to have a feel for the type of classroom atmosphere that supports productive group communication. This is in large part a perceptual skill. It entails an ability to know when environmental conditions are right for the kind of learning activity you are promoting. Environmentally sensitive teachers are quick to notice when student attentions are elsewhere, when they are fidgiting, glancing at one another, or working on an assignment for another subject.[4] They immediately sense when a group is slow to settle down or when they are in an inappropriate mental state.

A major impediment to classroom communication is unrestrained chatter, or the inclination of some students to talk impulsively, often to no one in particular. Impromptu talking has become an increasingly difficult management challenge for teachers in today's schools.[5] Otherwise competent teachers sometimes become conditioned to accept a certain amount of it as though it were normal conduct. These teachers' perceptual faculties seemingly become desensitized to behavior that is clearly detrimental to effective group communication.

There are several main reasons why teachers fail to attend to classroom conditions that are adverse to group learning. Understanding these can be the first step to dealing constructively with the problem. One reason, and the primary emphasis of this section, is the lack of finely tuned classroom sensitivities.[6] This usually involves a failure to work from an internalized image of appropriate classroom conditions and to recognize when these conditions are or are not being met.

Another possible factor, and the main focus of the preceding section, is the absence of an abiding resolve to develop and maintain a classroom atmosphere that contributes to a meaningful teaching goal.[7] This condition can of course contribute to the first one. Teachers who feel disorganized or uncertain may ignore inattention and minor forms of misbehavior out of their own confusion; or they may ignore it out of inability to see student behavior in relationship to a well-defined teaching objective.

Probably the most common reason why some teachers appear insensitive to inattentive and distractive behavior in their classes is a lack of confidence in their management skills. Such confidence deficiencies usually stem from failure to achieve an appropriate skill foundation for approaching class management.[8] The remaining sections of this chapter concentrate on basic techniques to help you control a modern classroom with finesse and self-assurance.

Application Exercise

1. As you observe classrooms in schools where you are involved, practice sizing up the classroom dynamic wholistically. Make an effort to notice not only what the teacher says and does, but what the students are doing, that is, where their attentions are, how they are responding, the attitudes they are reflecting toward the class, and so forth. Are there things you are seeing and hearing to which the regular teacher is failing to attend? If so, do they seem to be behaviors that the teacher is aware of but is choosing to ignore for one reason or another? Decide privately whether these would be appropriate learning environments for your own purposes as a teacher.

LOW-PROFILE MANAGEMENT TACTICS[9]

The most obvious requirement for competent classroom management is an appropriate set of techniques for structuring group activity and dealing with any behavioral problems that may arise. The best classroom managers possess an assortment of low-key tactics for gaining student attention, maintaining a smooth and productive flow of activities, and responding to inappropriate behavior.[10]

Once they have been mastered, many of these manuevers can be performed quite instantaneously and effortlessly, becoming subtle ingredients of your classroom style. Others are more deliberate, requiring a greater degree of calculation and planning to implement. Some of these teacher behaviors are essentially verbal moves, whereas others are nonverbal skills. These management behaviors can be categorized as (1) initiatory behaviors, (2) corrective maintenance behaviors, and (3) preventive maintenance behaviors.

Initiatory Behaviors	Corrective Maintenance Behaviors	Preventive Maintenance Behaviors
Cuing	Eye contact	Scanning
Tuning	Gesturing	I-Messages
Pausing	Moving in	Synchronizing
Restarting	Relocating	Prepping
	Broken-record	Renewing
	Defusing	Positive framing
	Time out	
	Conferencing	
	Referral	

ATTENTION-GETTING AND INITIATORY MANEUVERS

One of the first requirements for effective class control is to be able to obtain student attention with a minimum of effort. The moves you undertake to get a class period underway, to change the direction of class activities, or to reconvene a class after a break are crucial to your success in behavioral management. On these occasions you will need reliable techniques for bringing the focus of attention to the front of the class. Common mistakes are for teachers to attempt to begin lessons before they have everyone's attention or for them to move prematurely into activities before students are in a proper mental set. In these situations, teachers are failing to set the stage for harmonious group instruction.

Your attention-getting and initiatory maneuvers are indispensable preconditioners for what is to follow in a lesson.[11] The ability to perform these tasks skillfully and deliberately can make the succeeding job of controlling the class much less difficult. As such, they will deserve your concentrated attention as you seek to develop workable management strategies.

Cuing

Resourceful teachers sometimes rely on nonverbal cues to indicate that class is about to begin. This may involve positioning yourself on the edge of the desk in front of the class, placing the attendance slip in the door, or raising your hand as a signal for quiet. You may need to alert students to your expectation that this nonverbal sign will be considered equivalent to a call for group attention.

Skillful cuing can also be used as an initiatory device for other purposes, for example, holding a book in the air to accompany a request that the class take that book. The essence of good classroom management is getting students to work cooperatively and productively together in a group setting, so a large share of the task amounts to conditioning students to respond appropriately to indicators that certain behaviors are in order.[12] You can save yourself considerable management stress when you are able to bring students to perform these required behaviors simultaneously with a minimum of commotion or resistance.

Tuning

Although you may use cuing as a nonverbal signal for student attention, the act of initiating a class activity will normally be some sort of verbal opener. It is important that this be approached in a deliberate and purposeful manner. The concern at this stage is to get students in tune with you before any kind of group-centered activity begins to unfold. Teachers who are inclined to ignore this requirement, allowing class proceedings to evolve in a haphazard manner, may find it increasingly difficult to keep students on task for the remainder of the lesson.

In cases where it is necessary to verbally appeal for student attention, you should face the class and make that request in direct and emphatic terms, for example, "I'd like everyone's attention please." If students appear relatively settled at the beginning, teachers may initiate class with a message or an announcement, for example, "Just a reminder that we'll be meeting in the library tomorrow." Or you may begin with an appeal to the class for information of some kind, for example, "I'd like to take just a few minutes to get an idea of how you people are coming on your special projects."

When students appear ready to begin class without special prompting, one of the best ways to commence class activity is to move directly into a lesson set: for example, "Did any of you have occasion to watch the evening news on television last night?"; "I have a question I've been thinking about . . ."; or "There were several comments made during our discussion yesterday that I'd like to follow up on."

Whatever the means for initiating class proceedings, you should make a special effort to get students in sync with you at the beginning of a class period as well as at transition times when it may be necessary to refocus students' attentions. The investments made here will usually make the succeeding management task considerably less strenuous.

Pausing

Pregnant pauses can generally be used to good advantage when seeking group attention. You should use pauses to momentarily wait-them-out when students show an inclination to give competition for the floor. In cases where the competition is relatively mild, pausing for attention should be a first impulse. It is a low-key maneuver designed to provide a slight jar to the awareness of inattentive students. This tactic will normally be effective once you have established a moderately strong verbal presence with your classes. Teachers whose verbal presence is not as well developed may find it less effective.

To get the desired result, teacher pauses should be accompanied by a nonverbal demeanor that helps to communicate "I'm waiting" or "Please give your attention up here, now." You should be prepared to wait several seconds or longer for students to focus their attentions on you. In cases where pauses are ignored by students, you should emphatically announce your expectation that future efforts to wait for attention will bring more immediate compliance. When you continually pause for attention, yet allow students to ignore the stimulus, your conditioning efforts are having negative results. This would indicate the need for a change in management strategy.

Restarting

In keeping with the principle that teachers should insist on concentrated attention when addressing groups of students, another effective low-key move is for you to stop talking in the middle of a sentence and to restart as a sign of refusal to endure inattention, for example, "I'd like to read a short . . . I'd like to . . . I'd like . . ."

As with pausing, restarting is another subtle wait-them-out maneuver that will normally bring positive results when skillfully applied. If several attempts to restart should fail to gain attention, this is likely an indication that a brief time out (to be discussed in a later section) is in order.

Application Exercises

1. Determine several nonverbal cues you might employ as a classroom teacher to signal the need for student attention at the beginning of a class period.
2. As you observe teachers in the schools where you are involved, notice the techniques they use to start classes and to gain student's attentions. Do the majority of these teachers get students in tune with them before they attempt to teach? What attention-getting and initiatory maneuvers do the effective teachers employ most frequently? What do the less successful classroom managers fail to do or do ineffectively when they attempt to initiate classroom activities? Attempt to decide what specific initiatory moves you would use in some of these situations.

CORRECTIVE MAINTENANCE MOVES

To be a capable classroom manager you will need to possess an appropriate set of response behaviors for correcting minor or major instances of misconduct in your classes. You should learn to apply these techniques quietly and efficiently, yet firmly and persistently, while calling as little unnecessary attention to the problem as possible. By working to implement good low-profile corrective strategies, you can begin to insure that you do not inadvertently become a serious distractive influence in your own classroom.[13]

Eye Contact

With a reasonably well-established classroom presence you can usually extinguish minor forms of inappropriate behavior—for example, inattention, private conversation—by focusing your attention on the misbehavior.[14] In many instances the simplest and most effective corrective move is for you to be able to make solid eye contact with these students. Proficient classroom managers often rely heavily on their eyes as basic tools for keeping a class orderly and attentive.[15] This avoids the unnecessary use of the voice to deal with localized and relatively routine problems, thereby averting a potential distraction for students who are productively engaged. Once you have instituted a systematic management policy that includes predictable consequences for chronic misbehavior, a fixating stare is frequently all that is necessary to say "I want your attention" or "Please don't do that again."

Eye contacting as a corrective measure needs to be penetrating. It cannot be done superficially. A fleeting glance in the student's direction will usually be of no consequence. It requires an ability to hold the eye contact long enough to transfer some of the affect that accompanies it. As a beginning teacher, you would do well to rehearse your piercing stares as one of the first and most important management behaviors you will need to perfect.

Gesturing

Like sharp eye contact, well-placed teacher gestures can be beneficial low-profile maneuvers for effecting minor behavioral adjustments during a busy class session. By pointing emphatically to a student's seat, you may effectively signal "Sit down please." By extending an open hand toward one section of the room, you can use sign language to say "Please hold your comment for a moment until we've had a chance to deal with the one that presently has our attention." Or on a different occasion, a deft finger to the lips serves as a reminder to students that the present activity requires silence. Most exemplary classroom managers have cultivated their sign language to the point where they are able to save themselves and their students a lot of unnecessary verbalization, at the same time maintaining orderly and productive classrooms.[16]

Moving In

When for one reason or another eye contact or gesturing fails to remedy minor forms of inattention or distraction, you can often get positive results by moving calmly and deliberately in the direction of the misbehavior.[17] In such cases, your physical presence will generally serve as a corrective without the need for verbal intervention. It may be appropriate at times to culminate the moving-in maneuver by leaning over a student and whispering a quiet message, for example, "We need your attention too," or "I'd like you to put that other book under your seat."

Teachers who make it a practice to move toward and among their students during the course of a lesson tend to fill more psychological space in a classroom than those who remain planted in the front of the room for entire class periods. Among the many possible conditions thought to contribute to successful classroom management, a teacher's ability to know what is going on in the classroom, or "withitness," has been found to be a major factor.[18] Other things being equal, students are generally more respectful and cooperative toward teachers whom they regard as highly perceptive or "with it." They tend to create fewer and less serious management problems for teachers who demonstrate a moment-to-moment awareness of classroom behavioral patterns.

Moving in is a low-profile strategy, then, that can help to curb localized, nonextreme types of misbehavior and to increase the degree of withitness you are seen to possess.

Relocating

When you are aware of the ongoing social dynamics within your classroom, you may on occasion find it appropriate to make certain impromptu changes in seating arrangements. Relocating certain people can be an effective maneuver when you wish to impress on students the need for consistent attention and cooperation. When you have decided on such a change, the move should be made as expeditiously and goodnaturedly as possible, with a minimum of on-the-spot discussion.

Although seat changing is not a cure-all for classroom behavioral problems, if you can accomplish it without bruising a student's self-esteem or triggering more serious management difficulties, you may find it a useful strategy for breaking up unworkable student combinations or bringing inattentive students into closer proximity to the teacher's desk.

Broken-record

In order to maintain good credibility with student groups, there will be occasions when you will need to insist on prompt student compliance with your directives. For example, on asking a student to make a seat change or to refrain from sharpening a pencil in the middle of class, you have a stake in seeing to it that the behavior be carried out as quickly and smoothly as possible. When students are inclined to argue, the *broken-record technique*[19] is usually an effective device for stressing the nonnegotiable nature of the decision and the need for immediate compliance:

> STUDENT: But I need to sharpen my pencil.
>
> TEACHER (SOFTLY): Not now. Please sit down.
>
> STUDENT: But the lead's broken. I need to sharpen my pencil.
>
> TEACHER (CALMLY AND QUIETLY): Later. Please sit down.
>
> STUDENT: But, I . . .
>
> TEACHER (INSISTING, CALMLY AND QUIETLY): Sit down, now.

By persisting with the order (if necessary, up to three or four repetitions), you can normally expect compliance from the average student. It is important that the broken-record technique be applied as calmly and rationally as possible. If the technique does not cause the student to yield, this will ordinarily mean you have a more serious discipline problem on your hands, one that needs to be dealt with through other measures. If you find you have difficulty using the broken-record ploy without communicating negative or confrontational emotions, you should avoid this technique.

Defusing

Sensitive class managers have an eye for emerging situations that could put them in compromising positions or that might threaten the order and productivity of the class. You can usually divert or *defuse* a potentially distractive incident, for example, a student comment you consider a "hot potato," by casually ignoring it, by tactfully changing the subject, or by countering it with sharp wit. For example, when confronted by comments like, "Hey, let's have class outside today" or "Mrs. Smith do you want to come to our party after school," you may, if you prefer not to deal with the remark, deliberately ignore it in the expectation that it will simply dissipate into the woodwork.

In other instances, you can effectively counter an objectionable turn of events by meeting it head-on and resolutely refusing to allow the class focus to be moved in that direction. For example, perceptive class managers are normally able to detect evolving situations where they and their policies could become targets of group complaint sessions. They learn to avoid no-win situations where a few students may attempt to play on the sympathies of the rest of the group to initiate grievances over things like the grading system, homework policies, or class activities. A good tactic for heading off a developing ''get the teacher'' maneuver is to tell the class in firm and forthright language, ''I'm quite willing to listen to your thoughts about the homework assignments. However, I don't want to take class time to subject the whole group to what may well be the complaints of just a few people. If you're interested in talking to me personally about this, see me after class and we'll arrange a time.''

Time Out

Eye contact, gesturing, moving in, relocating, broken-record, and defusing are low-profile strategies for dealing primarily with individual cases of minor misconduct. Their usefulness is limited, however, when it comes to more serious or more pervasive management problems. You must be able to recognize when classroom noise or misbehavior is becoming too widespread to justify continued efforts to combat individual ''brush-fires.'' To attempt to deal with problems on an individual basis when new ones are emerging in other parts of the room can be an exercise in futility and frustration for a teacher. Under the circumstances it may be necessary to stop class proceedings momentarily for a brief ''understanding session'' with the whole group.

Particularly during the early stages of working with a new group of students, it may be appropriate to call periodic *time outs* to review certain behavioral ground rules with the class. When a time-out becomes necessary, it should be regarded as a vital step in the process of conditioning students to operate within the class rules. It should not be treated as an occasion to harangue the group, but rather as an opportunity to remind students of certain behavioral expectations and to review the consequences of continued failure to comply. You should attempt to take a clinical approach to these brief critique sessions. The message should be as positive as possible, with perhaps you yourself accepting some responsibility for the developing group atmosphere: for example, ''Some of you in the group have apparently misunderstood what's expected. Perhaps I haven't made myself clear. Let me review once again . . .''

Conferencing

Private *conferences* for discussing behavioral problems can be thought of as time outs with individual students. This should be the next move when students fail to respond constructively to low-profile stategies or timeouts from the lesson. As with group timeouts, you should be prepared to initiate early private conferences with individuals who are having trouble adapting to your system of expectations. It is to be anticipated that some students will require a measure of early special attention as a means of bringing them into compliance with behavioral requirements.

Depending on the severity of the problem, these private conferences may range from short, spontaneously arranged talks with individuals during or as they are leaving class, to more formal after school meetings with student and parents (see chapter 11). Whatever their degree of formality, they are investments that can serve to correct minor misunderstandings or personality conflicts before they have a chance to become serious behavioral problems.

Referral

In your efforts to maintain positive rapport with your students you should attempt to handle your own discipline problems to the extent this is possible. However, if an occasion arises when it is necessary to refer students to the administrator in charge of discipline, this should be accomplished in as firm, straightforward, and humane a manner as possible. You should make every effort to avoid insulting students, arguing with them, or otherwise creating an embarrassing scene in front of the class. It is also important for you to be well aware of any school-wide discipline policies that might apply, the person to whom you are sending students, and the kind of support you can expect to receive from the school administration.

Application Exercises

1. Based on the corrective maintenance strategies presented earlier, indicate which tactics you would consider appropriate for dealing with the following kinds of student behavior:
   a. Students slow to settle down when I want to start class.
   b. Students arguing with me when I ask them to do something or refrain from doing something.
   c. Students frequently out of their seats when they should not be.
   d. Students chattering impromptu when they should be listening.
   e. Some students not following directions very well.
   f. Students saying insensitive or off-the-wall things at the wrong time.
   g. Some students consistently failing to pay attention.
   h. Some students constantly wanting to converse with their neighbors.
   i. Some students being discourteous or openly hostile toward peers.
   j. Some students working on assignments for other classes.
   k. A student who is usually well-behaved talking to a friend at the wrong time.
   l. A student using foul language to protest an assignment.
2. Imagine that as a classroom teacher you are confronted with the following situation: Jesse and Allison, two of your seventh-grade students, have interrupted class with a loud argument over ownership of a pen. Each is adamant in insisting it belongs to them. It has taken you longer to quiet this disturbance than you would have wished, leaving you with a feeling of irritation that something like this could happen in the middle of an otherwise productive lesson. You have arranged a short private conference with Jesse and Allison to express your concern and to insure this kind of disruption does not happen again. Specify in some detail the substance of your message to these two students.

PREVENTIVE MAINTENANCE STRATEGIES

The majority of your potential discipline problems can be prevented if you takes steps to avoid the conditions that foster them. Generally speaking, students are most likely to become restless and disorderly when they are unsure of what is expected of them, when teachers are neglectful of group dynamics, and when teachers fail to model a positive and constructive approach to classroom activities.[20] Recognizing this, you can anticipate situations that lead to management problems and take actions to prevent these situations from arising. There are certain identifiable strategies that will not only enhance your instructional effectiveness, but will serve as preventive maintenance measures to minimize instances of student misbehavior.

Scanning

As mentioned earlier, one of the main attributes of effective classroom managers is their ability to remain acutely aware of what is going on in their classrooms. Such teachers are able to use their eyes (in concert with their ears) to scan the classroom and instantly size-up behavior, while at the same time attending to other teaching tasks, for example, attendance taking, helping individuals with seatwork, presiding over a discussion.[21] It is crucial that you develop the visual prowess to be able to glance at a class and immediately assess students' state of attention and activity.

Also, as indicated in discussing the perceptual requirements of competent behavioral management, teachers sometimes possess psychological sets that militate against broader awareness of classroom conditions. However, given an appreciation of its importance as a preventive maintenance skill, the ability to use your eyes effectively in the classroom can normally be developed through concentrated practice.

I-Messages

It is important to be firm and direct in communicating your expectations to students. When you are able to assertively state, "I like that" or "I don't like that," you convey a sense of personal responsibility and natural authority that tends to foster student cooperation.[22] Confidently delivered *I-messages* have a personal quality that indicates to students your commitment to obtaining the desired behavior: "I'd like everyone to have completed this project by Friday."

I-messages should be stated as concisely and sincerely as possible, going directly to the area of concern without any hint of ambiguity or equivocation. Some examples:

"Drew, I'd like you to stop talking to Kipp and get back to work." (as opposed to, "You two are being too noisy back there.")

"Shannon, I'd like you to take this first seat in the second row, and Antonio I'd like you to move two seats forward." (as opposed to, "Class, we're going to need to move some seats because you can't stop talking. Shannon and Antonio can you both move away from Kipp?")

"These interruptions are irritating to me. I expect you to wait your turn." (as opposed to, "You're always interrupting. Why are you so rude?")

Synchronizing

As you work to develop an effective class management system, you should take deliberate steps to insure that student groups learn to function in harmony with you. This is especially crucial when beginning to work with a new class (see chapter 5). It is important that when you ask students to pass forward a homework assignment, the group be able to accomplish this in unison without a lot of unnecessary movement or conversation. It is to be expected that when you call for students to locate a particular passage in a textbook, the group be able to do this relatively quickly with a minimum of noise and confusion.

During the first several days with a new group you should find occasions to walk through certain precisely structured activities with the class as a whole. You might, for example, request initial information from students on a three-by-five card. This is an opportunity to give students practice in following simple teacher directions. You should attempt to be as focused and deliberate as possible, using this as an appropriate time to monitor group compliance. By moving briskly among the group and indicating "I'd like to have you do this quickly and quietly please," you set important precedents for future group behavior.

The primary value of such an exercise is to help the students learn to perform as a group within the expectation system you have installed. It is an opportunity for you to begin conditioning the group to work in unison with you, to learn to respond appropriately to your voice, your mannerisms, and your directions.

Prepping

When departing from a traditional teacher-centered format, it is important that students be adequately briefed on relevant procedures and responsibilities before they are expected to perform effectively in more learner-centered activities. With certain kinds of class activities it is especially necessary that you do a thorough job of "prepping" before releasing students to their own devices. Some examples:

1. Students are required to give formal speeches before groups of peers in an English class. This can turn out to be a negative experience for teacher and students if the teacher fails to take prior measures to insure that those making up the audience know their proper roles, that students know the ground rules for evaluating their peers, that individual performers have reasonable "safety valves" in cases of extreme anxiety, and so forth.
2. Classes are divided into a number of individual teams to play half-court basketball on separate outdoor courts during physical education class. Problems can be anticipated if students fail to receive a sufficient briefing on specific objectives and ground rules for these particular games, expectations for etiquette and fair-play, rules for settling disputes, and so forth.
3. Students are broken into groups to discuss a current-events issue in history. Teachers can expect disorganized, nonfocused discussions if this activity is initiated without a detailed scheme for attacking the issue or without provisions for keeping the groups on task during the allotted time, and so forth.

Renewing

Proficient classroom managers are inclined to begin and end class sessions with brief attempts to identify where the class is, where it has been, and where it is going in relation to its learning activities.[23] It is important to regularly renew learning perspectives with your students so class activity does not become stale routine. Losing your grip on the direction of student learning can serve to weaken your effectiveness in behavior control.

Particularly in classes where students become accustomed to working in subgroups or on independent projects, it may take extra effort to maintain a strong sense of class goals and teacher leadership. In activity-based subjects where classes tend to become disjointed, it is advisable to bring students together at the beginning and end of the class period to provide group feedback and reorientation to learning objectives. Besides the educational value of such continued renewal of direction, it is good for you to regularly assert your managerial presence so as to maintain a close working relationship with your students.

Positive Framing

In your role as a teacher you are a central influence on the prevailing atmosphere in your classroom. The attitudes you demonstrate toward day-to-day activities will have a large bearing on the nature and frequency of the management problems you encounter. When your inclination is to construe the business of teaching and learning in positive and constructive terms you stand to avoid much of the negativism and ill-feeling that often characterizes today's crowded classrooms.[24]

There are several specific areas where a positive approach can make a valuable contribution to preventive class maintenance. One has to do with your attitudes toward rules and regulations. Teachers who frame class ground rules in terms of "Do's" rather than "Don't's" show a preoccuption with positive rather than negative behavior. When you use "please walk" as opposed to "don't run" you are modeling a more constructive approach to desired behavior than when you couch your prescriptions in negative language. This can have an important effect on the attitudes and dispositions of young people who are destined to spend long hours in your presence.

Another area where positive methods have preventive maintenance value is in the evaluation of student attitudes and performances. When you go out of your way to notice and comment on desirable aspects of student behavior, you are making investments that can reap important benefits in classroom management terms. For example,

> "I appreciate the efforts you people have been making to get to class on time. The short space between classes makes it difficult for you. I hope you'll all continue to do your best."
> "I thought most of you did a good job with your demonstration speeches today. I also felt you evaluators had some excellent comments to offer. I appreciate all of this good work."

A third way in which you can accentuate the positive rather than the negative is in your customary attitudes toward the day-to-day activities you share with your students. By demonstrating good humor and a reasonable sense of personal control over situations you encounter, you help convey the attitude that school life does not have to be as oppressive and dispiriting as some would have it. On the other hand, teachers who consistently display patterns of irritation and frustration with their students and with the school environment are communicating negative attitudes toward the teaching–learning situation that will tend to rub off on these students. Such an orientation becomes a prime contributor to classroom management problems.

Application Exercises

1. Discuss the advantages of natural authority as opposed to role-based authority when implementing preventative maintenance as a classroom management strategy. What are some of the key indicators of natural authority in teacher–student relationships? What are the main signs that teachers are depending primarily on role-based authority in managing a classroom? Detail some of the interpersonal investments teachers must be prepared to make if they are to work from natural authority in a classroom.
2. Using positive framing, specify the kinds of behavioral expectations (or rules) you would want to communicate to your students as they are being introduced to your classroom management system. Which would have the highest priority?
3. Select a learning activity in your teaching area that would ordinarily call for some teacher ''prepping'' before students are allowed to begin. Plan a short presentation, indicating as precisely as possible what instructions you would give to a group of students who were about to engage in this activity.

A SUMMARY OF CLASSROOM MANAGEMENT GUIDELINES

A summary of basic guidelines and strategies for effective classroom management in today's schools includes the following:

1. Always attempt to have an activity that is meaningful to you and that you anticipate will be meaningful to your students. Have confidence that given a fair chance you can bring it off. This gives you an air of resolve you do not have otherwise.
2. Be aware of the attitudes you are projecting toward class activities. Are they attitudes of confidence, enthusiasm, purpose? Or are you communicating uncertainty, frustration, superficiality? Learn to take inventory of your own moods and to get yourself mentally ready to face a class.
3. Work to avoid falling into a mechanical, matter-of-fact approach to teaching. Be enough of a risk-taker that you are not afraid to put a substantial amount of yourself into your teaching.
4. Make a serious effort to come to grips with the question of what is and is not desirable and tolerable behavior in your classroom. As a teacher of groups of young learners you need to take a stance in favor of what is reasonable and acceptable group behavior as opposed to what is thoughtless and irresponsible.
5. Learn to keep your fingers on the ''pulse of the class.'' Move swiftly and purposefully to control behavior that threatens to distract from the lesson. Do not get in the habit of ignoring minor behavior problems in the hope they will simply go away. In most cases they will not disappear.

6. Get students in tune with you before you attempt to carry on with your teaching agendas. Be careful not to allow slippage here. Do not attempt to talk over the competition. Use pauses, restarts, or lowering of the voice to cause students to attend. Walk through exercises periodically with your students to keep them used to working harmoniously with you.

7. Learn to use silence to advantage and to cultivate your sign language. Your eyes and your gestures are critically important to you here.

8. Anticipate likely consequences of what you ask students to do. Try to avoid always being in a reactive (corrective) position with your classes. Learn to use preventative maintenance to keep yourself out of the corrective mode as much as possible.

9. When it becomes necessary, use corrective maintenance calmly and confidently, but make it penetrate. Do not interrupt the whole class to reprimand one offender whenever it is possible to avoid it.

10. Tell the class in clear terms what you are up to and the behavior you expect of them. Learn to recognize signs that adjustments in strategy are necessary.

11. Make a determined effort to combat uncontrolled chatter in your classes. It is disconcerting to you and to students trying to attend. Teach your students to recognize when impromptu talking is acceptable and when it is disruptive.

12. Do not get in the habit of doing classroom management on the run. Take time to plan for it as a key aspect of your teaching.

SUGGESTED ACTIVITIES AND QUESTIONS

1. What are some of the popular theories of classroom management? What essential differences do you see in these approaches? Attempt to describe the philosophy of classroom management that you have brought with you into teaching. How has the approach presented here supported, changed, or extended your ideas on classroom management?

2. Based on your own experiences with education, take a position on each of the following statements:
   a. Students in today's schools need more discipline than they are presently getting.
   b. Young people should be allowed a maximum of self-expression in the classroom. When students spend most of their time quietly attending to the input of others, they cannot be expected to learn much of importance.
   c. Lack of effective discipline is a major reason for low achievement in our schools.
   d. One of the teacher's main responsibilities is to keep the classroom quiet and orderly for those who want to learn. Students who disrupt the learning atmosphere should be removed from the school.
   e. Teachers need to be more sympathetic toward the predicament of students in today's schools. Most school discipline problems result from the difficult conditions young people have to endure in our crowded, boxlike classrooms.

3. Have you had experience in situations where you were responsible for structuring the behavior of other people, either individuals or groups (e.g., previous teaching, recreation programs, youth camps, babysitting)? How well did you handle this kind of responsibility? Were you able to communicate directions, expectations, dissatisfactions, and so forth, with firmness and confidence? Were you able to use your voice, eyes, and gestures to good advantage in these situations? What has been your experience when it comes to critiquing and correcting the

behavior of other people? What particular feelings, anxieties, or reservations do you have about being in a position of authority like this?

4. What do you anticipate will be your most difficult challenge in terms of classroom management? Based on your present experience, what kinds of behavior problems constitute the most serious challenges to teachers who are striving to have orderly classrooms in today's schools?

5. It has been emphasized that one of the key roles of teachers is to be an effective climate-setter in their own classroom. Discuss some of the things a classroom teacher can do to help develop an appropriate environment for learning.

6. Take the position that classroom management is to a large extent an expression of a teacher's personality. What kinds of personality traits are most functional for carrying out the classroom management system presented here? What sorts of personality characteristics would be least appropriate for implementing the behavioral management strategies outlined in this chapter?

NOTES AND REFERENCES

1. Fritz Redl and William Wattenberg, *Mental Hygiene in Teaching.* New York: Harcourt, Brace and World, 1959, see chap. 9.

2. C. M. Evertson and E. Emmer, "Preventive Classroom Management." In D. L. Duke (Ed.), *Helping Teachers Manage Classrooms.* Alexandria, Va.: Association for Supervision and Curriculum Development, 1982, pp. 22–30.

3. Jere E. Brophy and C. M. Evertson, *Learning From Teaching: A Developmental Perspective.* Boston, Mass.: Allyn and Bacon, 1976, see chaps. 3 and 12.

4. Jacob Kounin, *Discipline and Group Management in Classrooms.* New York: Holt, Rinehart and Winston, 1977, pp. 79–83.

5. Neil Postman, *Teaching as a Conserving Activity.* New York: Delacorte Press, 1979, see chap. 4.

6. For an in-depth treatment of this subject see Thomas L. Good and Jere E. Brophy, *Looking in Classrooms,* 3rd ed. New York: Harper and Row, 1984, chap. 2.

7. Lee Canter, "Be An Assertive Teacher." *Instructor,* 88, no. 60, pp. 96–97.

8. E. T. Emmer, C. M. Evertson, and L. M Anderson, "Effective Classroom Management at the Beginning of the School Year." *Elementary School Journal,* 80, pp. 219–31.

9. The expression "low-profile classroom controls" has been used by Carl Rinne to contrast this approach to classroom management with more conventional high-profile control measures that distract students' attention *first* before focusing on lesson content. See Carl H. Rinne, "Low-Profile Classroom Controls." *Phil Delta Kappan,* September 1982, pp. 52–54.

10. Frederic Jones, *Positive Classroom Discipline.* New York: McGraw-Hill 1987, see chap. 1; and Kounin, op. cit., see chap. 4.

11. A. Weber, "O.K. Kids, Let's Quiet Down." *Teacher Education* 13, no. 2, pp. 23–32.

12. Jones, op. cit., pp. 10–12.

13. Rinne, op. cit., p. 52.

14. Jones, op. cit., p. 26.

15. Ibid.

16. Ibid.

17. Ibid.

18. Kounin, op. cit., pp. 80–81.

19. Lee Canter, *Assertive Discipline: A Take-charge Approach for Today's Educator.* Seal Beach, Calif.: Canter and Associates, 1976., p. 65.

20. Kounin, op. cit., see chap 6.

21. Ibid.
22. Canter, op. cit., p. 62.
23. Kounin, op. cit., pp. 109–115.
24. Jere E. Brophy, *Child Development and Socialization.* Chicago: Science Research Associates, 1977, p. 435.

PART THREE

Following up Instruction

CHAPTER 10

Evaluating and Grading Student Performance

AN INTEGRAL PART
OF EFFECTIVE TEACHING

In designing strategies that allow maximum control of the teaching–learning process, you will want to develop effective procedures for determining whether or not your teaching goals are being met. This will require regular judgments of where you are in relation to where you want to be with respect to student learning. Along with planning and conducting lessons, evaluation of learning progress should be regarded as an integral part of teaching, as an ongoing activity that is present at all stages of instruction.

Although the topic of evaluation has direct relevance to quality control in teaching, it seldom gets the concentrated attention it deserves. Too often it is viewed by teachers as an onerous chore that is peripheral to the instructional process, and a task that requires very little theoretical or practical knowledge. Because of felt pressures to emphasize measurable results of learning over the learning process itself, educators are prone to reducing evaluation of student learning to postinstructional testing. Evaluation thus becomes an activity performed ad hoc in order to assign grades.

There are some good reasons for avoiding this overly simplistic approach and employing a broader concept of evaluation in your own teaching. First, students learn more effectively when evaluational processes are used not just to assess ultimate learning outcomes, but to aid learning activity in all of its stages.[1] In addition, teaching becomes a great deal more efficient and less hit-or-miss when teachers make it a practice to assess students' preknowledge before beginning instruction and their progress throughout the learning cycle.[2]

Moreover, in adopting a broadly based concept of educational evaluation you become less apt to misuse tests and testing when you are able to see evaluational processes in large perspective, as a means to appropriate educational goals. And finally, a balanced, well-designed approach to the assessment of student learning can have a decidedly positive effect on student attitudes toward test taking. One team of educational psychologists has found that students usually object less to evaluation itself than they do to bad testing practices:

It has been our experience that most complaints about testing stem from poor test construction and poorly conceived evaluative strategies in general rather than testing or grading per se. We cannot stress enough the importance of having a clear rationale upon which an evaluation strategy should be founded.[3]

The advantages of a properly conceived system of classroom evaluation will become increasingly apparent to you as you delve further into the subject. This chapter should assist you in developing a functional theory of evaluation by exposing you to some ideas and terms that are fundamental to the topic. It also provides practical suggestions for constructing, administering, and scoring classroom tests, and guidelines for grading student performance.

MEASUREMENT AND EVALUATION

In attempting to assess the learning progress of your students, it is important for you to recognize the difference between measuring and evaluating student performances. A measuring instrument like a formal test can provide you with quantitative data that you may wish to take into consideration when making evaluative judgments about student achievement. But a particular measurement has no meaning until you assign a value to it. A score of sixty-five on an exam says very little about the quality of the student's performance. That must first be interpreted, or compared with a *standard,* before it becomes an evaluation. In short, measurement is a *descriptive* activity, whereas evaluation involves a *judgment* based on values and standards. Or, as Gage and Berliner summarize the distinction, "Measurement gives us numbers. Human judgment, concern, and interpretation turn those numbers into evaluations."[4]

This distinction has some important implications for the evaluative decisions you will make in teaching. For one thing, it cautions against the tendency to equate evaluation with testing. In recognizing evaluation to be the larger concept and the end toward which testing is a potential vehicle, we are reminded that a test is not the only means, nor in many cases the best means, of sampling learning progress. Depending on the subject, the grade level, and the kind of learning being promoted, teacher's informal observations, student projects and written assignments, and other kinds of learning input, may provide more pertinent information for evaluative decisions than a written test. Learning objectives in the affective domain, for example, will normally require informal rather than structured means of evaluation. Test scores and other measurement data have no inherent meaning until we as teachers give them meaning, so the responsibility lies with us to determine their relevance to our professional purposes. In order to do this you will need to know what constitutes a good test.

As you become aware of the critical difference between measuring and evaluating learning progress in your teaching, you become conscious of the importance of the standards we use to interpret the data obtained from tests and other samples of learning performance. How much importance then should we attach to a particular performance sample? Should our evaluations of learning achievement involve comparisons of students with one another or should our ratings be based on fixed standards? What are the circumstances that would cause you to choose one approach rather than the other? Are there occasions when it would be appropriate to base your evaluations of student learning on individual progress or improvement?

Two Kinds of Evaluation

As indicated, there is often a tendency for school people to treat evaluation as primarily testing, and to regard it as something teachers do at the end of courses or units to measure what students have learned for purposes of assigning grades. This prevalent and necessary form of evaluation attempts to summarize and appraise students' knowledge after they have learned. Appropriately enough, educators have come to refer to this type of assessment as *summative* evaluation.[5] It is not always necessary to depend on written tests as a basis for summative evaluations. Depending on the subject, grade level, and inclinations of the teacher, it may be deemed appropriate to use oral conferences, research papers, long-term creative projects, or physical performances of one sort or another to measure achievement at the end of a concentrated period of instruction.

Another important function of teacher evaluation is to obtain initial and ongoing information that will assist students to learn better and help you to teach better. These are assessments you make of student aptitudes and abilities prior to instruction and while learning is in its developmental stages, determinations that allow you to make good strategic decisions as you proceed with a lesson or unit. Accordingly, they have been labeled *formative* evaluations.[6] The feedback you receive from formative evaluations is helpful in deciding whether changes in subsequent learning experiences are needed and in determining specific learning errors that need to be corrected.

Pretesting is an attempt to assess student knowledge and abilities before undertaking a particular lesson or unit as a means of determining particular strengths or skill weaknesses that need to be taken into consideration. Information from such tests can be used to place students in appropriate groups, to assign suitable tasks to students, or to review prerequisite lessons with students who lack these prerequisites.

Observational methods, in addition to paper-and-pencil tests, are also useful in monitoring student progress. There is evidence to show that student learning is aided by well-placed teacher feedback throughout the learning process (e.g., discussing correct answers after a quiz).[7] Several factors have been cited in an effort to account for this, including, (1) it enables students to monitor their own progress toward educational goals, (2) it focuses student attention on what is important, and (3) it raises the students' level of interest.[8]

ORGANIZING YOUR EFFORTS

As you plan each unit of instruction you should give some concentrated attention to the various means you will employ to assess student learning. There will ordinarily be a number of sources of input available to you in your efforts to gain information on student progress and development, including both formal and informal means of evaluation.

Informal Observations

Your system of informal assessment will normally entail day-to-day observations of student behavior to determine such things as:

1. The amount and quality of their participation in class activities
2. The kinds of questions they ask both during and after class
3. The cooperative learning skills they demonstrate while working on group projects
4. The way they receive directions and other important information
5. The way they respond to teacher questions
6. Their ability to follow tasks through to completion
7. The kind of initiative they demonstrate in seeking information and attacking problems
8. The kinds of verbal skills they demonstrate in expressing thoughts and explaining ideas
9. Their ability to manage time and to complete assignments promptly

This type of informal evaluation requires observation skills that often take a period of time to develop. It will involve monitoring the behavior of individual students while performing other classroom activities.

You can take steps to make your classroom observations as objective and reliable as possible by (1) determining in advance what to look for, and (2) setting up a checklist, rating scale, or some other written guide to help organize these observations.

Formal Sources of Evaluation

Besides written exams, the following are some of the more prominent sources of formal evaluative input available to classroom teachers:

1. Written Work—including themes, lab reports, workbook exercises, book reports, math exercises, poems, research papers, and journals
2. Oral Work—including individual reports, class discussions, panels and debates, simulation games, and oral recitations
3. Special Projects and Performances—including shop projects, arts and crafts projects, athletic activities, speech and drama performances, and music activities

The most widely used means of formal evaluation are written tests. Test construction and test utilization are treated in considerable depth in succeeding sections of this chapter.

Announcing Your Policy

Having determined what your basic approach to evaluation will be, it is important that you do not keep this information to yourself. Students need to know how, when, and on what criteria their work will be judged. This can help to reduce some of the anxiety students typically experience over evaluation and test taking. It is advisable to furnish students with an initial written statement of the testing policies you plan to follow. Your statement should include the following kinds of information:

1. When you plan to give tests or quizzes. Whether you intend to have weekly or monthly tests. The amount of advance notice that will be provided. Necessary

distinctions between regular unit quizzes, surprise quizzes, and larger summative exams.

2. The type of tests to be expected. Examples of previous test items and indications of the amount of material to be covered will be helpful information to students.

3. Your standards of evaluation. Whether you plan to include spelling, grammar, and neatness in marking exams. How test scores are related to the course or subject-matter grade?

4. Your policy toward makeup exams. What students can do to make up a test following an absence. Whether students will be allowed a second chance after a poor performance on a particular exam.

5. Any other important general information about procedures you plan to follow in reviewing for tests, in administering, scoring, and returning exams, and in dealing with dishonesty during a test.

Insist that students understand these criteria and share this information with their parents to insure that both students and parents will be familiar with your evaluation policies.

WHAT IS A GOOD TEST?

Validity

Once we understand that there are important qualifications to be met before a particular sample of student learning can be used as a basis for evaluation, one of the first questions we need to ask is what in theory makes a good test? First, the test must be *valid,* or in other words, capable of measuring what it is supposed to measure. Although this may sound self-evident, it turns out that without careful attention to this requirement a test can easily be extraneous to the learning you are or should be attempting to promote. For example, in an English class unit on public speaking, written tests of cognitive knowledge may be invalid if your purpose is to make judgments about speaking ability.

A valid test should also sample the various elements of knowledge that were taught, in proportion to the emphasis that was placed on them. If a group of students had spent the bulk of their class time memorizing rules of grammar with very little time devoted to application, it would not be valid to follow up with a test that stressed the ability to use these rules in context. This points up the need to have clearly stated instructional objectives so both you and your students will know precisely what knowledge is being evaluated.

Reliability

Another major consideration in judging the adequacy of tests is the consistency with which a particular test can be expected to produce useful data. If you give a student a test on Monday and a similar test on Friday, and the resulting scores prove the same or close, you could judge the tests to be *reliable.* If the scores differ significantly, you would have some legitimate doubts about the test's reliability. To do the job for which it is intended, a test must provide consistent and dependable measurement. When a test is reliable one can say that its measurement is fairly accurate because chance errors and other inconsistencies have been largely eliminated. The reliability of tests can also be affected by factors external to the test itself, such as the test environment or the state of mind of the test-taker. The physical condition or anxiety level of the student, or a student's preferences for oral, written, or activity tests, can each affect the ability of a test to deliver accurate and consistent results. There are a number of things you can do to enhance the reliability of the tests you use.

Objectivity

A good test should also be *objective*. A test can be considered objective to the extent that the personality of the examiner does not affect the way it is scored. In other words, there should be precautions taken to insure that the biases, prejudgments, or personal feelings of the scorer have no bearing on the results. A truly objective test would have to be scored in exactly the same way by every scorer. The category of measurement devices commonly referred to as *objective tests* attempts to build-in objectivity by allowing one clearly established right answer per item, and by a scoring system that allows for no ambiguity or examiner bias in marking the exam. At the same time, one of the reputed shortcomings of essay examinations is their subjectivity, or their vulnerability, to reader biases and changing dispositions while scoring.[9]

As we begin to apply the criteria of validity, reliability, and objectivity to various types of tests, we become aware of the difficulty in locating or constructing an instrument that adequately satisfies all three criteria. A test that is long on objectivity, may turn out to be short on validity. For example, while touting the inherent objectivity of true–false or multiple-choice tests, we must also recognize the relatively narrow range of knowledge they can adequately test. When we attempt to use them to sample other than memory-level knowledge, their validity immediately becomes suspect. Similarly, whereas reliability is an important property for measuring instruments to have, it does not guarantee a good test.

The indispensable quality that all good tests must have is validity. "As long as validity is not sacrificed, the more objective the instrument the better. However, a valid instrument may be a good instrument even though it is not objective, while an objective instrument that is not valid is always worthless."[10]

Concrete suggestions for making classroom tests as valid, reliable, and objective as possible are treated in more detail in the following sections on test construction.

CONSTRUCTING CLASSROOM TESTS

General Guidelines for Test Construction

The following are some general guidelines to keep in mind as you approach the work of test construction.

1. Have some questions that are easy enough for every student in the class to answer correctly. Begin with the least difficult question so all students will get a good start and will be encouraged to go on to the following questions.
2. Make test items reflect instructional aims and the content taught. Test teaching

objectives in proportion to their importance. If the test overemphasizes, under-emphasizes, or omits representative portions of learned content, it will not be valid.

3. Watch the vocabulary level of test items. To be valid your test should measure the content students have learned, not reading ability (unless previously stated).

4. Make it easy for students to demonstrate what they have learned. Do not allow glibness, writing ability, or speed in test taking to be a factor in student success. Everyone should have a chance to do well on the test.

5. Make sure test directions are entirely clear to students. Determine that no student should miss an item because they misunderstood the details for answering it. Tricky, obscure questions spoil the test's validity.

6. Use only a few types of items, for example, true–false, multiple-choice. Too many different types of items may confuse the students. Place all items of the same type together so students are not confused.

7. Include several test items for each objective. This will give students ample opportunity to demonstrate competence, thus avoiding the possibility that a chance error could give a false assessment of ability.

8. Include all the information and material students need to complete each item. When you must interrupt to provide missing information or when students find it necessary to stop working to seek clarifications, the reliability of the test is affected.

9. When one of your purposes is to determine differences in students' achievement, do not allow choices in the questions to be answered. You must use exactly the same measuring instrument for everyone, otherwise you jeopardize validity.

10. Make more items than you will use. Select only the best items, then rework them as necessary to make the test reflect your best professional effort. The final product off the ditto or copy machine should be neat, grammatically perfect, and a clear format to follow.

Choosing and Preparing
Individual Test Items

The preceding guidelines for constructing tests in general apply specifically to the development of objective tests. Among the most common varieties of objective test items are true–false, completion, multiple-choice, and matching questions. Following an examination of these objective test items, we focus on essay (or subjective) test questions.

True–False Questions.   In this familiar type of objective test item, students are given statements they are to judge for accuracy. This kind of test can be useful for finding out if students can discriminate fact from opinion and valid from invalid generalizations. You may increase difficulty and discourage guessing by asking students to qualify their answers with a sentence telling why they answered one way rather than another. On the surface, a true–false test seems simple to construct, but it is usually a challenge to produce true–false items that are free from ambiguity or false leads. By taking the following precautions, you can avoid some of the main difficulties in making good true–false tests:

1. Avoid making broad generalizations into questions. Words like *always* and *never* can serve as clues that statements are false.
2. Attempt to keep a balance between true (T) and false (F) statements.
3. Avoid trivial items that may obscure the main ideas, for example, ''The color of your textbook is blue.''
4. Make the test long enough so that guessing is not a major factor in its reliability.
5. Avoid using negative statements as items when possible. If you do use negatives, be sure the key word is underlined or capitalized to call attention to it (i.e., NOT, NEVER).
6. Make the true items the same average length as the false items. Students sometimes discover a pattern of false items being short and general, whereas true statements often contain qualifications that make them longer.
7. Use conversational phrasing for questions. Textbook wording is likely to test memory power but not understanding.
8. Avoid any discernable pattern of true–false answers. Scatter the true and false items randomly throughout the test.

True–false tests have the following major strengths:

1. Items can be scored easily and objectively.
2. Directions to true–false items are easy for students to understand.
3. A good number of items can be answered in a short time.
4. They are good for initiating discussions and for pretesting.
5. They are a quick way to test for simple factual knowledge.

These are the main weaknesses of true–false tests:

1. It is difficult to avoid simplistic or ambiguous items because statements are seldom entirely true or entirely false.
2. Student performance is subject to guessing and chance effects.
3. True–false tests tend to overemphasize rote memorization.

Completion Questions.   These are statements with important words or phrases left out that are to be written in by the test-taker. These items are useful in testing for specific information because they require that the student supply information that is not included in the test. The following ideas should be helpful to you in developing completion questions:

1. Be sure students know what is expected in terms of length and detail in their answers.
2. Attempt to word the item so only one correct answer is possible. A poor question is, ''Michelangelo was a famous _____ .''

3. Supply enough context in the statement to give the item meaning. The following is an example of an item with an inadequate ratio of words provided to words omitted:

    "The _____ protects _____ , liberty, and _____ ."

4. Avoid grammatical clues such as a blank following the letter *a,* which indicates that the missing word(s) would begin with a consonant.

5. Design questions so only significant words are omitted. A poor example would be, "Washington (crossed) the Delaware to defeat the Hessians."

6. Use a direct question if possible, avoiding textbook language.

These are some main advantages of completion items:

1. They are easy to construct and relatively easy to mark.
2. They allow a rapid survey of information over a large area of content.
3. Students find it difficult to guess right answers.
4. They are especially appropriate when recall is important.

Some of the central weaknesses of completion tests are:

1. It is difficult to construct items that call for only one correct answer.
2. When used exclusively, completion items may encourage memorization without understanding.
3. They cannot be scored mechanically.

Multiple-choice Questions.   This is the most commonly used form of objective test, and is generally applicable in all subject areas. A multiple-choice item contains two major components, its stem and its alternative answers. The *stem* may be phrased as a question or a simple statement: "Most automobiles are propelled by." Of the alternative responses, one is the correct answer and the others are the *distractors,* so-called because they are intended to distract or mislead students who are not certain of the correct answer. In this case, the alternative responses might be:

a. a steam engine
b. an electric storage battery
c. an internal combustion engine
d. a solar cell

Multiple-choice questions are relatively versatile types of test items because, depending on the complexity of the item, they can assess memorization learning and also higher-level cognitive objectives. To produce good items requires considerable skill and attention to detail. The following guidelines apply to the development of multiple-choice tests:

1. The stem of the question should be clear and contained separately from the possible answers. If the stem is in the form of an incomplete statement, it

should provide enough meaning so students will not have to read the answers to understand the question.

2. At least four responses should be provided. This will decrease the likelihood of guessing correctly and increase the validity of the item by requiring students to be more discriminating.

3. Questions that call for "best answers" are more useful for measuring higher thought processes than those that call for correct answers.

4. Make all the responses plausible, and when testing at higher levels, increase the similarity in the choices under each item in order to better test the powers of discrimination.

5. If you can, avoid the use of negatively stated items. These tend to be somewhat more ambiguous than positively stated items.

6. Distribute the order of correct answers randomly and equally, avoiding any discernable pattern such as favoring first or last choices.

7. Each item should test individual information that gives no clues to other items in the test.

8. Use a level of English that is simple and clear. The language should be understandable enough for the poorest readers to comprehend.

These are the primary strengths of multiple-choice items:

1. A wide range of subject matter can be tested in a short time.

2. They can be administered and scored quite rapidly.

3. Student guessing can be neutralized by using four or five alternative answers in each question.

4. Items can be written to test for relatively fine discriminations in students' knowledge in a number of subject areas.

5. They can be used to test both simple memory and higher mental processes.

The most significant disadvantages of multiple-choice tests are:

1. Good items are difficult and time consuming to write.

2. Like all structured response items, they do not require students to generate information in their own language.

3. They normally require a level of concentration and discrimination on the part of the test-taker that may make them inappropriate for use with younger learners.

4. Mechanical scoring of items requiring complex thinking provides no basis for checking the thought processes of students.

Matching Questions.   Matching items are appropriate means of testing for correct associations between related classes of information, such as names-dates, people-events, authors-books, terms-definitions, laws-illustrations, and the like. They are well-adapted to testing *who, what, where,* and *when* areas but not to measuring understanding as distinguished from mere memory. In constructing these items, two lists are drawn up and the test-taker must match each item in the first list with the one in the second list to which the relationship is closest. The following are suggestions for constructing good matching items:

1. Include no more than ten to twelve items to be identified or matched. Lengthy matching questions can be confusing and will take too long to complete.
2. There should be more items in the "answers" column than in the "questions" column. If the numbers are equal, students will be helped to make correct choices at the end through a process of elimination.
3. All items in each column should be in the same general category. For example, events and their dates should not be mixed with events and the names of famous persons.
4. Directions should clearly state what the basis for matching is. The directions should specify if choices may be used more than once.
5. You should attempt to keep both columns on one page to avoid the confusion of flipping back and forth for answers.

The main advantages of matching questions are:

1. Their compactness allows you to test a good deal of factual information in a short period of time.
2. They are particularly appropriate for surveying knowledge of definitions, events, personalities, and so forth.
3. They are easy to score.

The most prominent weaknesses of matching items are:

1. They are not well-suited to measuring the understanding of concepts or the ability to organize and apply knowledge.
2. It is difficult to avoid giving clues that tend to reduce validity.
3. The format requires the use of single words or very brief phrases.

Essay Questions.   Essay tests require the learner to supply an extended written response to a stated question or problem. They are appropriate for measuring ability to select and organize ideas, writing abilities, and problem-solving skills requiring originality. The student must create an answer from memory or imagination, so these items are capable of testing a higher level of knowledge than most objective tests. Essay tests are still widely used, particularly by high school teachers, although they are often criticized for their subjective nature.

The following are guidelines to be used in writing essay questions:

1. Make your wording of the question as clear and explicit as possible. It should precisely define the direction and limits of the desired response. It is important that all students interpret each question in the same way; otherwise, you may have them writing good answers to the wrong question.
2. Include more items requiring shorter answers rather than a very few questions

requiring long answers. This will allow a better sampling of subject-matter knowledge and encourage more precise responses.

3. Make a conscious decision about whether or not to include grammar and sentence structure in your evaluation of answers. You may wish to give two marks, one for the substance of the answers and the other, less crucial grade, for form and writing style. Be sure to announce your decision to the class before they begin the exam.

4. Provide students with guidance on how to use their time in answering the items. Suggest approximate time limits and answer lengths for each question so students will distribute their time appropriately.

5. Write the question while planning the unit of instruction rather than near the conclusion of the unit. This will help you to focus more clearly on the objectives of the unit as you are constructing the test.

6. In general, do not allow students a choice on essay items unless there are different objectives for different students in the course. All students must take the same test if you are to have a sound basis for comparing scores.

7. In general, do not ask questions that only sample a student's opinion or attitude without having the student justify the answer in terms of the cognitive content of the course.

8. Have a colleague critique the test as a means of alleviating ambiguity and misinterpretations.

Essay questions have the following main strengths as evaluative instruments:

1. They can measure more than the ability to remember information.
2. They encourage students to learn how to organize their own ideas and express them effectively.
3. Students tend to use better study habits when preparing for essay tests.
4. They permit teachers to comment directly on the reasoning processes of individual students.
5. They require writing only a few items for a test.
6. The problem of guessing is greatly reduced.

The following are the most prominent disadvantages of essay tests:

1. Answers may be scored differently by different teachers or by the same teacher at different times.
2. They are usually very time consuming to score.
3. Only a relatively few questions on limited areas of knowledge can be answered in a given period of time.
4. They do not efficiently measure purely factual information.
5. Students who write slowly may not be able to complete the test even though they may possess adequate knowledge.

Application Exercises

1. Read each of the following test questions to determine whether they qualify as good items. If you identify deficiencies in a particular item, rewrite that item to make it a better test question.
   A. Multiple-choice Questions:
      1. Good multiple-choice items (a) are easy to write; (b) can only test memorized content; (c) are better than essay items; (d) there is no such thing; (e) can test a wide range of content.
      2. Which of the following characteristics is not true of completion test items, but is an important distinguishing attribute of matching tests, multiple-choice questions, and true–false items?
         a. They are objective test items.
         b. They require knowledge recognition but not production.
         c. Much more difficult to construct.
   B. Matching Question:
      1. Completion items   a. Depend on good distractors
      2. Multiple-choice items   b. Most susceptible to guessing
      3. Matching items   c. Best for testing associations
      4. Objective tests   d. Usually simple to score
      5. True–false items   e. Tend to resist one correct answer
   C. True–false Questions:
      1. The advantages of true–false tests include the ease with which they can be constructed and scored, the simplicity of their directions, their ability to test the discriminatory powers of students, and the relative number of items that can be answered in a short time.
      2. Because of the everpresent potential for guessing, true–false tests should always contain at least twenty-five items.
   D. Essay question:
      1. Discuss essay tests compared to objective tests.
2. Construct an essay question to test knowledge of some section of this chapter. Write a model answer for that question. Share your question with at least two of your peers and ask them to answer it. Compare their answers with your model answer, and then respond to the following questions:
   a. Was the question clearly stated? Did you get comparable answers from each of the other people?
   b. Did any of the responses include ideas other than those in your model answer?
   c. Did this exercise provide any insights into the writing and scoring of essay questions that might be helpful to you as a teacher?
3. Produce eight to twelve objective test items over material covered in this chapter. Include items from each of the four formats: true–false, completion, multiple-choice, and matching. ask one of your peers to answer these test items. After providing this person with the correct answers, give them an opportunity to critique your test.

ADMINISTERING AND SCORING TESTS

Guidelines for Administering a Test

To administer formal tests in a systematic and controlled manner will require some careful preplanning on your part. You will also need to use your best classroom management skills to insure that test security and proper testing atmosphere are maintained throughout the exam. Your first effort should be to incorporate a proper routine for test taking in your classes. This will entail establishing certain "test-day" expectations, then conditioning students to perform according to the procedures you have set up. The following are steps you can take to make the testing process as smooth and efficient as possible:

1. Once the test has been prepared, do a careful job of proofreading to be sure it contains no errors. The test should be neat and highly legible with no typos or spelling errors. You should also be certain that all directions are clear and make special note of any items that need to be further explained before students begin the test.

2. Decide on an appropriate seating arrangement. Plan to have students spread out as much as possible to remove any possible temptations toward cheating. Have students place books, notebooks, and other extraneous material under seats or away from the test area before starting the exam.

3. Make sure the physical condition of the room is conducive for test taking. Improper heat, light, or ventilation, as well as distracting noises or interruptions, can affect student concentration and thereby reduce the reliability of the test.

4. Be sure students have everything they need before the test begins. Check to see that each student has a good copy of the complete test. Any other materials, such as maps, extra paper, or special pencils should be supplied prior to beginning the test.

5. Have a controlled procedure for distributing test materials and beginning the exam. To allow all students to start at the same time you may want to have them keep tests face down on their desks until everyone is ready to begin.

6. If it is necessary to explain last-minute corrections, do this before the test begins and also write the explanation or correction on the chalkboard so students can be reminded after the test begins. Try to avoid interrupting with announcements once the test is underway.

7. Ask students to look carefully at the test and ask questions before the test begins so they will have less need to ask questions once they have begun.

8. Make a conscientious effort to monitor test-taking behavior throughout the exam. Be sure all students are occupied with the test and that everyone's eyes remain on their own work. Regardless of the maturity level and trustworthiness of the group, it is not good practice to ignore the class once the test begins. By standing strategically at the back of the room, then quietly roaming among the rows from time to time, you help to insure proper test-taking behavior on the part of your students.

9. Have students raise their hands to receive assistance if a question arises once the test has begun. Try to avoid discussing questions aloud with a student while other students are working.
10. Be sure students know what they are to do with their tests and their time if they finish early. Insist that early finishers respect the needs of those who are still working.

Procedures for Scoring Tests

The procedures you will use to score students' tests should be determined in advance. It is usually advisable to prepare an answer key, indicating the acceptable answers, as you are constructing the test. This is when you are highly focused on the specific objectives you are testing and the most appropriate responses. One of the easiest ways to make a key for an objective test is to fill in the proper responses on a blank test, which can then be placed against the answer column of the tests you are scoring.

Essay exams will require a more strategic approach. As indicated earlier, objectivity in scoring is a major concern with essay questions. However, there are some basic measures you can take to make your scoring of essay items as objective as possible, including:

1. Be sure you have appropriate responses firmly established before you begin scoring the exams. Write these out as though you were taking the exam yourself. Determine the number of points each answer is worth and show on your model answer how these points will be distributed. Use this material as your key.
2. Score only one question at a time for all papers. This increases the likelihood that you will use the same standard for every student. If you decide to give credit for points not included in your answer key, be sure to reread papers already scored to insure everyone is given credit for the additional point.
3. Attempt to read all papers without knowledge of the "author." One way of keeping papers anonymous is by asking students to write their names on the back rather than the front of the test. Another is to number the tests, then provide a separate sheet of paper on which the student signs his name and test number. Whatever you can do to counteract potential biases or preconceptions as you read essay exams will help to make them more objective and reliable measures of student learning.
4. If there are a large number of papers, do not attempt to score them all at one sitting. If possible, take several sessions to read all of the questions. This will help you to prevent "reader fatigue" and a resultant lack of consistency in your scoring pattern.

METHODS OF GRADING

Once you have obtained scores from a test or other sample of student achievement, the scores must be compared with some available standard in order for you to assign grades to those performances. There are three basic standards of comparison you can use in evaluating and grading student learning: (1) the performances of other students, that is, the norms of the group, (2) performance criteria contained in set objectives, and (3) a student's own past learning performances.

When evaluation is based on comparisons with the work of other students, the evaluation system is said to be *norm-referenced.* When student performance is rated according to a preestablished standard, this type of evaluation is called *criterion-referenced.* If teachers have occasion to use the previous performances of individual students as the basis for judging learning achievement, this approach is referred to as *self-referenced* evaluation. Each of these three evaluation standards commonly used in our schools has its distinct advantages and disadvantages. It will be important for you to have a general understanding of these different approaches to grading and to be acquainted with some practical methods for arriving at student grades.

Norm-referenced Evaluation

The traditional way of assigning grades has been to divide students into categories based on what was conceived to be a natural distribution of abilities in any normal population. According to this bell-shaped classification system, approximately one-sixth of the students receive As and Bs, the middle two-thirds are assigned Cs, and the bottom one-sixth either fail or barely pass. In recognition of its shortcomings, the bell-shaped curve is seldom used in our present schools, although most teachers still adhere to a modified and generally more liberal grading curve that judges student learning performance in terms of comparisons and competitions with peers.

Norm-referenced evaluation continues to be popular because it reflects the entrenched expectations of educators, employers, and society at large that academic learning will be a competitive endeavor. Also, the system of letter grades it produces is one that has come to be well-understood by students and parents and is useful in keeping school records. Some good examples of norm-referenced evaluation instruments are the standardized achievement tests prepared by test publishers and national assessment agencies. These tests compare academic performances of individual students, classes, or schools with what are considered normal or typical performance levels for students throughout the country.

In the final analysis, scores made by a student on a norm-referenced test can tell us something about that student's performance compared with the average student, but they give little insight into the student's learning strengths and weaknesses. Unfortunately, these scores and grades do not have a universal meaning to the educators and others who are called on to interpret them. The meaning of letter grades will often vary greatly from teacher to teacher and from one school or school system to another.

Criterion-referenced Evaluation

Criterion-referenced evaluation systems rate student performance against an absolute standard. The emphasis here is on mastery of prespecified skills or information rather than on meeting or exceeding group norms. Thus, it is conceivable that everyone could pass, or, by the same token, everyone could fail. Some advocates of mastery learning have proposed strategies whereby all students in a class could achieve close to 100 percent success in satisfying stipulated learning criteria.[11] However, because criterion-referenced evaluation seldom produces the spread in scores that is obtainable with norm-referenced systems, many educators would consider it less appropriate for assigning grades.[12]

Others have argued for more criterion-referenced evaluation in our schools, claiming it has these merits:

1. It enables students to tell at a glance how they have progressed in a given area of learning.
2. It can be used in ways that are more individual–student–centered than norm-referenced tests (e.g., standards can be adapted to ability levels of students).
3. It makes it more possible for educational administrators to control what students learn and the rate at which it is learned.
4. The goals of mastery learning can be stated in behavioral terms, thus making it easier for agencies outside the school to monitor accountability.[13]

Self-referenced Evaluation

There have long been serious criticisms of both norm-referenced and criterion-referenced evaluation systems in terms of their appropriateness for assigning grades. Some educators have considered both approaches to be based on arbitrary standards, and thus to be unfair to students.[14] Many humanistically oriented critics have maintained that the only justifiable form of educational evaluation is one that allows learners to be in competition with themselves.[15] From this point of view, a teacher's evaluative judgments should be based on the progress or improvement students have made in their learning performances since the beginning of instruction. Depending on the amount of pressure teachers feel to meet group norms or preset standards, there is probably room for more self-referenced evaluation in our schools, particularly in areas where external standards of achievement are less pronounced.

Finding Your Own Method

After examining some of the underlying theory together with advantages and disadvantages of different standards of evaluation, you will need to make some important practical decisions regarding a grading system for your classes. The pressing need to have an effective method of assigning grades will become apparent to you as you prepare to mark your first set of papers.

The Fixed-percentage System. One widely used method of grading is a criterion-referenced approach that assigns letter grades on the basis of percentages of correct answers. Using this system, you might, for example, determine that a score of 87 to 100 percent is necessary for an A, 73 to 86 percent for a B, and so on. When the standard is preestablished, it tends to remove any surface ambiguity from the evaluation process insofar as the student is concerned. Although some students may find it difficult to meet the criteria for a top grade, there can be no question in their minds concerning these criteria. Students are competing with an absolute standard rather than with one another, so it is theoretically possible for all students to do well. It is also conceivable that everyone could fail on a particular test or assignment.

The popularity of this fixed-standard method of grading is due in large part to its perceived objectivity and the belief that the standard determines the grade, not the teacher's subjective preferences or the student's ranking within the group. However, teachers' subjective influence is still very much present at the point where they determine the difficulty of the test and the percentage of correct answers required for a top grade.

For your purposes as an evaluator, a criterion-referenced system such as this makes the work of grading relatively cut-and-dried. Once you have designed and scored the test and stipulated the standard, grading becomes mostly a matter of mathematics. This fact could convince you to seek a system of grading that is less absolute, one that allows more last-minute control over the grading process once you have had a chance to scrutinize test results.

The Flexible-distribution System.   Another method of assigning grades to student tests or papers is to start with a general idea of the proportions of students you want to receive As, Bs, Cs, and so on. Then use the score distribution pattern to help you decide how to apportion these grades. This is essentially a norm-referenced method of grading, but one that allows you considerable flexibility in determining how the grades are apportioned. It is most appropriate when you have a relatively small number of papers or tests to grade, the distribution of scores is quite random, and you want to retain some last-minute discretion in assigning grades. The procedure works as follows. Suppose that after tallying the scores of a forty-five-item test for a class of twenty-eight students, you end up with the following distribution pattern:

```
                                36
            26          32    35 36 38 39 40        42
   13  17  23  26  28  31  32  33  35  36  38  39  40  41  42  43
                        32          36          40
```

On examining this layout of scores, you discover that the lowest score was less than half of the highest (probably confirming that there should be both As and Fs). You also note that the middle or "median" score was thirty-six (scores that fall around the median in norm-referenced systems would ordinarily be assigned Cs). The only significant breaks in the distribution pattern were at the lower end, where the two or three lowest scores tended to stand out (natural breaks in the distribution are often good places to establish grade breaks). Finally, you notice that close to two-thirds of the class scored in the thirty-five to forty-three range, showing a relatively large proportion of high scores, but no perfect scores.

Before attaching grades to the scores you might also take into consideration the difficulty of the test or assignment, student attitudes approaching the test, whether it is early or late in the school year, and any other factors that might cause you to want to send a particular kind of message in grading these performance samples.

Based on your initial sense of appropriate grade proportions, the score distribution pattern you have discovered, and other relevant considerations, you might well decide to have the majority of the grades fall in the B and C categories, with a relatively small number of As and Ds, and one or two Fs:

42–43	A	15%
41	A –	
40	B +	25%
38–39	B	
36	C +	
32–35	C	40%
31	C –	
28	D +	
26	D	11%
23	D –	
below 23	F	8%

This method of grading is basically norm-referenced in that comparisons among performances are being used to make grade determinations, but it does allow you to examine the score distribution pattern before deciding on the norm. If everyone does well and the test is significant, it is possible that the average grade might fall in the B range, with no Ds or failures. In other instances you may decide no one did well enough to receive an A. Or, on examining the pattern of scores, you might find gaps in the score distribution that would suggest assigning mostly Cs, with some As and Fs, and few or no Bs and Ds.

In the eyes of some testing experts this method of grading may appear unjustifiably arbitrary. You will notice, however, that it is arbitrary in a different sort of way from the fixed-percentage system. It undoubtedly gives you a great deal of subjective leeway in assigning grades once you have scored the test, whereas an absolute standard approach to grading introduces arbitrariness and subjectivity at the point where you determine the fixed standard.

In effect, then, whatever method of grading you adopt, you will always have important subjective decisions to make at some critical juncture in the process. Evaluation inevitably reflects the values and preferences of the evaluator, thus complete objectivity is always an illusion.

Figuring Combined Grades

When it comes time to report student progress at the end of a marking period, you will need to combine scores from tests and other measures of achievement in order to determine a summary grade for each student. This process can be a relatively simple one if you are averaging norm-referenced performance samples, all of which carry the same value. If you attempt to combine raw numerical scores before they have been converted to standard scores or grades, you will be combining measures that are likely to be incompatible. Averaged ungraded raw scores do not take into consideration a student's standing with the rest of the class. It is possible, for example, that of two raw scores, a seventy-two and an eighty-five, the first could be the better comparative score because of a low class average on that particular test or assignment and an exceptionally high class average on the other. If these scores are combined in their present form, we lose valuable information about how students performed in relation to one another. There are certain well-established procedures for converting raw test scores to standard scores for purposes of grading.[16] However, we will recommend that you first consider some simpler methods of arriving at summary grades.

Also, if your practice is to record percentage scores on tests and other measures of achievement, simply averaging the percentages will result in some measures affecting the grade more than other measures. To illustrate this, imagine you are averaging the scores of two tests, one test consisting of eight items and the second test containing thirty-two items. If a student received a score of 100 percent on the first test and 50 percent on the second one, she would have averaged 75 percent. If another student earned a score of 50 percent on the first test and a score of 100 percent on the second, he would also have an average of 75 percent. Yet, the first student would have answered twenty-four out of forty items correctly on the two tests, while the other student would have thirty-six out of forty correct answers. It is obvious that the two students did not perform equally on these two achievement samples. The best way to combat this problem is to assign different weights to the various measures of performance that you use. In this particular case, the second exam, with four times the number of items as the first, should be accorded four times the weight of the first test.

There are two relatively easy-to-apply methods of assigning final grades that take into consideration the potential difficulties in averaging student performance samples.

Reducing Accumulated Grades to Final Grades.   If your approach during the marking period has been to attach letter grades to the various samples of student performance, there is a simple procedure for combining these grades into a final grade. It involves the following steps:

1. Determine the weight that is to be given to the different kinds of marks you will be averaging. (Hopefully, this will have been done when you designed your evaluation plan.) For example, you may decide that tests will count 50 percent, special assignments like papers and themes, 25 percent, and daily work, 25 percent in calculating final grades.
2. Change all letter grades to numerical values, using these conversion factors: A = 4; B = 3; C = 2; D = 1; F = 0.
3. Determine the average grade for each sample area, as in the following example:

Daily work: (six samples)	Special assignments (of equal value)		3 tests: (of equal value)	
C = 2		A = 4		B = 3
B = 3		B = 3		C = 2
B = 3		A = 4		B = 3
A = 4		C = 2		8/3 = 2.67
C = 2		13/4 = 3.25		
C = 2				
16/6 = 2.67				

4. Combine the averages:

Daily work	2.67	2.67
Special assignments	3.25	3.25
Tests	2.67 × 2	5.34
		11.26/4 = 2.81 or C+

(Note: Tests were to have twice the weight of daily work and special assignments, so you would need to take this into account in the final averaging process. This accounts for the divisor of four rather than three.)

Basing Grades on Total-performance Scores.   Another recommended method is to use a point system for assigning grades. In this case you would attach a certain number of points to each of the various performance activities in which students engage. Each component is accorded a maximum number of achievement points, based on its relative importance in the evaluation scheme. For instance, students might receive a maximum of ten points for both recitation and homework, fifteen points for quizzes, twenty-five points each for two unit tests, and fifteen points for term papers, for a possible total of one hundred points during the marking period. You and the students would each keep a running count of earned points throughout the marking period. Your task in determining grades would be to calculate point totals for each student, then apply either a norm-referenced or criterion-referenced scale to the accumulated scores. You might assign grades according to a preestablished performance standard like this:

90–100 total points = A
80–89 total points = B
70–79 total points = C
60–69 total points = D
less than 60 total points = F

Or you could use a norm-referenced approach to *classify* students on the basis of their total performance scores, utilizing a scheme such as the following:

Top 15 percent   A
Next 20 percent   B
Next 45 percent   C
Next 15 percent   D
Bottom 5 percent   F

Application Exercises

1. Consider each of the following test attributes listed and determine whether they are characteristic of norm-referenced or criterion-referenced measures.
    a. Students are compared to a set standard.
    b. Most appropriate when performing formative evaluations.
    c. Results in a more or less equal distribution of letter grades.

d. Determines whether a student is in the top or the bottom of the group.
e. Most suited for teaching mastery of knowledge or skills.
f. Puts students in competition with one another.
g. Makes it possible for all students to receive As.
h. Allows students to know their standing within the group.
i. Represents the more traditional way of assigning grades.
j. Is clearly established prior to the test.
2. Using the flexible-distribution method, determine letter grades, A, B, C, D, and F for the following group of test scores:

```
                                      X
                                      X
                          X       X  X              X
                  X       X  X    X  X  X        X       X
          X       X       X  X    X  X  X     X  X    X  X
  1   2   3   4   5   6   7   8   9  10  11  12  13  14  15  16  17  18  19  20
```

SUGGESTED ACTIVITIES AND QUESTIONS

1. It is sometimes claimed that tests encourage an elitist attitude on the part of academically able students while discouraging low-achieving students from trying. As a teacher, how would you attempt to minimize these unfavorable potentials of testing and grading? What do you see to be the principle purpose of tests and grades? Which grading model best realizes that purpose?
2. Have you had any particularly unpleasant experiences with testing and grading during your years in school? How have grades affected your performance as a student? Can you think of testing or grading practices that you believe unfair or irresponsible? What basic principles of evaluation or test construction did they violate?
3. Are you able to cite important objectives of high school or elementary school education that tend to be overlooked by the types of tests that are commonly used in our schools? What kinds of evaluation strategies would you use to measure these objectives?
4. Could universal criterion-referenced evaluation ever become a reality in U.S. education? What are the most persuasive arguments in favor of a criterion-referenced approach to measuring learning achievement? Does it have significant disadvantages? Elaborate.
5. Identify teaching situations where you believe self-referenced evaluation would be most appropriate. What are some of the main advantages and disadvantages of this approach to evaluating student learning?
6. What are some of the main arguments in favor of a pass–fail approach to evaluation in contrast to the grading system currently being used in our schools? Can you think of any serious disadvantages to a pass–fail system of reporting student progress?
7. What are some basic steps a teacher can take to enhance the validity of teacher-made tests?
8. Evaluation experts have maintained that the decision to use essay questions on a test implies a tradeoff between the inherent advantages and disadvantages of this testing format. If so, what kinds of measurement values are you exchanging when you choose to use essay items to sample learning achievement? Could it also be argued that a decision to use objective test items involves similar tradeoffs? Elaborate.
9. Would you be inclined to assign more weight to tests or to homework assignments when it

comes to grading learning achievement in your classes? What factors would you take into consideration in making this decision?

NOTES AND REFERENCES

1. William L. Goodwin and Herbert J. Klausmeier, *Facilitating Student Learning: An Introduction to Educational Psychology.* New York: Harper and Row, 1975, pp. 256–60.
2. Robert M. Gagne, *Essentials of Learning for Instruction.* Hinsdale, Ill.: Dryden Press, 1974, p. 4.
3. Nelson F. DuBois, George F. Alverson, and Richard K. Staley, *Educational Psychology and Instructional Decisions.* Homewood, Ill.: Dorsey Press, 1979, p. 364.
4. N. L. Gage and David C. Berliner, *Educational Psychology,* 4th ed. Boston: Houghton Mifflin, 1988, p. 572.
5. Benjamin S. Bloom, J. Thomas Hastings, and George F. Madaus, *Formative and Summative Evaluation of Student Learning.* New York: McGraw-Hill, 1971, p. 20.
6. Ibid.
7. Henry C. Lindgren and W. Newton Suter, *Educational Psychology in the Classroom,* 7th ed. Monterey, Calif.: Brooks/Cole, 1985, p. 379.
8. Ibid.
9. Ibid., p. 383.
10. Leonard H. Clark and Irving S. Starr, *Secondary and Middle School Teaching Methods,* 4th ed. New York: Macmillan, 1981, p. 291.
11. Bloom, Hastings, and Madaus, op. cit., pp. 45–53.
12. Clark and Starr, op. cit., p. 297.
13. Lindgren and Suter, op. cit., p. 404.
14. Jean D. Grambs, John C. Carr, and Robert M. Fitch, *Modern Methods in Secondary Education,* 3rd ed. New York: Holt, Rinehart and Winston, 1970, p. 329.
15. See Carl R. Rogers, *Freedom to Learn.* Columbus, Ohio: Charles E. Merrill, 1969, pp. 91–93; and John Holt, "I Oppose Testing, Marking, and Grading." *Today's Education,* 60 (1971), pp. 76–82.
16. See Norman E. Gronlund, *Measurement and Evaluation in Teaching,* 4th ed. New York: Macmillan, 1981, chap. 14.

CHAPTER 11

Communicating with Students and Parents

A HELPING RELATIONSHIP

In your role as a teacher you will have many occasions to interact with students on a one-to-one basis over subjects ranging from common interests to personal problems. You will also be called on to meet with parents from time to time to discuss mutual concerns relating to students' school life. The communication skills that will allow you to be effective in these personal encounters are likely to be considerably different from those you use to teach your classes. They will involve the ability to relate sensitively and authentically to these clientele on a nonacademic level. The capability to enter into genuine two-way conversation over matters of feeling as well as matters of fact is one of the things exemplary teachers have in common with good counselors. For most of us, the skills and attitudes necessary to perform well in a helping relationship do not come naturally. They need to be deliberately cultivated.[1]

Many teachers never acquire the aptitudes to conduct productive meetings with students and parents over delicate issues.[2] For these teachers, serious parent conferences and emotion-generating interactions with students are sometimes a dreaded part of the job. Yet, in a service profession like teaching, a willingness to take the lead in arranging and directing such meetings is necessary to maintain positive working relationships with those you are serving. Your ability to establish authentic communication with these people on a personal level will greatly enhance your success in teaching.

This chapter discusses fundamental principles of one-to-one communication in a helping relationship. It will also provide specific strategies and techniques for effective interaction with students and parents on a personal level.

Some Underlying Principles

There are some fundamental principles of human interaction that will have a direct bearing on the quality of your personal communication with students and parents. They are:

1. *People tend to withdraw from close interaction when fear, uncertainty, or suspicion is present.*[3] This is an important consideration to keep in mind when it comes to arranging conferences with clientele, particularly when the purpose is to discuss a problem or to give an evaluation. It is natural for people to feel anxious and apprehensive about a situation that poses a possible threat to their security or self-esteem. When placed in that situation, most of us tend to play it close to the vest until we are able to feel more confident and comfortable.

2. *People are much more likely to share their true selves when they feel they are being understood and accepted.* There is much evidence to confirm that individuals are more inclined to be honest and self-revealing in the presence of those who accept and appreciate them for what they are.[4] This points to the need for unconditional acceptance and positive regard as preconditions for getting people to be open and trusting in their interactions with us. Unconditional positive regard means a willingness to respect and value the personhood of the other individual with no strings attached, in spite of behavior that may be difficult to tolerate. It is also important to exhibit a caring, nonjudgmental attitude when people attempt to share their deepest feelings and concerns. Other individuals are more likely to be self-revealing when they sense we are attempting to see things from their point of view.[5] Carl Rogers stresses the importance of nonevaluative listening when he asserts that "the major barrier to mutual interpersonal communication is our very natural tendency to judge, to evaluate, to approve (or disapprove) the statements of the other person."[6]

3. *Feelings and emotions are generally more powerful than facts and reasons in human interaction.* Someone who is experiencing physical or emotional pain, or feelings of affection, fear, or disappointment is unlikely to be receptive to appeals to rationality, particularly if they involve an unsympathetic effort to discount the emotion. The feeling is often a more dominant reality to that person than the competing consideration someone would attempt to impose. "Denying or ignoring the existence of feelings in communication is like building a house without a foundation or framework."[7] To undertake to judge or talk someone out of an emotion is folly. The best way to gain entry to the psychic space of someone who has just expressed a strong feeling (e.g., an attraction, a distaste, a wish), is to enter at the feeling level.[8] That is to say, expressions of feeling should receive feeling-level responses (e.g., an understanding gesture, an expression of empathy).

4. *Your body language communicates a great deal more than what you say.* Experiments have shown that people generally consider nonverbal, bodily messages to be a great deal more reliable than verbal messages. It has been claimed that as much as 90 percent of the feeling conveyed by verbal messages comes from the vocal tone and facial expression of the speaker.[9] "A student is much more likely to attend to a teachers' face than to his words for indications of approval or acceptance."[10] Unfortunately, in human interaction our body language very often contradicts what we are able to verbalize. We are telling people one thing, but our physical being is conveying something quite different. Rogers discusses the need for congruence in the messages we communicate to another person. To Rogers congruence means being "genuine and without 'front' or facade,

openly being the feelings and attitudes which at that moment are flowing in you." Although no one ever achieves total congruence, we can begin to approach it by being attuned to what is going on inside us, by being able "to *be* the complexity of our feelings without fear."[11]

5. *Words do not carry meaning, people do.* This is a reminder that words symbolize thoughts and images that people have inside them. In and of themselves they have no meaning. Particular words may have significance to some people and mean nothing to others. Or the same words may be meaningful to a number of people, but in very different ways (e.g., love, education). To be effective communicators we must be able to place ourselves in the situation of the listener, to be able to imagine the other person receiving our message. Ambiguous terms like "good student" or "quality education" leave room for many possible interpretations. They can lead to serious misunderstandings when we use them as though they carried the same meaning for everyone. The best assurance we can have that the other person is receiving the meaning we intend is to be as descriptive as possible in the messages we send. Rather than characterize someone as a "good student," we communicate much more effectively when we describe that person as someone who listens attentively in class, completes assignments on time, and scores well on comprehension exams. The realization that words themselves carry no meaning should caution us to be careful of specialized language (jargon) when talking with people who are not teachers themselves.

6. *Telling someone something does not insure they have heard you.* This may appear on the surface to be an obvious truth about communication. The fact is, however, educators are especially prone to violating this principle. With so much emphasis on "delivery systems" and teacher presentations, it is easy for school people to imagine that a message well-sent is one well-received. However, effective communication also entails a concern for how the other person is receiving our messages. What really determines whether your idea gets into the mind of the listener is his level of mental activity while he is listening.[12] He must be actively processing the message for it to have any real meaning to him. One of the best ways to stimulate another person to think about what you are saying is by asking certain well-placed questions to encourage him to talk about your ideas:

"What do you think would be the consequences if we were to try this?"
"Do you know of any examples of this?"
"Where do you suppose I got this idea?"

When one person presents an idea and the other person does not talk about it (at least internally), there is no real penetration.[13]

PERSONAL INTERACTION WITH STUDENTS

Knowing Your Goals

Maintenance Conversation. It is important to be aware of what you are trying to accomplish in your personal communications with students. Many of your one-to-one encounters with these young people will be of the informal variety. They will occur spontaneously without much thought as to the objective. Generally, however, there will be an underlying purpose to the conversation: Ideally, it will be designed to establish or maintain a certain kind of relationship with that student. Regular *maintenance encounters* are essential to a constructive helping relationship. They let students know you are interested in them and that you are a person with whom they can share personal thoughts and feelings. Some of your best teaching may be done during brief one-to-one exchanges with students where you help them to clarify thoughts and feelings, to deal with contradictory emotions, or to examine points of view other than their own. There is a body of evidence suggesting that healthy emotional development in young people (i.e., depth of feelings and meanings) is dependent to a large extent on the quality of the interaction they have with significant adults in their lives (e.g., parents, teachers).[14] Studies have also demonstrated the importance of facilitative relationships to a youngster's intellectual achievement.[15]

Problem-based Meetings. The other main type of personal interaction you will have with students will be prompted by the need to discuss a problem or concern identified by either you or the student. It is especially important for you to develop an effective, client-centered pattern for handling *problem-based encounters* of various kinds in your professional life. The occasion may be to discuss some student difficulty with classroom behavior, academic performance, or peer relations. Or, a student (or parent) may ask to talk with you about a perceived problem with some aspect of your behavior (e.g., one of your teaching techniques). In any case, you should make a concerted effort to treat the problem in a reasonable and respectful manner, one that does not ignore the feelings, needs, and agendas of the other person.

This takes considerable patience and interpersonal sophistication, because there are often strong emotions and tensions involved, sometimes initial tendencies toward suspicion, defensiveness, or withdrawal. Problem-centered discussions generally require a more strategic approach than maintenance-type interactions. From a practical standpoint, your concern must be not only to solve the problem to your own satisfaction, but to sustain a positive helping relationship for the future. This requires that your methods be consistent with the goals you would hope to achieve. By having a firm sense of what you, the helper, are trying to accomplish in the encounter, you are less likely to sabotage your own purposes.

Tuning in to the Student's Agenda

Free and honest communication between two people generally involves some risk for these individuals. In personal interactions with students where strong feelings are involved, you can normally expect some reluctance on their part to share themselves openly until they are made to feel they are in the presence of an interested and understanding listener. It is important that you not move too quickly to present your own thoughts and agendas. Your initial effort should not be to impose your ideas or to resolve a problem, but to open the channels of communication.

Questions as Conversation Enhancers. You can begin to accomplish this by showing a genuine interest in students' situations, including important thoughts and feelings they may be holding. Simple, nonthreatening questions are usually very helpful at the beginning of such discussions. You can help to relax students by asking questions that are easy to answer. These may be simple factual questions that can be answered with little elaboration (e.g., "Are you still working after school?"), or they may be open-ended questions that allow students to warm up to the discussion by talking about something they know well and would have little reluctance to share (e.g., "How does the school year seem to be going for you so far?"). Be prepared to tolerate some initial wandering into areas that have no direct bearing on the point of the meeting. Although your time is important, so is the need to establish the groundwork for a fruitful discussion.

Reflective Listening.   You communicate genuine interest and respect through your willingness to listen attentively and empathetically to the other person's messages. One effective indicator of active listening is the ability to reflect back to the speaker through a simple paraphrase the essence of the message as you understood it:

> "You're saying school is becoming hard to cope with these days."
> "You believe students should have more elective classes to choose from."
> "So you and Jessica have become good friends."

Paraphrasing as a reflective listening technique is intended to convey one's effort to hear and understand. To have its proper effect as a conversation "lubricant" it should be offered in a low-key and neutral (not inquiring) tone that does not suggest disagreement or disbelief.

Nonjudgmental Responding.   Teachers who can attend nonjudgmentally as students express feelings and personal concerns will have more success in talking with students at this level than teachers who are quick to offer advice and criticism.[16] Some of the nonverbal accompaniments to empathetic listening are a comfortable posture, a sympathetic facial expression, and affirmative nods that signal "Yes, I'm hearing you." The ability to resist interrupting is also very important.

Responding analytically to student expressions of feeling is generally counterproductive. Appeals to rationality when the other person is in a nonrational mood may only serve to intensify the feeling and create defensiveness. When students say privately, "I dread this test. I'm just not ready for it," your first impulse may be to respond with rational statements like "You did have plenty of notice," or "Don't worry about it, you'll do all right." A better reply would match the feeling level of the student. A nonevaluative paraphrase is often the best response: "You don't feel prepared for this one," or "You're especially nervous about this test." In a case where a student remarks sincerely to a teacher, "I really wish we could get out of school earlier for the summer vacation," an appropriate feeling-level response would be, "You'd like to have a longer summer," or "You're ready for a break."

Nonjudgmental paraphrasing is especially appropriate in one-to-one situations where personal problems or interpersonal tensions exist. If a student is willing to share the feeling that "Nothing is going right for me lately," teachers do well to respond at that level rather than to react with information or advice. By simply reflecting, "You've had some bad days lately," or "This just isn't your week," teachers indicate a willingness to begin the conversation on the student's wavelength rather than their own. Although you may feel a desire to get to the heart of the problem and to move more quickly to impose your own agenda (e.g., a student has been violating an important class ground rule), if one of your purposes is to establish two-way communication with the student, your agenda should temporarily remain in the background. It is imperative that you avoid criticizing at this point in the conversation if your concern is to stimulate open, trustful interaction with the student.

By initially resisting judgment or advice, teachers do not give up their right to an opinion, nor do they abdicate their position of influence. Instead, these nondirective responses will usually turn out to be communication enhancers. By allowing their initial responses to match students' level of concern, teachers communicate to students that they are in the presence of teachers who are able to suspend their own agendas long enough to entertain those of the students. Under these circumstances, students will not only be more willing to confide in such teachers, but will be more receptive to teachers' influence.

Providing Feedback and Support

Accepting and Encouraging.   Once you have made progress in engaging the other person in open and trusting conversation, it is important for you to offer something of your own in the way of a substantive response. You help to sustain the momentum of the conversation when you are able to provide positive, nonevaluative feedback to that individual. Students who have begun to share a part of themselves—their thoughts, their feelings, their intentions—should have that willingness reinforced by expressions of acceptance and encouragement from you. Sometimes it is a matter of directly conveying your appreciation and support for their efforts:

> "I appreciate your willingness to be honest with me about that."
> "I imagine it's difficult for you to talk about that—I'm glad you made the effort."
> "I've never been in that situation before—I'll bet it was quite an experience."
> "It sounds like something that's worth pursuing—I'd like to be of some help to you if I could."

By taking opportunities to offer supportive statements, or ego boosters, that communicate respect and positive regard you can do a great deal to promote the student's confidence and good feelings toward self, prerequisites to the authentic sharing of that self with others:[17]

> "That's an interesting point. You seem to have some good insights."
> "I can see why you have so many friends in this group. Many of the others in the class seem to respect you and look to you for leadership."
> "As I listen to you talk, I can't help but think how well you express yourself."

Giving Input.   In providing your own input during a conference or discussion, you will want to remain mindful of your main role in a helping relationship, namely to be of assistance to others rather than use this as an opportunity to promote your own needs and interests. You should be sensitive to any tendencies you may have to introduce irrelevancies, to moralize, to use unnecessary jargon, or to talk too much about yourself. Here are some suggestions for making your input relevant and understandable:

1. Stick to the point. Offer only ideas that contribute to the idea-pattern you are trying to convey.
2. Space your ideas by keeping your speeches short. This gives your listener time to think about each idea as it is presented.
3. Do not tell the other person what he or she already knows. Repeat your meaning but not your words, and avoid saying the obvious.
4. Use concrete words whenever possible. Whenever you use abstract words illuminate them through use of concrete ones.
5. After presenting ideas, stimulate the other person to think by asking questions.

If your encounter with a particular student is essentially maintenance-based (i.e., generally informal; aimed at promoting openness, trust, or self-disclosure), you may have no need to move to a problem-solving stage in the conversation.[18] The communication enhancers embodied in these first two interactive phases will have been instrumental in making the relationship one of mutual trust and respect. Students are likely to feel comfortable in your presence and regard you as a person who is generally interested in them as people.

Addressing Problems

When the central purpose of the conference is to address a problem or concern you have identified, the time should now be ripe for you to bring the discussion to a head by making your agenda clear. Essentially what you want to communicate at this point is, "I respect and value you as a person with purposes and agendas of your own. Meanwhile, I have a concern I want to call to your attention." Your positive support and willingness to consider the other's thoughts and feelings should have earned you the opportunity to bring attention to the problem without eliciting troublesome defensiveness. If it is a behavioral problem you are attempting to resolve, you should now be able to elicit the student's attention and cooperation without having to invoke your authority.

Of course, it should be anticipated that the student may have things to say that conflict with your own values or reality perceptions as they apply to the situation (possibly reflecting the basis of the problem or disagreement that occasioned the meeting). However, it is important that you not allow these differences and accompanying feelings to jeopardize the positive flow of the discussion. There are ways you can respectfully disagree without being confrontational or authoritarian. Your effort should be to show that you support the other's right to a particular feeling or opinion, without necessarily subscribing to the substance of the view:

"Yes, I hear what you're saying. . . . On the other hand, this is how I see it. . . ."
"I can understand how you might feel that way. . . . My own experience has been rather different. . . ."

''I respect your position on this . . . I also think there's something else we need to understand about the situation. . . .''

Low-key, nonconfrontational disagreement is best achieved when your voice tone reflects a concern to understand rather than to be right, and when you are able to leave expressions like ''Yes . . . But . . .'' and ''I disagree'' out of your conversation. Such language tends to carry adversarial overtones, usually causing the other person to dig in and defend a chosen position rather than listen to your point of view.

Problem-solving Maneuvers.   By stimulating in-depth, two-way communication during the early stages of the discussion, you hope to have set the stage for a reasoned, cooperative approach to the problem that necessitated the meeting. Having arrived at the place where both parties are aware of some difficulty that needs to be resolved, there are at least three kinds of approaches you can use to instigate action. One is to invite an action proposal by asking directly, ''What do you think we should do about this?'' or ''Would you like to think some more about what we've discussed and let me know tomorrow what you propose to do?'' This approach attempts to place the responsibility on the student to come up with a solution. It conveys the message that ''I think of you as a basically reasonable and responsible person and I'd like to give you first opportunity to suggest a way of dealing with this.'' This method is not suitable if the student has broken a clearly defined rule for which there is a preestablished penalty.

A second alternative is to offer a possible solution that involves shared responsibility for action on the problem. It contains a provision that you would be willing to contribute something to help students resolve the difficulty, if they will do the main part:

''If I remove these last two tardies, will you make it a point to show up on time for the rest of the semester?''

''If you would get that assignment to me by 8:00 tomorrow morning, I'd be willing to give you credit for it.''

''I'll allow you to keep that seat if you can show me you won't talk privately with people around you during group lessons.''

This strategy is particularly appropriate in the case of a student who would benefit from a slight nudge to action or a second opportunity to demonstrate proper behavior. It represents a show of good faith on your part, saying in effect, ''I'm willing to contribute something to help you resolve this because I believe you will follow through with your part of the bargain.'' It is less appropriate a second time, after your first expression of good faith has not borne fruit.

The third approach to problem resolution is a straightforward teacher directive that describes in precise terms the expected behavior:

''The rule about throwing food in the lunchroom is quite clear, Emilio. I'll expect you to eat lunch in the classroom for the rest of the week.''

''Jennifer, you know what my standard is for neatness in your written work. I'd like you to redo this assignment.''

''Trevor, it wouldn't be fair to the other players for you to miss practice to attend to this other business. You'll need to make all of our practices this week if you want to play in the game on Friday.''

A teacher directive is most appropriate when you decide there is no room for negotiation. This may be the case when a clearly defined rule or standard has been violated, or when you feel the student's behavior does not merit further discussion or a second chance. When using this direct and unilateral approach to problem resolution, it is important that you be as objective as possible in defining proper behavior and reasons for a particular decision. Consistent with the need to maintain unconditional positive regard in a helping relationship, it is essential that in criticizing behavior you not attack the personhood of the student. By being as descriptive as possible when discussing appropriate and inappropriate behavior, you avoid labeling students as nasty, inconsiderate, sloppy, or other characterizations that can be damaging to the person and to the teacher–student relationship.

Application Exercises

1. For each of the following student comments, provide brief responses that would serve to accomplish the specified purpose (assume in each case that you are alone with the student):
   a. "I'm afraid I won't make the team. There are so many people trying out this time." (Realizing the student probably is not talented enough to make the team, you want to be sympathetic, but also positive.)
   b. "Wow! I got the shaft today. Two failure notices—one in math and the other in English." (You want to find out more about the problem without being judgmental.)
   c. "This is the best score I've had so far. I'm really feeling good about this one." (You want to share in the student's good feeling.)
   d. "What's so wrong about missing a day of school once in a while? My dad is able to take days off from his job; you teachers can take personal leave days. Students shouldn't be treated any different." (You want to offer a different point of view without seeming disagreeable or defensive.)
   e. "For a while I was doing O.K., but now I'm worse than ever. Nothing I do seems to help. What's the use of trying?" (You want to show empathy and a desire to be helpful.)
   f. "I'm sick of school. I need a vacation." (You want to accept the expressed feeling without being judgmental or moralistic.)
2. Imagine yourself as a teacher in each of the following personal encounters with students. Specify the purposes you might be seeking to achieve and the main communication strategies and techniques you would employ in each instance.
   a. As a junior high school teacher, one of your students approaches you to discuss a problem he is having with test taking in your class. This boy, a cooperative and seemingly average student, manages to perform satisfactorily on homework assignments and in-class recitations, but has had little success with the first several written tests. He is preoccupied with the thought he might fail the class.
   b. As a fifth-grade teacher, you have decided to talk privately with a girl in your

class who has recently been disrupting other student's games during recess. This student, a relatively well-behaved participant in regular in-class activities, has been teasing other girls and kicking their gameballs on the playground. She has on one other occasion confided to you her feeling that girls in the class have been slow to warm up to her because of her outsider status as a recent transfer student.

c. As a popular high school teacher, you have been invited to join a small group of students with whom you have very positive relationships for an upcoming Saturday afternoon picnic. You are reluctant to accept the invitation for two main reasons. First, that you would like to spend a quiet weekend at home after a hectic week at school. Second, you do not feel quite prepared to extend the relationship to this level of informality, in spite of the fact that these are especially enjoyable and loyal students. One of the students has cornered you during lunch for the purpose of trying to talk you into accompanying them in this weekend outing.

CONDUCTING PRODUCTIVE PARENT MEETINGS

Setting the Stage

There are several things you should do in preparation for a parent conference. One is to settle on an appropriate time and place for the meeting. If you are initiating the conference, the best method is a phone call to make the first contact personal. However, some parents may be difficult to reach during the times you might call. A second choice is to send a written request home with the student. Try to find a time that is convenient for both you and the parent. After school may be your best time. For parents who work, early morning, lunch hour, or evening meetings may be necessary.

An important consideration will be the setting in which you hold the conference. Unless you are sharing a classroom with other teachers, the most natural place for the meeting will be your own classroom. If so, make an effort to insure privacy. Students taking tests or moving in and out of the room can be a bothersome distraction, as can calls from the office, street noises, and so forth. If an empty classroom or teacher's office is not available, frequently an administrative office or nurse's room will afford the necessary privacy. Make an effort to insure the time and place for the meeting are well understood by the parent and that you have these firmly set in your schedule. Mixups or missed meetings can be especially embarrassing for both parties when you are trying to establish a good working relationship.

Wherever you hold the conference, it is advisable to provide comfortable and appropriate seating. Generally the less formal and more personal the arrangement, the better. You seated behind a desk with the parent in a student's chair on the opposite side tends to reflect impersonality and is not conducive to the interpersonal atmosphere you want to create.

In short, to be perceived as a sensitive professional it is important that in arranging parent conferences you reflect a concern for the time, the privacy, and the comfort of the parent.

Overcoming Initial Barriers

As you begin a parent conference you should be aware of some of the possible psychological barriers that could work to make free and open discussion difficult.

Parent Anxiety.   For one thing, parents sometimes feel apprehensive about meeting teachers within the school environment to discuss matters over which the teacher has the greater knowledge and authority. This can be a distancing factor when it comes to teacher–parent relations. Also, within the larger society, teachers are generally thought of as relatively well-educated people with above-average language skills. In contrast, some of the parents with whom you meet may have less formal education and less verbal facility in formal conversation. As a result, you may notice some initial anxiety and reluctance on the part of the parent to enter into easy conversation at the beginning of a meeting.

Stereotypes.   As a related consideration, based on their own school experiences parents may be harboring stereotypes of teachers and the kinds of behavior to be expected from them, preconceptions that affect a parent's ability to relate to a teacher on a personal level. They may expect teachers to dominate the conference with their explanations and prescriptions, and come prepared to simply listen and endure. Some parents may regard teachers as primarily academic in their orientations and interests, with little inclination to be interested in them and what they might contribute to the meeting.

Adversarial Feelings.   Sometimes parents (or even teachers) have a tendency to see the relationship as adversarial rather than cooperative. In the eyes of the parent, teachers are authority figures who function primarily as critics and evaluators. Particularly if they or their children have had a history of difficulties with schools and their representatives, they may tend to view teachers in an unfavorable light. Teachers themselves may unintentionally contribute to this feeling. Being highly sensitive to the need to maintain system and control in their work, teachers are liable to construe conferences with students or parents over school problems as encounters with those who would disrupt that system. When the occasion for such meetings is a difficulty with student behavior or achievement, or dissatisfaction with the teacher's methods, each party may approach the interaction with blinders, with a tendency to see only their side of the problem.

When confronted with behavior in these conferences that suggests resentment, prejudgment, or distrust, it is critical that you not respond in kind or allow yourself to be drawn into a battle of egos. As the professional in a helping relationship, one of your priorities should be to provide a positive and constructive tone to the meeting.

Providing Direction and Focus to the Meeting

Once you have completed the process of greeting parents and expressing your appreciation for their willingness to meet, you should make an effort to size up their readiness to enter into a productive dialogue. Being mindful of some of the potential obstacles to open and trustful communication, you will want to allow sufficient time at the beginning to set a positive tone for the meeting and to give the parent an opportunity to warm up to the discussion. Your ability to be a good listener is critical here, effective listening being the single most important skill you can bring to a parent conference.

Conversation Lubricants.   It is often helpful to begin the meeting with a limited amount of small talk to stimulate conversation. Unless the parent shows an interest in moving directly to the main agenda, you should work up to any sensitive issues by employing the same sorts of communication enhancers that were discussed in connection with teacher–student interaction (i.e., nonthreatening questions, reflective listening techniques, support statements, positive feedback). In the case of self-confident, highly social people, the dialogue may be relatively free-flowing from the beginning.

Taking the Lead.   Time limitations will usually require that you limit a parent meeting to one or two main agendas. You should take the intiative to insure that the discussion moves in a direction that allows you to meet the objectives you have set for the conference. During all phases of the conference you should make a strong effort to demonstrate the interpersonal dispositions essential to any productive helping relationship (i.e., positive regard, empathy, congruence). Here are some additional suggestions for making the meeting a mutually beneficial experience for both you and the parent:

1. Take responsibility for maintaining a pleasant and respectful tone throughout the conference.
2. Be willing to tolerate some irrelevant conversation during the warm up period, but thereafter do not hesitate to redirect the discussion if you find it to be moving in a nonproductive direction.
3. Do not use the conference to talk about yourself or your problems.
4. Emphasize the positive. Be mindful of the emotional investment parents have in their children. The things you say about a son or daughter will reflect on them and their abilities as parents.
5. Tell anecdotes that "catch" the student demonstrating the kind of behavior you are trying to describe. Instead of mentioning that "Jamie has a good attitude," elaborate by saying, "Jamie always comes into class with a smile on her face. Yesterday, for example, she kept that smile all through a test we were taking."
6. Be prepared to take notes on important items parents may mention during the conference.
7. Do not allow yourself to appear hurried or preoccupied during the conference. Nervous glances at your watch or toward the door will give a parent the impression you are too busy to give them your full attention.

Concluding and Following up the Conference

You will seldom have unlimited time in a parent conference. When it becomes necessary to conclude the meeting, you should take the initiative to get closure on the discussion in a way that will seem natural and fitting to the parent. It will usually be appropriate to provide a brief review of the purpose and the main highlights of the conference, including any conclusions that were reached. Parents should leave the meeting with a clear understanding of what was discussed and any action to be taken. If there will be a need for further discussion or a follow-up meeting, this is the time to schedule another conference. The closing phase of the conference should allow time for you to end the meeting in a cordial and unhurried fashion.

At the conclusion of a parent conference it is a good idea to make a written record of what transpired. You may want to design a conference form with spaces for various kinds of information that you will want to have on hand for your own record (e.g., date, reason for conference, relevant background information on student, action to be taken). This form could include a bottom line for your signature and that of the parent once the conference was concluded.

MANAGING DIFFICULT CONFERENCES

From time to time you may find yourself involved in a conference with a parent whose behavior makes it especially difficult for you to establish a productive dialogue. You can anticipate several kinds of parent behaviors that may be tension producing and/or disruptive of your efforts to lead a fruitful meeting, including: (1) extreme withdrawal, (2) unusual aggressiveness, (3) debilitating emotion, and (4) self-centered monologue.

Extreme Withdrawal

In this first instance, you may encounter parents who become completely bogged-down once the conference has begun and have a particularly difficult time articulating ideas or concerns. They may appear accepting of what you have to say, but essentially unable to offer anything of their own. You realize very quickly that the conference has turned into a one-person show. When this is the case, you will want to make the parent as comfortable as possible, then use some simple conversational lubricants to get this person talking.

You may attempt light humor as a means of loosening them up. Also, use low-pressure questions to draw parents into casual conversation on a topic with which they feel comfortable. Then by employing reflective listening techniques to show genuine interest and support, you can usually begin to stimulate two-way conversation.

The key idea here is for you to resist dominating or attempting to move the conference to a quick conclusion without parent participation. Otherwise this will end up being just a token conference. It is also critical that you not show discomfort or impatience with this parent's reticence to talk. As a teacher and a helping professional it will be important for you to be able to deal effectively with shyness and withdrawal in your personal interactions.

Unusual Aggressiveness

Dealing with an overly assertive or hypercritical parent can also be difficult. This person may attempt to take the lead and offer a premature perception and resolution of the situation. Generally aggressive people will have a need to be heard and to vent what is on their mind. They may begin the conference by being unreasonably critical of your behavior or that of the student. Or they may show an inclination to interrupt and disagree with points you are making. If this aggression seems aimed at you, very likely they have entered the meeting with preconceptions of you and/or the school based on past experiences with teachers or on stories their child has brought home.

In managing encounters with overly aggressive parents (or students) it is imperative that you avoid overreacting or arguing. The longer you can remain outwardly calm and in control of your own emotions, the better chance you have of maneuvering them into a reasonable mood. As in any personal encounter where other people have pressing concerns they need to get off their chest, your listening skills are paramount. Your ability to employ reflective, empathetic listening techniques (e.g., affirmative nods, confirmatory paraphrases, supportive feedback) can do wonders to turn a confrontational situation into one of mutual sharing and understanding. This will take the personal security and confidence to be able to say, "You may be right," "I understand your feeling," or "I can see how you might get that impression." By rolling with the punches and not arguing, you effectively disarm combative people in their efforts to do battle.

When you provide no immediate resistance to their aggression, their next move is likely to be a show of willingness to temper their strong position. When this happens, you should make an effort to redirect the discussion to talk about factual matters (e.g., the student's failure to complete six out of eight homework assignments). If it is apparent that there is a conflict in values (e.g., the school favors more homework, the parent wants less), point up the conflict, make a case for the school's position, but indicate your ability to understand their point of view. Again, avoid arguing—it is important that you come off as reasonable, whether the parent is or not.

Debilitating Emotion

A conference where the parent becomes upset or distraught in the meeting can create unusual discomfort and indecision for a teacher. Even highly trained counselors sometimes have trouble knowing how to proceed with clients who lapse into weeping and despair. Assuming a nonextreme case, where you can expect the parent to eventually gain emotional control, there are some reasonable steps you can take to deal with the situation and to salvage something worthwhile from the meeting. If you sense ahead of time that this could be a stressful session, it is good to have a box of tissue on hand. Beyond that, it is of course critical not to attempt to force your agenda. An expression of empathetic understanding and support is also important (unless you have good reason to regard the show of emotion as a characteristic ploy to avoid responsibility or to influence you in a particular direction).

Often the most effective strategy for helping these parents regroup and begin functioning in a rational manner is an attempt to refocus the conversation to something they are more comfortable discussing. If the debilitating emotion resulted from a discussion of their son's failures in school, it could be settling to get them talking about something he excels in outside of school. Above all, in a conference like this it is important for you to be able to maintain your own composure. In a case where you perceive the parent's emotional state is too extreme to justify continuing the conference, you should have the presence of mind to suggest postponing the meeting until a later time.

Self-centered Monologue

It may also be difficult to cope with parents who are self-centered and attempt to dominate the conversation with references to personal status, accomplishments, tastes and distastes, and so forth. The biggest problem with ego-involved parents is their tendency to keep the conversation focused on themselves rather than on the main topic of the meeting. Some self-centered parents will want to use references to their child's school performance as opportunities to talk about their own school experiences and achievements. Like the overly aggressive parent, they have a need to be heard. They are usually looking for occasions to tell someone about themselves.

After demonstrating an initial willingness to listen and entertain this person's agendas, you will want to assertively redirect the conversation to the main topic of the meeting; for example, "I'd like to focus for a moment on something I've observed about Nathan." In conferencing with a parent who shows a disposition toward self-centeredness, it is essential that you maintain the lead in the discussion. It will be up to you to keep the conference focused on the business at hand.

Application Exercises

1. Discuss the basic strategies you would consider appropriate to use in conducting each of the following teacher–parent conferences. Give reasons for the approach you would take in each case.
   a. The father of one of your eighth-grade students has made an appointment to talk with you about a nonpassing grade his son has earned in a basic math class. Your preliminary inquiries would indicate this parent is a strong-willed person who is primarily interested in keeping his son eligible for athletics.
   b. You have arranged to meet with the mother of one of your third-grade students to discuss her daughter's continuing aloofness toward you and many of her peers in the class. This girl has been reluctant to join in some class activities (e.g., music, square dancing), claiming her mother objects to her participation in some aspects of the school program. To date you have not been able to find out what the reasons are, or if in fact they exist.
   c. You have arranged a conference with the mother of one of your exceptionally talented tenth-grade art students to discuss this girl's interest in pursuing a college scholarship in the area of art. It seems that the mother, a person with limited formal education, has shown little support for the idea, and has left the girl feeling discouraged about her chances of achieving this goal. In the past you have been unsuccessful in getting this parent to come to school to discuss her daughter's situation.

SUGGESTED ACTIVITIES AND QUESTIONS

1. Define *communication* in your own words. When can it be said that one has communicated? Is communication the process of transferring a message or conveying meaning? Compare your ideas with those of other beginning teachers. What are some main similarities and differences?

2. How effective do you consider yourself to be as an interpersonal (face-to-face) communicator? List some of your communication strengths. Also list any communication weaknesses you might possess. List specific measures that can be taken to overcome these weaknesses.

3. It has been claimed that although most of us are born with the capacity to hear, we must learn how to listen. What do you take to be the difference between the two processes? Discuss some of the main reasons for poor listening in person-to-person interaction. Considering its fundamental importance to human communication, would it be appropriate to provide instruction in listening as well as reading and writing in our schools?

4. Consider the following hypothetical criticism of nonjudgmental listening as a communication skill in teacher–student interactions: "If I allow students to use me as a sounding board to vent silly, irresponsible feelings, I'll lose my standing as an authority figure and behavior management will become that much more difficult." Present an argument showing how this attitude can actually lead to more rather than fewer behavioral problems for a teacher.

5. Look for opportunities to interact on a one-to-one basis with students in schools where you are involved (e.g., during tutoring sessions, lunch periods, after school activities). Use these occasions to deliberately practice some of the main interactive skills presented in this chapter. In particular, make it a point to utilize reflective listening techniques when sharing ideas, experiences, and feelings with these young people. Do you notice differences in the way these students respond to you when you take time to show genuine interest in and support for their personal agendas as well as your own? What are these differences?

6. When interacting with other people, both in a school setting and elsewhere, make a concerted effort to keep the "Yes . . . Buts" and "I disagrees" out of your conversational patterns. Do you perceive differences in the emotional climate of a discussion when your manner of disagreeing is low-key rather than confrontational?

NOTES AND REFERENCES

1. Carl R. Rogers, *On Becoming a Person.* Boston: Houghton Mifflin, 1961, see chap. 3.

2. Robert R. Carkhuff and Bernard G. Berenson, *Beyond Counseling and Therapy.* New York: Holt, Rinehart and Winston, 1967, p. 11.

3. Bonaro W. Overstreet, *Understanding Fear in Ourselves and Others.* New York: Harper and Row, 1951.

4. Haim G. Ginott, *Teacher and Child.* New York: Macmillan, 1972, p. 69; and Carl R. Rogers, "The Interpersonal Relationship: The Core of Guidance." In Carl R. Rogers and Barry Stevens (Eds.), *Person to Person: The Problem of Being Human.* New York: Pocket Books, 1971, p. 69.

5. Rogers, *On Becoming a Person.* op. cit., p. 332.

6. Ibid., p. 330.

7. George I. Brown, *Human Teaching for Human Learning.* New York: Viking Press, 1961, p. 6.

8. Ginott, op. cit., p. 64.

9. Joseph Morris, *Psychology and Teaching: A Humanistic View.* New York: Random House, 1978, p. 363.

10. Ibid.

11. Carl R. Rogers. "The Interpersonal Relationship: The Core of Guidance." In Carl P. Rogers and Barry Stevens (Eds.), *Person to Person: The Problem of Being Human.* New York: Pocket Books, 1971, p. 73.

12. Jesse S. Nirenberg, *Getting Through to People.* Englewood Cliffs, N.J.: Prentice-Hall, 1973, p. 109.

13. Ibid., p. 116.
14. William Glasser, *Reality Therapy*. New York: Harper and Row, 1975, p. 196; and Carkhuff and Berenson, op. cit., p. 4.
15. Carkhuff and Berenson, op. cit., p. 11.
16. Ginott, op. cit., p. 70.
17. Rogers, *On Becoming a Person*. op. cit., chap. 3.
18. An exception would be an apparent maintenance-level encounter that uncovers a personal or behavioral problem that needs to be resolved.

CHAPTER 12

Managing Your Own Development as a Teacher

THE TASK OF SELF-MANAGEMENT

Teaching affords personal growth opportunities like few other professions. The job will provide ongoing occasions for you to increase your interpersonal skills, your decision-making abilities, your verbal and rational powers, your time-management skills, and your basic self-confidence. These potential fringe benefits often become apparent to perceptive newcomers to the teaching profession:

> Teaching has helped me develop a kind of self-confidence I've never had before. It's especially good for increasing your interpersonal skills since you're constantly interacting with people of different ages and different ability levels. I feel I'm becoming just basically more comfortable presenting my ideas to other people after only a few weeks of teaching.

> I didn't realize teaching was going to require so much of me at a personal level. In many ways this is the most challenging thing I've ever done, but it's also without a doubt the most fulfilling. I've never been involved in anything where my personal skills increased so rapidly.

> Teaching can be good basic training for other things I might want to do later on in my life. The best way to learn something well is to have to teach it to someone else. Another thing you can gain from teaching is the ability to plan and organize activities within certain time limits. This type of skill should be useful to a person in many other kinds of work.

The most fulfilled and successful teachers find ways to take advantage of these growth opportunities. They insist on being responsible for their own progress as professionals, thereby avoiding the need to rely on external prescriptions and supervisor's evaluations to keep them focused and productive. Yet, because of the complex and fast-paced nature of the work, new teachers often find themselves coping rather than growing (see chapter 2). This fact of life points up the desirability of developing a viable plan for engineering your own professional growth.

This chapter centers on ideas for managing and monitoring your personal development as a teacher. It will offer self-governing strategies in three important areas: (1) developing a clear sense of professional direction as you begin teaching, (2) monitoring your own skill development as a beginning teacher, and (3) expanding your horizons as a professional educator.

FIRMING UP YOUR GUIDELINES

As you assume responsibility for your own classroom, the direction you take in developing lessons and managing classes will be largely up to you. At that point it will be important for you to have a reasonably clear notion of the role you wish to play as a teacher and how you will proceed to implement your goals in teaching.

Clarifying Your Philosophy of Teaching

What Does Research Say About Good Teaching?   In formulating a serviceable philosophy of teaching, it will be instructive for you to take into consideration the studies that have been done on effective teaching. The research on proficient teaching has tended to yield results that make it difficult to offer easy prescriptions for sound instruction. For example, studies aimed at determining whether indirect strategies are superior to direct methods of instruction have, as you might imagine, concluded that it depends on the objective. Direct methods are generally more effective when your goal is to teach basic information or skills, whereas an indirect teaching style is more suitable for promoting understanding and higher-level thinking.[1] One frequently cited review of the research on teaching has identified several teaching characteristics that have been consistently associated with gains in student achievement.[2] These characteristics are:

Enthusiasm: exhibiting vigor, involvement, excitement, and interest during classroom presentations through vocal inflection, gesturing, eye contact, and animation

Clarity: logical, step-by-step order; clear and audible delivery free of distracting mannerisms

Variety: variability in instructional materials, questioning, types of feedback, and teaching strategies

Engagement: businesslike orientation; ability to keep students on task; limiting opportunities for distraction; getting students to work on, think through, and to ask questions about the content

Another attempt to summarize the literature on effective teaching has produced the following list of recommended teacher behaviors:

1. Willingness to be flexible, to be direct or indirect as the situation demands
2. Ability to perceive the world from the student's point of view
3. Ability to personalize one's teaching
4. Willingness to experiment, to try out new things

5. Skill in asking questions (as opposed to seeing oneself as a kind of answering service)
6. Knowledge of subject matter and related areas
7. Provision of well-established examination procedures
8. Provision of definite study helps
9. Demonstration of appreciative attitudes (evidenced by nods, comments, smiles, etc.)
10. Use of conversational manner in teaching—informal, easy style[3]

Summarizing Your Own Views. The concept of "good teaching" that guides your professional life will be one that you have chosen, so it would be advantageous for you to attempt to clarify your present thinking as you make the transition from student to teacher. As a vehicle for summarizing your current views on teaching, you might allow yourself to reflect on the following questions:

1. Now that I have the opportunity to see teaching from the "other side of the desk," has this changed my conception of the teacher's role? In what ways?
2. How do we determine what constitutes good teaching? Are there certain teacher behaviors that are inherently right or desirable regardless of measurable outcomes, for example, beginning a lesson with a "set," or should "good teaching" always be defined in terms of the amount of learning it produces?
3. Is teaching primarily a science or an art? What is the difference? What are the implications for learning to teach?
4. What is my conception of the ideal teacher? Is it reducible to certain fundamental human qualities, to technical abilities, to intellect, or to a combination of the three? Should anyone with demonstrated knowledge in a particular subject area be able to teach that subject?
5. What particular communication skills are fundamental to my concept of good teaching? Are these skills unique to teaching?
6. How much importance will I attach to information transfer in the subjects I teach? What will be the role of inquiry methods in my teaching?
7. As a classroom teacher, where does my ultimate responsibility lie? To the subject matter? To the students and their parents? To the school system? To the teaching profession? To myself?

Consolidating Your "Game Plan"

You can enhance your ability to be self-governing as a teacher if you will take time prior to entering the classroom to construct a strategic plan for gaining control of the job. Your "plan of attack" should include a summary of the main rules of procedure from which you will be working. This will likely take some careful thought and organization on your part. Considering the variety of theories and methodologies you will have been exposed to during the course of teacher training, it may require considerable effort to sort it all out and to distill from it a concise set of prescriptions for your teaching. Your ability to "own" the principles that guide your school behavior will allow you to achieve what Joyce and Showers call *executive control* over your teaching strategies.

Executive control "involves understanding an approach to teaching, why it works, what it is good for, what it's major elements are, how to adapt it to varying content and students—the development of a set of principles that enables one to think about the approach and to modulate and transform it in the course of its use."[4]

To help you prepare your initial game plan, the following summary of recommendations and rationales represents a synthesis of some of the central ideas and strategies offered in previous chapters of this handbook.

Becoming Established

1. Make a special effort during the first few days of teaching to get students used to attending to you and cooperating with your system of expectations. You should place a high priority on having them give you undivided attention when you are addressing the class. Refuse to begin class until all students have settled down and are focusing on you. This is one of the first and most important principles of classroom management.

2. Work to make your classroom communications deliberate and penetrating. Nervous anxiety may cause a tendency to hurry through explanations or instructions. Recognize when you are too fast-paced or mechanical in your teaching. If students sense you are simply going through the motions of teaching, they will be inclined to tune you out.

3. Find occasions to "walk" your students (as a group) through some short tasks or exercises so they can get into the habit of responding to your voice and following your instructions. Take this opportunity to carefully monitor compliance. Respond quickly and goodnaturedly when you notice students who lag or become inattentive. Be patient, but deliberate and insistent, when it comes to keeping individuals on task with you and the rest of the group. The precedents you set here during these early stages of teaching will be crucial to your success with a particular group.

4. Do not expect everything to fall perfectly into place during your first days of teaching. Classroom teaching is often hectic and unpredictable. Things will not always work out as logically and precisely as you had planned. A sense of humor and a good night's sleep will usually do wonders after "one of those days."

Relationships with Students and Supervisors

1. Strive to develop natural authority, the approach that allows you to gain cooperation and respect from students because they respect you as a person rather than as someone filling a role. This will require that you be as authentic as possible in your interactions with students. It is important to avoid coming across as too stiff and subject-centered at the one extreme or too wishy-washy and ingratiating at the other. Attempt to be honest and unpretentious in all your relations with students, and be ready to take personal responsibility for anything you ask them to do.

2. Do not allow a desire for natural authority to lead to peer-level relationships with your students. Whereas students usually prefer teachers who are friendly and approachable, they seldom expect teachers to behave toward them like

peers. Try to avoid behaviors that would signal an inclination on your part to be just one of the gang. Most young people have more friends than they do stable adult models in their lives. Addressing groups of students as "you guys" or allowing them to call you by your first name is not recommended.

3. Recognize that you are the "spiritual leader" in your own classroom. You will generally create the mood for the day. Try always to be positive, but not phony, in your approach to classroom business. Use positive rather than negative phrasing when stating expectations or when reprimanding (e.g., "I'd like everyone's attention up here at the front of the room," rather than "You people are going to have to stop talking back there"). When you feel you are doing your part to promote a positive and constructive classroom environment, you have a right to expect students to reciprocate. Make a deliberate and sincere attempt to compliment students for their well-intended efforts in that regard.

4. Make a strong effort to maintain an interest in and respect for individual personalities, in spite of the tendency for personalities to be obscured within the group atmosphere of the school. Your ability to consistently show patience, understanding, and appreciation toward individual students will go a long way toward earning the trust and cooperation of the young people with whom you work.

5. Find ways to clear the necessary space in your life to enable you to devote your best energies to teaching. Be able to manage personal problems and outside agendas that could compete for your time and attention as a teacher. In your relationships with other adults in the school, work to project an image of yourself as a resourceful adult who is able to handle routine problems and adversities with a minimum of distraction.

Getting Students Involved in Learning Activities

1. Attempt to personalize your teaching as much as possible. Appeal whenever you can to students' imaginations, curiosities, personal experiences, moral sensitivities, problem-solving abilities, and desires for competence when introducing new learning. The more abstract and impersonal your teaching, the more difficult it will be for students to learn; and the more fidgety and distractive behavior you can expect.

2. Work to avoid communicating to your students the idea that everything that goes on in the classroom is simply a game played to satisfy the needs of an impersonal system. When you begin a class by saying, "OK, let's take out learning objective number twenty-three," "Don't forget we have a test on chapter 5 on Friday," or "All right, we have to start our demonstration speeches today," you allow yourself to feature classroom routines rather than the substance of the learning you are there to promote. You are unwittingly contributing to the dullness, impersonality, and artificiality that many students have come to associate with classroom learning. It makes for a better learning situation when you appeal to the internal motivations of students rather than relying on grade anxieties, perceived needs to get into college, or other forms of external leverage. As a general rule it is better to start a class by asking, "What were several things we learned from the lab experiment we did yester-

day?''; ''Did any of you notice the headline on the front page of yesterday's local paper?''; or ''What would you do if you were faced with this situation?''

3. Plan your lessons so your instruction converges on main points or ''big ideas'' (or definable skills). Be able at any stage in a lesson to say, ''This is the point I'm trying to make here,'' ''This is what we're leading up to,'' or ''This is what I'd like everyone to be able to do when we're finished.'' Make an ongoing effort to achieve clarity and simplicity in your instructions and in your explanations. Be as conversational as possible without resorting to slang or inappropriate colloquialisms.

4. Give some attention to the pacing of your teaching. A deliberate, unhurried approach is the thing to strive for. The abundant use of questions, pauses, and opportunities for thought and humor helps create an environment where students are comfortable and genuinely involved with learning tasks.

5. Do not hesitate to put a good deal of yourself into your teaching. Your personality cannot be left out of the teaching–learning process. Students will be more interested and attentive when you present yourself as a whole person. You can share personal thoughts, experiences, and humor with your students and still retain dignity and an orderly classroom provided you do not come across as corny, eccentric, or easily sidetracked.

Application Exercises

1. Using the questions on page 231 as a basis for your ideas, develop a one-page summary of your philosophy of teaching? On examining your statement, indicate some of the ways your beliefs about teaching will affect what you do in the classroom.

2. Carefully review the summarized prescriptions presented on pages 232–234 to determine how well this suggested game plan represents an extension of your present philosophy of teaching. Highlight those rules of procedure that you feel prepared to implement in your own teaching. Modify or reconstruct this set of recommendations to make it best represent your own plan of attack.

MONITORING YOUR OWN SKILL DEVELOPMENT

Making the Necessary Investments

Competent teaching calls for complex skills that do not come easily and naturally for most new teachers. As a prime example, the ability to interact effectively with groups of students while also performing a control function involves multiple behaviors that normally require new investments in attention control and interpersonal communication. For most beginning teachers it entails considerable unlearning of old patterns before new skills can be properly mastered. In the process of acquiring complex teaching behaviors, there will normally be a point at which you can expect to get worse before you get better. As in the learning of athletic maneuvers requiring high levels of coordination (e.g., a proper golf swing), dysfunctional tendencies must first be eliminated. This may mean a retreat to "square-one," before that person can advance to higher levels of competence.

During this period of unlearning, it is normal for learners of complex skills to feel awkward and off balance. As teachers-in-training often testify, this can lead to feelings of vulnerability and defensiveness:

> I grew up in a family where the adults were the authorities. When I'm working with younger people, I tend to be better at delivering information than I am at sharing ideas. Learning these new communication skills is not going to be easy for me. At times I feel like I'm being moved away from what I do best.

> I tend to be a practical-minded person, so I'm feeling a need to get on with the action. Taking time to examine the reasons for what we do in the classroom hasn't exactly been my cup of tea. I know I'm feeling threatened by the fact that others in the group seem to be better with theory than I am.

When the new behavior does not come easily and quickly, the tendency is to revert to the old and more comfortable pattern. This accounts for the fact that many people fail to advance beyond a relatively low-level of performance in learning various complex skills (e.g., driving, tennis, reflective listening). It helps to explain why some teachers remain fixated at the level of information giving and assignment checking as the sum and substance of their teaching repertoires.

If you understand and accept the fact that complex skill development is an arduous task, you will be more psychologically prepared to master the requirements of competent teaching. According to psychologist Joseph Russo, the route to "creative behavior change," such as that required to learn new teaching skills, includes the following main steps:

1. An *awareness* of the need for new behaviors, including a recognition of the inadequacy of existing behaviors or skills
2. The willingness to uncritically affirm your present level of skill as the place from which you must start. Such *affirmation* is important to maintaining a positive self-concept, a vital ally during difficult periods in complex skill development
3. The assumption of personal *responsibility* for any present skill lacks, rather than blaming other persons or the environment (e.g., your teaching schedule, the makeup of a class of students) for your inadequacies
4. The *identification* of the new behaviors you wish to acquire and formulation of a plan for achieving your goal
5. The experience of some *frustration* (and perhaps demoralization) when it is discovered that the previous four steps have not automatically produced change
6. The strengthening of resolve or commitment to give *vigilant attention* to the goal implementation process until the new behavior begins to be automatic. This is the step at which goals are translated into intentions
7. The process of *acting* on one's intentions over and over again. This is the step at which intentions are translated into actions
8. The decision to accept and live through the vulnerable stage, or in other words,

to learn to *support yourself* through the period of awkwardness and frustration that occurs right after you let go of an old, familiar behavior and up to the point where you begin to feel secure with the new behavior[5]

Using Available Mirrors

There are several good ways of obtaining self-initiated feedback on your classroom performance. One is to get tape-recorded samples of your teaching. Another is to solicit information from your students. A third means of gaining insight into the quality of your teaching is to invite observations by fellow teachers.

Audio and Video Recordings.   One of the quickest and easiest means of finding out how you are coming across in your classes is to get an audiotaped sample of you interacting with a group of students. It is normally a simple matter to obtain audiorecorded teaching segments whenever you have a desire to know how you might be sounding to groups of students. In listening to a simple audio recording of your teaching you are able to screen out other classroom events and to concentrate on one main indicator of the quality of your performance, namely, what you are saying to students and the way you are saying it. It is generally a good idea to acquire samples of your teaching voice at some early point in the school year. By listening to an audiotaped segment of your teaching, you can determine:

> The quality of your teaching voice—Is it clear and understandable? Is it well-paced and unhurried? Does it include a full-range of expression? Are you projecting loudly enough to be heard throughout the classroom?
> The adequacy of the directions and explanations you are giving—Are you being deliberate and emphatic in stressing important points? Are you giving students a chance to ask questions? Are you meeting stated criteria for good explanations?
> The nature of your questioning patterns—Are you asking only one, easily understood question at a time? Do you pause at the end of a question to allow students to think? Are you using different types and levels of questions during a lesson?
> The overall mood you generate—Does your voice reflect personal confidence? Does it sound positive and encouraging? Are you using humor or other verbal ploys to lighten the atmosphere?

It is a fairly simple matter to obtain these audiotaped samples. Usually you will want to place the recorder in some inconspicuous spot at the front or side of the room and to nonchalantly turn it on when you wish to record. In the event there is another teacher in the room with you, you might ask that person to do the taping. You should be sure to use a good quality tape as well as recorder. If you have to strain to hear your voice while analyzing the tape, you are making this process more difficult than it need be.

A videotaped segment of your teaching will of course allow you to do a more complete postmortem after you have taught a lesson. Many schools presently have video equipment for this purpose. You can usually arrange to have a fellow teacher (or a mature student) videotape one of your lessons during a free period. One possible drawback to videotaping as a means of performance analysis is the potential for this equipment to be a distracting influence for you and/or your students, resulting in a nonrepresentative teaching sample. However, once you and the students are accustomed to having a video camera in the room, it becomes less distracting.

Studies on the use of video- and audiotape for reconstructing teaching performances have shown that, if used appropriately, these tapes can help teachers analyze and improve their teaching. However, because the behavior on the tape is rapid and complex, it is necessary at first to have help in critiquing your performance. "If teachers do not know what to look for, they will not see very much. . . . When teachers view tapes with a colleague or supervisor who can provide specific feedback or with materials describing what to look for, positive change occurs. . . . Such materials are effective only if specific teaching behaviors are highlighted and discussed."[6]

Obtaining Feedback from Students.   Another easily available method of getting useful feedback on your teaching is to draw on student perceptions of your class and its activities. Students can provide helpful data on how your teaching is being received. They can tell you whether they are understanding your explanations, whether they are having time to complete your assignments, whether they are comfortable with your interpersonal style, and so on. From this kind of information you can make inferences about the effectiveness of a particular teaching approach. It can help you decide whether specific methods are producing the results you had hoped to achieve.

Probably the easiest way to find out what students think of your teaching is to observe their reactions to your classes. If students appear apathetic, bored, restless, or ill-tempered, this is an indication that something is wrong. Although it may not reflect directly on your teaching, this kind of behavior should alert you to the possibility that a particular approach is ineffective. Interested, attentive classes, on the other hand, are usually a sign that something is working well for you.

Another way of obtaining ongoing feedback during the course of a lesson, is to periodically ask your students, "Are you hearing me in the back of the room?"; "Does everyone understand the point I'm making?"; "Does what I'm asking you to do seem fair and reasonable?"; "Will you now be able to complete the rest of this assignment on your own?" Although it may take some experience to know just how to interpret the feedback (or lack thereof) that you get in these situations, once you have developed productive rapport with a group of students, such inquiries will usually result in sincere efforts on the students' part to provide accurate feedback.

Besides methods that involve keeping your fingers on the "pulse of the class" during instruction, you can also get useful information on your teaching by periodically asking students to respond to questionnaires or rating sheets that you have prepared for this purpose. If the responses are to be candid, you should take measures to assure students that their ratings will remain anonymous. With this in mind, forms that call for check marks are sometimes more appropriate than those that ask for handwritten comments.

It will be important in soliciting student feedback on your teaching that you ask the right questions. Students have no training in pedagogy, so they can only tell you how they are being affected by your teaching. They cannot tell you how to teach. It would not be appropriate, for example, to ask students whether a particular concept would be best taught through direct or indirect instruction. However, it would be useful to know which of these approaches students are finding more interesting and understandable. These are some of the kinds of questions that you might use with students beyond the primary level to obtain useful feedback on your teaching:

> Are students in the class treated fairly?
> Does the teacher seem interested in the students?
> Does the teacher keep good control in the class?
> Are the assignments and explanations clear?
> Are you having enough time to finish assignments?
> Is the teaching interesting and stimulating?
> Do you feel free to participate in the class?

Utilizing a Neutral Observer.   A fellow teacher or supervisor of your own choosing can also be a source of helpful feedback on your teaching. You should attempt to find someone with whom you feel comfortable to attend your class and gather data on a designated area of your teaching. It will entail finding a time when this other person is available, then settling on a focus and a format for the observation. Considering the number of concurrent happenings in a typical classroom, it is important that you pinpoint ahead of time what is to be observed. There are several kinds of focuses that a neutral observer might adopt. For one thing, you could ask this person to collect information on the behavior of students during the class period. From a strategic spot in the back of the room, a disciplined observer might, for instance, notice particular points in the lesson when a sizable number of students begin to lose interest, starting to fidget or gazing out the window.

Or, you might ask an observer to concentrate on dominant tendencies that you exhibit in your teaching, patterns to which you may be oblivious. For example, it would be useful to be made aware of an inclination to teach primarily to one side of the room, or of a disposition to favor certain students in a discussion and to ignore others. It could also be important for you to get descriptive feedback on inappropriate verbal mannerisms such as a habit of overusing "O.K.s" or "you knows" in your speech, or a tendency to slur your words at the end of sentences.

Interaction Analysis.   A more formal approach to the examination of teaching patterns is *interaction analysis*. Here the observer might record who talks during the class and how often, the types of questions being raised, or other kinds of data relating to the nature and frequency of both teacher and student input during the lesson. Some interaction analysis techniques are relatively easy to use, making it possible for you in certain instances to do the analysis yourself with taped samples of your teaching. One simple method allows you to determine the ratio of teacher-talk to student-talk in your classes by recording a "T" for every instance of teacher-talk and an "S" for every time a student talks. If one of your overriding objectives is to have students actively involved in your classes, this kind of feedback can be an indication of whether or not you are meeting that objective.

A more sophisticated interaction analysis technique is a well-known scheme developed by Flanders (Flanders' Interaction Analysis) that attempts to categorize all verbal interactions that occur between teacher and students in a classroom setting.[7] Using this system to analyze a segment of teaching, an observer would make a tally every three seconds to indicate what the teacher is doing. For example, the teacher might be giving directions, praising a student, criticizing, or asking a question. The Flanders system contains a number of categories, some of which reflect *direct* teacher influence during instruction (lecturing), others representing *indirect* teaching behaviors (accepting or using ideas of students). This technique is a systematic way of gaining a comprehensive picture of what is happening in a class. It is especially worthwhile for determining the extent to which you are allowing indirect as well as direct influence to be a part of your teaching strategy.

A good source of in-depth information on techniques for classroom observation is *Looking in Classrooms,* written by Thomas Good and Jere Brophy.[8]

A Summary of Criteria for Assessing Teaching Ability

As you proceed to develop techniques and skills for assessing live teaching, whether your own or someone else's, it would be good for you to possess a comprehensive set of criteria for evaluating teaching ability. These criteria can then become the basis for an evaluation form or rating scale that represents your concept of good teaching. This gives you a solid basis for self-evaluation, and a frame of reference for discussing your teaching with other interested parties (like administrators and parents).

The following group of questions represents a set of general criteria for assessing the quality of instruction in most areas of teaching:

Classroom Presence:
Does the teacher demonstrate a strong enough personal presence to be able to gain the attention and cooperation of the class?
Is the teacher able to develop relationships with students based on natural authority rather than on power or position?
Does the teacher show a calm, confident, unhurried approach to the demands and pressures of the classroom?
Is the teacher able to maintain a focus and a sense of direction in the face of interruptions, unexpected happenings, and other potential distractions?
Is the teacher able to effectively handle discipline problems in a confident, low-key manner so as not to create unnecessary anxieties and distractions for other members of the class?
Does the teacher model genuine interest, enthusiasm, and good humor with regard to learning tasks and activities?
Is the teacher able to keep his or her fingers on the "pulse of the class" and to recognize the need for adjustments in technique when appropriate?

Clarity of Communications:
Does the teacher communicate the objectives of the lesson clearly?
Does the teacher provide a sufficient context for new learning by using "advance organizers" or references to previous learning?
Do the teacher's lessons center on main ideas or skills. Does the teacher use internal summaries and other techniques for establishing emphasis in lessons?
Does the teacher use terms that are unambiguous and within the students' experience? Does the teacher clarify and explain terms that are potentially confusing?
Does the teacher provide sufficient examples, illustrations, and analogies in explanations?

Does the teacher take time at the end of class periods to achieve proper closure on the lesson?

Interactive Skills:

Does the teacher begin lessons with lead-ins or "grabbers" that appeal to students' curiosities, imaginations, past experiences, or problem-solving interests?

Does the teacher address and respond to students in a manner that conveys respect, support, and concern for them as individuals?

Does the teacher demonstrate a thoughtful, well-paced approach to teaching that features the use of questions, pauses, and challenges to student thought processes?

Does the teacher show an ability to engage students in learning by appealing to internal needs and interests in preference to authority, grade anxiety, or extrinsic rewards?

Does the teacher attempt to personalize instruction by using second-person references to engage students in learning (e.g., "Can *you* imagine . . . ," "Have any of *you* ever seen . . . ," "What do *you* think about . . . ," "What would *you* do if . . . ?").

Application Exercises

1. Obtain an audio recording of one of your teaching performances. Do a self-analysis based on a set of criteria you have devised for assessing the verbal aspects of your teaching.
2. Using the teaching prescriptions on pages 232–234 as your frame of reference, construct a comprehensive rating scale you could use to assess your own teaching, based on videotaped samples and/or feedback received from a classroom observer.
3. Find opportunities to observe two or three other teachers in discussion activities with students. (You might use videotapes for this purpose.) Focusing exclusively on the teacher's behavior, make a tally each time the teacher (1) asks a question, (2) gives an instruction or an explanation, (3) praises or acknowledges a student idea, or (4) criticizes or arbitrarily corrects a student. At the end of the class period total the number of tallies in each category. What kind of balance do you find between direct and indirect teacher influence based on these interaction samples?
4. Devise a practical scheme for doing an interaction analysis (see pages 238–239) of your own teaching based on data that you would be able to obtain from audio- or videotapes in which you determine the focus of the analysis.

MAINTAINING YOUR PROFESSIONAL COMMITMENT

As you enter teaching, you are in the beginning stages of your occupational development. You will need to continue to expand your professional knowledge and capabilities in order to reach your optimum level of performance in teaching. The strength of your commitment as a teacher is reflected in the kinds of professional growth activities you continue to undertake out of your own initiative. There are several kinds of ongoing pursuits that will help keep you vital and up-to-date as a teaching professional. These include (1) substantive professional reading, (2) membership in professional organizations, (3) continuing education and in-service work, and (4) familiarity with new trends and technologies.

Professional Reading

Comprehensive professional reading is perhaps the most fruitful way to continue to expand your horizons as an educator. Regular reading in the area of education not only allows you to be in touch with the best minds in the field, with all the attendant possibilities for new ideas and new perspectives, but stimulating professional reading is a primary means of sharpening your languaging skills as a teacher. As you become actively involved with educational literature, you are in effect able to dialogue with people who are entertaining some of the same questions and experiencing some of the same problems. In addition to its potential practical value, stimulating professional reading can be reassuring and empowering for you at times when you are beginning to feel isolated and powerless within the confines of your own classroom.

There are several kinds of educational literature that will have relevance to you as a classroom teacher. The first type is reading in your own teaching area. You would be well advised to subscribe to at least one good professional journal in your field(s) of concentration.

A second category of professional reading offers new concepts and approaches in the area of curriculum and instruction (i.e., content development and general teaching methods). One well-recognized and very worthwhile curriculum journal is *Educational Leadership,* prepared by the Association for Supervision and Curriculum Development. Reading in curriculum and instruction can help you become attuned to new ideas and trends having to do with teaching methods.

The third general type of educational literature is material of a more theoretical nature. This would include reading in philosophy and sociology of education, educational research, and current issues in education. Although articles of this kind may at first glance seem abstract and impertinent to your concerns as a new teacher, there is much to be gained from reading that explores basic questions and issues underlying your work as a teacher. The ability to comprehend and analyze foundational matters related to teaching and learning is critical to your status as a professional educator. Probably the most comprehensive monthly journal for teachers at all levels, one containing a good mixture of theoretical and practical articles of current interest, is the *Kappan* magazine published by the Phi Delta Kappa organization.

Participating in Professional Organizations

Membership in professional organizations is another way to keep abreast of new ideas and developments related to your teaching. Organizations that are specifically concerned with various subject matters include the National Council of Teachers of English, the National Council of Teachers of Mathematics, and many others. Some organizations, such as the the National Middle School Association, are oriented toward a particular level of schooling. The activities of professional organizations usually include regular meetings (involving discussions or speakers), conferences, conventions, and various service projects. These meetings, which often include experiences with other teachers who have similar problems and concerns, can be energizing and inspiring. In many cases such memberships will entitle you to receive the professional journal of that particular organization.

When you take a teaching position, you will normally be expected to belong to the local teacher's association and its state and national parent organization. Two large professional organizations are the National Education Association (NEA) and the American Federation of Teachers (AFT). Both organizations are politically active in promoting working conditions and higher salaries for teachers through collective bargaining. The NEA also attempts to play a role in promoting the professional development of teachers and the improvement of educational practices. In some school districts you may have a choice between joining one or another of these organizations. Before making a decision on which association to join, you should look carefully at the goals and programs of both organizations to determine which is more closely oriented toward your own professional philosophy.

Continuing Your Formal Learning

A third means of remaining motivated and up-to-date in your teaching is to continue to be involved in education classes and workshops that will help you to increase your professional knowledge. If your teaching job is within commuting distance of a local university, you should seriously consider taking graduate courses in professional education. These courses should be chosen with specific goals or applications in mind. Relevant courses can help you to increase your teaching skills in areas of perceived weakness. They can also alert you to new methods and materials, as well as provide you with new insights into the students with whom you work.

Some states require a certain amount of graduate work as a condition for the periodic renewal of teaching certificates. It is important for you to be aware of any such requirements when you take a teaching position. Also, most districts will allow teachers graduated salary increases for completion of a specified amount of graduate work, with larger increases for advanced degrees.

In addition to university graduate courses, you will have opportunities to be involved with in-service programs sponsored by your school system. Most school districts budget a certain amount of money each year for the in-service development of teachers. They frequently provided on-site classes or workshops aimed at helping teachers increase their competence in some aspect of instruction (e.g., classroom management, questioning techniques). Teachers are often allowed some choice in selecting programs pertinent to their needs.

The quality and usefulness of such in-service programs varies greatly among school systems. With the help of highly motivated teachers, some districts put a great deal of effort into offering practical and relevant in-service workshops. Other districts do relatively little to encourage the in-service development of their teachers. It will be worth your while to inquire about district-sponsored in-service opportunities whenever you interview for a new teaching position. The seriousness with which school districts approach the in-service education of their teachers can be an important indicator of the vitality of that school system.

Keeping Up with New Trends in Education.   Your endeavors to keep yourself up-to-date as a teacher should include efforts to be familiar with important new developments in the field of education. Comprehensive professional reading is one way to maintain a good feel for the current status and future direction of public education.

School Reform.   As one preparing for a career in teaching, it is important, for example, that you be cognizant of some of the recent widespread criticism of U.S. schools. Several highly publicized national reports issued in the 1980s have advocated major reforms in the U.S. education system. One of the reports, entitled *A Nation at Risk* presented in 1983 by the federal government's National Committee on Excellence in Education, contains an appeal for measurably stronger academic standards and graduation requirements. Certain of these reports have recommended longer school days and years, better discipline, and more homework for students. Also, some influential national panels have advocated the tightening of requirements for achieving and maintaining teaching certificates. In many cases state legislatures have responded to the growing calls for school reform by proposing laws that would produce significant changes in school practices and teacher education.

Computers in Education.   You should also make yourself aware of significant technological developments that have the potential to affect your life as a teacher. One such technology that has made sweeping inroads in schools in recent decades is the microcomputer. A main objective has been to make students computer literate, or, in other words, to provide them with a basic understanding of what computers are and how they work. In recent years, computer literacy has become a part of the curriculum of many schools at all grade levels. Some schools have included an introduction to computer programming in their computer literacy classes.

As teaching aids, computers are able to serve two main functions.[9] One is to assist you in the activity of teaching (computer assisted instruction). This includes specially designed programs for engaging students in drill-and-practice sessions, simulation activities, and certain kinds of games. The drill-and-practice programs are not designed to teach new material, but to offer practice on skills that have been previously taught. It is possible to obtain tutor programs that provide skill instruction along with a practice component. Simulation programs attempt to imitate aspects of real-life situations, giving students opportunities to cultivate problem-solving skills and other thought processes.

The other main service a computer can offer you as a teacher is to help you manage the extensive paperwork that accompanies classroom teaching (computer-managed instruction). Computer-managed instruction assists teachers with the large number of their record-keeping chores. Programs would allow you to record student scores on quizzes and tests, after which they automatically calculate averages and assign appropriate weights, based on data you have initially fed into the system. With an ongoing record of tests and assignments, these programs make it simple to keep students informed of their progress through instant printouts and to figure grades at the end of the marking period. Computer-managed instruction is also useful in test construction. You are able to place test items into the system, then quickly analyze the items after the test to determine how many students missed particular items, if there is a pattern to the errors, and whether certain items should be used a second time. These programs make it possible to create convenient *test banks* that can be modified and improved over a period of time, thus allowing you to create better tests with less effort.

SUGGESTED ACTIVITIES AND QUESTIONS

1. Mention several aspects of classroom teaching that you find most challenging. What are some things you can do to prepare yourself to meet these challenges?
2. Consider the best teachers you have had during your years in school. Attempt to list shared qualities (or behaviors) that made these teachers exceptional? Compare your list of characteristics with the teacher behaviors that research has found to be most indicative of effective teaching (refer to page 230).
3. Is it ever appropriate to say a teacher has taught when the students have not learned? Can you think of arguments for both sides of this question? Does it make any practical difference how we answer the question? Elaborate.
4. Why is it that teachers have a difficult time being aware of everything that occurs in the classroom? Mention some specific strategies you intend to use to enhance your awareness of classroom behavior, and particularly your own teaching behavior?
5. What are some things you can do to insure that your efforts at self-evaluation do not disrupt the natural flow of classroom events, and thereby invalidate the self-assessment?
6. What are some of the pros and cons of using students' evaluations to judge teaching performance? Mention several guidelines for obtaining and making best use of student evaluations.
7. Think of several kinds of information about your teaching that a discerning classroom observer might be in a more advantageous position to provide.
8. Investigate one or more professional journals in subject areas that you teach. Also find opportunities to examine the content of several popular educational journals of a more general nature (e.g., *Kappan, Educational Leadership, Educational Forum, Instructor*). What kinds of articles within these journals do you find to be of most interest to you? To which of the journals would you be most likely to subscribe?
9. Investigate the availability of computers in a school where you are presently involved. What are some of the ways computers can be of service to you in your teaching?

NOTES AND REFERENCES

1. Ned A. Flanders, *Analyzing Teaching Behavior.* Reading, Mass.: Addison-Wesley, 1970, pp. 401–27.
2. Barak Rosenshine and N. F. Furst, "The Use of Direct Observation to Study Teaching." In R. M. Travers (Ed.), *Second Handbook of Research on Teaching.* Chicago: Rand McNally, 1973, p. 167.
3. Don Hamachek, "Characteristics of Good Teachers and Implications for Teacher Education." In J. Michael Palardy, *Teaching Today: Tasks and Challenges.* New York: Macmillan, 1975, p. 36.
4. Bruce Joyce and Beverly Showers, "The Coaching of Teaching." *Educational Leadership,* 40, no. 1, (October 1982), pp. 4–10.
5. Adapted by permission from the teaching files of Joseph Russo, Department of Psychology, California State University, Chico.

6. Thomas L. Good and Jere E. Brophy, *Looking in Classrooms,* 3rd ed. New York: Harper and Row, 1984, p. 43.
7. Flanders, op. cit., p. 34.
8. Good and Brophy, op. cit., see chap. 3.
9. For more detailed information on the use of computers in teaching, see P. Coburn, P. Kelman, N. Roberts, T. F. Snyder, D. H. Watt, and C. Weiner, *Practical Guide to Computers in Education.* Reading, Mass.: Addison-Wesley, 1982; and H. F. O'Neil (Ed.), *Computer-based Instruction: A State-of-the-Art Assessment.* New York: Academic Press, 1981.

Index